REDESIGNING
THE AMERICAN
DREAM

BY THE SAME AUTHOR

Seven American Utopias:
The Architecture of Communitarian Socialism, 1780–1975 (MIT Press, 1976)

The Grand Domestic Revolution:
A History of Feminist Designs for American Homes, Neighborhoods, and Cities
(MIT Press, 1981)

W·W·NORTON & COMPANY·New York·London

DOLORES HAYDEN

REDESIGNING THE AMERICAN DREAM

THE FUTURE OF HOUSING, WORK, AND FAMILY LIFE

For Peter Marris

CONTENTS

ACKNOWLEDGMENTS

Financial support for this essay came from a Rockefeller Humanities Fellowship, a Guggenheim Fellowship, and a National Endowment for the Arts Fellowship. Special intellectual and institutional support for my investigations of women and the city came from Harvey Perloff and Martin Wachs at UCLA. The two designers who first sparked my interest in housing were Shadrach Woods, my teacher at the Harvard GSD, and John Habraken, the head of the Architecture Department at MIT when I was an assistant professor there. During the last decade many conversations with colleagues have contributed to this project. The people I especially wish to thank for perceptive, detailed comments on the manuscript are Jeremy Brecher, Robert Healy, Temma Kaplan, Susan Kreiger, Jacqueline Leavitt, Ann R. Markusen, Peter Marris, Kitty Sklar, Susana Torre, Martin Wachs, Peter and Phyllis Willmott, and Gwendolyn Wright. I am also grateful to Janet Abu-Lughod, Laura Balbo, Thomas Bender, Eugenie Birch, Manuel Castells, Francesco Dal Co, Phil Donahue, Margaret FitzSimmons, John Friedmann, Sherna Gluck, Patrick H. Hare, Mui Ho, Kevin Lynch, Margarita McCoy, Jean Baker Miller, S. M. Miller, Martin Pawley, Jan Peterson, Mary Rowe, Arie Schachar, Donna Shalala, David Thompson, and Gerda Wekerle, who contributed valuable criticisms of earlier articles or ideas. I would also like to thank Martha Nelson and Catharine

Stimpson, as the editors of *Signs* who first asked, "What would a non–sexist city be like?", and Carol Houck Smith, my editor at W.W. Norton, who showed me how many choices I had about what to do with the answers to that question.

Dolores Hayden
July 1983

Cities, like dreams, are made of desires and fears, even if the thread of their discourse is secret, their rules are absurd, their perspectives deceitful, and everything conceals something else.

Italo Calvino

Space is political and ideological. It is a product literally filled with ideologies.

Henri Lefebvre

To study the history of the American family is to conduct a rescue mission into the dreamland of our national self-concept. No subject is more closely bound up with our sense of a difficult present—and our nostalgia for a happier past.

John Demos

part I

The Evolution of American Housing

Does our housekeeping raise and inspire us, or does it cripple us?

Ralph Waldo Emerson

1

HOUSING AND AMERICAN LIFE

Mired in spring mud, striped with the treads of bulldozers, Vanport City, Oregon, is a new town under construction. Concrete trucks pour foundations and give way to flatbed trucks that deliver cedar siding from the forests of the Northwest. Carpenters, plumbers, and electricians try to stay out of each other's way as they work evenings, Saturdays, and Sundays. Architects from the firm of Wolff and Phillips confer on the site six, ten, a dozen times a day. "All my life I have wanted to build a new town," the project architect confides to a reporter, "but—*not this fast.* We hardly have time to print the working drawings before the buildings are out of the ground."

Near the town site, steel deliveries arrive at several shipyards on the Columbia River, where production is geared to an even more frenetic pace. Twenty-four hours a day the yards are open; cranes move against the sky, shifting materials. Tired workers pour out the gates at 8 A.M., 4 P.M., and midnight, each shift replaced by fresh arrivals—women and men in coveralls who carry protective goggles and headgear. The personnel office is recruiting as far away as New York and Los Angeles. They want welders, riveters, electricians. They offer on-the-job training, housing, child care, all fringe benefits. They also advertise for maintenance workers, nursery school teachers, elementary school teachers, and nurses. In ten months the personnel office does enough hiring to populate a new town of forty thousand people, white, black, Asian, and Hispanic workers and their families. This is the first time that an integrated, publicly subsidized new town of this type has ever been built in the United States.

The chief engineer from the Federal Public Housing Authority is checking the last of the construction details as the residents' cars, pickup trucks, and moving vans start to arrive. It has been ten months from schematic designs to occupancy. The project architect is exhausted; never has he had a more demanding design program to meet, never a more impossible timetable. He has had to rethink many basic questions in very little time, especially every idea he has ever had about normal family life, about men, women, and children. The program specified that he design affordable housing for all types and sizes of households, including single people, single-parent families, and nonfamily groups. He also had to design for low maintenance costs, and for energy efficiency, to make the maximum use of very scarce natural resources. He was directed to emphasize public transportation by bus. His housing also had to be positioned in relation to several child care centers and job sites: "On a straight line," said James Hymes, the client in charge of child care,[1] because he didn't want parents to have to make long journeys to drop off or pick up their children.

"They certainly should become famous for that," the architect asserts, considering the large child care centers, open twenty-four hours a day, seven days a week (just like the shipyards), complete with infirmaries for sick children, child-sized bathtubs so that mothers don't need to bathe children at home, cooked food services so that mothers can pick up hot casseroles along with their children, and, most important of all, large windows with views of the river, so that children can watch the launchings at the yards. "There goes mommy's ship!" said one excited five-year-old. It all seems to work very well. And it costs seventy-five cents per day for each child.

It is March 1943. This new town, a product of World War II, is nicknamed Kaiserville after the industrialist who owns the shipyards. Everywhere, at home and abroad, Americans are singing a song at the top of the wartime hit parade:

1.1 Women working as riveters and welders, 1944.

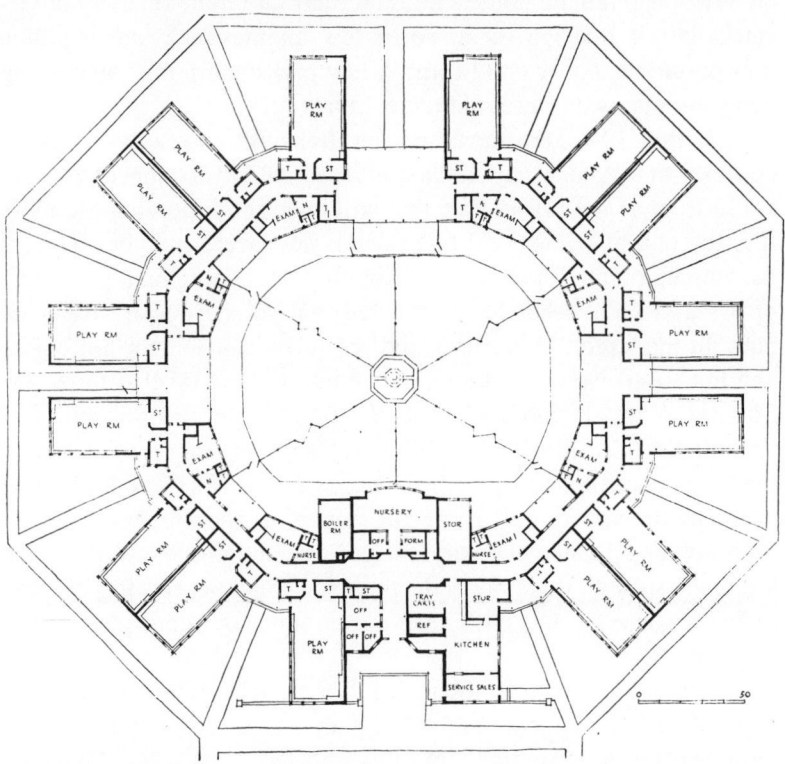

1.2 Kaiser and Wolff, architects, plan of a day-care center at Vanport City, Oregon, 1944. This project represents the industrial strategy of building housing as a support for the female and male workers in the industrial labor force.

All the day long whether rain or shine,
She's a part of the assembly line . . .
She's making history, working for victory,
Rosie the Riveter!

This amazing American woman has been the client as much as Henry J. Kaiser, who has built this town for her: Rosie the Riveter.

Six years later, another new town for seventy-five thousand people is being built at the same frantic pace in Hicksville, Long Island. In Hicksville, nothing is on a straight line. Roads curve to lead the eye around the corner, but every road is lined with identical houses. There is no industry in Hicksville except the construction industry. Each new Cape Cod house is designed to be a self-contained world, with white picket fence, green lawn, living room with television set built into the wall, kitchen with Bendix washing machine built into the laundry alcove. Every family is expected to consist of male breadwinner, female housewife, and their children. Energy conservation is not a design issue, nor is low maintenance, nor is public transportation, nor is child care. A few parks and public swimming pools are planned to provide recreation.

In March 1949, the developer in Hicksville is ready to sell his houses. On a Wednesday the first prospective buyers appear to camp out in front of the sales office that will open the following Monday. It is the end of winter on Long Island: raw, wet, and cold. One of the women on the line of buyers camping out is pregnant; the developer's assistant rushes her to the hospital so she doesn't have her baby in the street. He returns and sets up a canteen for hot coffee and hot soup. News photographers come by and take pictures. On Monday night, in three and a half hours, the developer sells $11 million worth of identical houses. His company emerges as one of the great business successes of the postwar era. His Cape Cod house becomes the single most powerful symbol of the dream of upward mobility and homeownership for American families. Because of mortgage subsidies and tax deductions for homeowners, it is cheaper to buy a house in Hicksville than to rent an apartment in New York City.[2]

The creator of this new town, Bill Levitt, acknowledges that Levittown is not integrated, and he explains to a reporter that this is "not a matter of prejudice, but one of business. As a Jew I have no room in my mind or heart for racial prejudice. But, by various means, I have come to know that if we sell one house to a Negro family,

1.3 Dream house for a new homeowner, with wife and children, Levittown, New York, 1948. This housing represents the haven strategy of building homes as retreats for male workers and as workplaces for their wives. (Bernard Hoffman, LIFE Magazine, © 1950, Time, Inc.)

then 90 to 95 percent of our white customers will not buy into the community.''[3] In fact, the Federal Housing Authority does not, at this time, approve mortgage funds for integrated communities, or mortgages for female-headed families.[4] The prospective customers do not get a chance to make this choice for themselves.

This second new town—Levittown—becomes known all over the world as a model of American know-how just as the first new town— Vanport City—is being dismantled, some of its housing taken apart piece by piece. Yet both of these ventures had great appeal as solutions to the housing needs of American families, and both made their developers a great deal of money. Vanport City met the needs of a wartime labor force, composed of women and men of many diverse racial and economic groups. The builders of Vanport City responded to the need for affordable housing, on-the-job training and economic development for workers. They recognized that single parents and two-earner families required extensive child care services in order to give their best energies to production. The site design and landscaping of Vanport City were good, the economic organization was good, and the social services were superb (down to maintenance crews who would fix leaky faucets or repair broken windows), but the housing lacked charm. It looked like a ''housing project,'' and the residents were renters not owners. Yet it was the most ambitious attempt ever made in the United States to shape space for employed women and their families. The U.S. government supplied $26 million to build the housing. Kaiser made only a $2 profit on it, but he made a fortune on the ships the war workers built for him.[5]

Levittown met rather different needs from the ones provided for by Vanport City. Levitt's client was the returning veteran, the beribboned male war hero who wanted his wife to stay home. Women in Levittown were expected to be too busy tending their children to care about a paying job. The Cape Cod houses recalled traditional American colonial housing (although they were very awkwardly proportioned). They emphasized privacy. Large-scale plans for public space and social services were sacrificed to private acreage. Although they were small, a husband could convert his attic and then build an addition quite easily, since the houses covered only 15 percent of the lots. Levitt liked to think of the husband as a weekend do-it-yourself builder and gardener: "No man who owns his house and lot can be a Communist. He has too much to do," asserted Levitt in 1948.[6] His town was as ambitious as Vanport City, but Levitt aimed to shape private space for white working class males and their dependents. The pressures of war and the communal style of military barracks living made suburban privacy attractive to many veterans, especially those with new cars to go with their new houses. Levitt made his fortune on the potato farms that he subdivided with the help of both federal financing programs for FHA and VA mortgages and federal highway programs to get people to remote suburbs. And as the landscaping matured, Levittown began to look better than the acres of little boxes some visitors perceived at the start.

Ironically, although Kaiser's highly praised wartime town lost the public relations battle to Levitt's postwar suburb, Kaiser himself was not a loser in this contest. He understood changing federal subsidy programs for housing, and after receiving wartime Lanham Act funds for Vanport City, which enabled him to expand his shipyards with new workers, Kaiser entered the post–Warld War II housing arena with new housing developments suited to FHA and VA subsidies. On the West Coast, he built thousands of single-family houses in subdivisions much like Levitt's.[7] "Vets! No down!" read his signs. The losers were not the housing developers but the skilled white female and minority male and female workers, who lost their wartime jobs to returning white male veterans and found there were no postwar housing subsidies designed to help them find new jobs, new homes, and mortgages with easy terms.

In the same era a third new town was launched—Baldwin Hills Village, in Los Angeles, California. It did not make anyone a fortune: neither an industrialist like Kaiser nor a developer like Levitt.

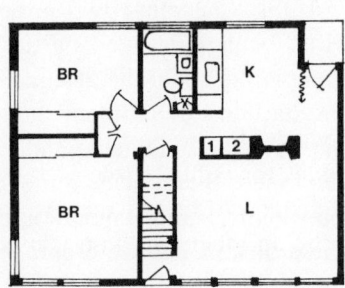

1.4 Plan of a Levitt house, 1952 model. (1) Bendix washing machine; (2) water heater.

1.5 Levittown, 1955.

Funded by FHA and the Reconstruction Finance Corporation, its designers had sophisticated professional ambitions: to reinterpret the tradition of common land at the heart of New England's Puritan communities in a way that could be copied throughout the United States; to adapt the best low-cost European public housing designs of the previous decades to American housing programs and life styles; and to keep the car in its proper place for the sake of air quality, children's safety, and open space design.

Unlike the other two projects, the construction of the Baldwin Hills Village dragged on in the early 1940s. City engineers made complaints about the designers' refusal to cut roads through the site; the building department didn't like the great variety of apartment and townhouse layouts, and the plans had to be redrawn no less than ten times. Budget cuts removed three child care centers and a shopping center; land acquisition problems canceled the second phase of the project; Clarence Stein, the overall designer, discovered that his proposal for community kitchens had not been funded.[8]

Yet when the project finally opened as subsidized rental housing, several of the collaborating local architects moved to Baldwin Hills Village. As a statement of support for their values about good housing, they left elegant private homes in other parts of Los Angeles to be part of the new experiment and to make sure it worked. They felt extremely pleased that they had created low-rise, medium density housing with generous floor plans, sunlight, and lush landscaping. The cost was almost as low as that of other local public housing "projects." The residents enjoyed a belt of three parks running through the center of the site, as well as smaller landscaped courtyards, tot lots, and private fenced-in outdoor space for each family. There were common laundries and drying yards, common garages, and a community center with a swimming pool.

Baldwin Hills Village was integrated at the start, but within ten years many white tenants left and were replaced by nonwhite and female-headed households who were considered "problem families" in comparison with the homeowners living on suburban quarter acre plots around them.[9] Eventually a group that was formed to rescue the buildings turned the Village into condominiums, prohibited children under eighteen, tore out the tot lots, and installed a miniature golf course on the central green. Today the children for whom the village was designed are gone, and many of the elderly residents are still too afraid of crime to use its three magnificent parks. Yet the Baldwin Hills Village is not as much of a ghost town

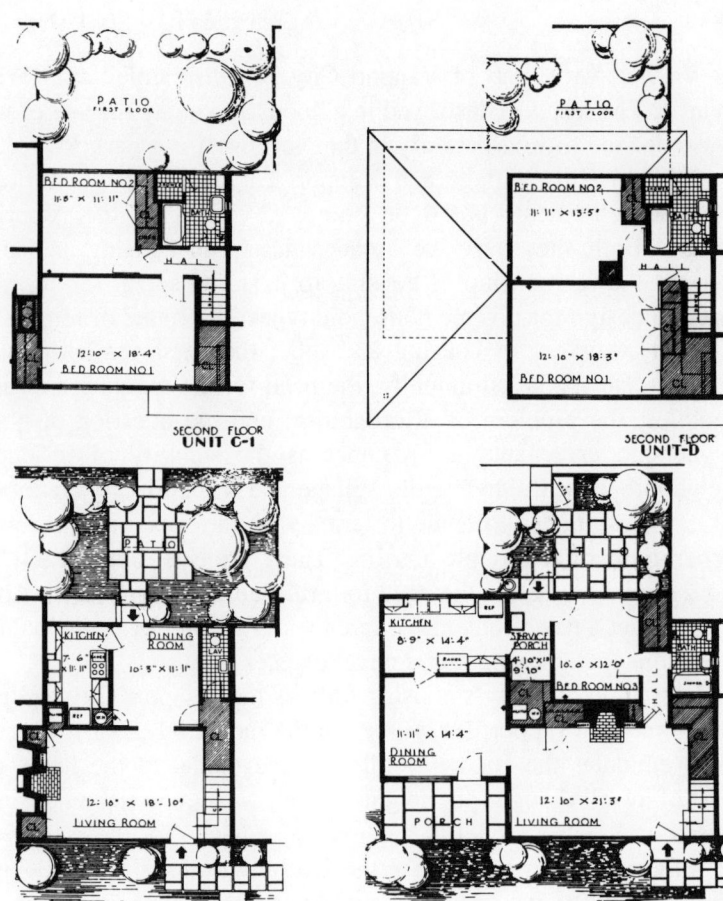

1.6 Clarence Stein, Robert Alexander, et al., Baldwin Hills Village, Los Angeles, 1938–1942. Baldwin Hills represents the neighborhood strategy of building homes. The one-bedroom (*A*), two-bedroom (*C*-1), and three-bedroom (*D*) houses were subsidized, rental units organized around shared open spaces.

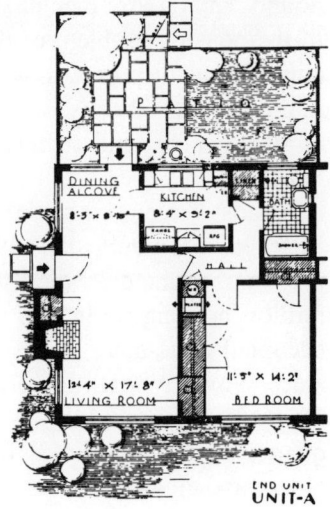

as Vanport City. Part of Vanport City was dismantled after World War II. The rest was destroyed in a flood, and today the site of what was once the fifth-largest city in the Northwest is a park.[10]

Baldwin Hills Village and Vanport City whisper the stories of planned settlements based on complex visions of the American dream. Both sites raise the broadest issues in housing and urban design: the relationship of housing to jobs and social services, the need to design for diverse household types, the rights of female and minority workers to housing and jobs, the need for both spatial privacy and spatial community, the need for the regulation of automobiles, the problem of affordability, and the question of home-ownership or tenancy as it concerns the stability of residential neighborhoods. Baldwin Hills Village and Vanport City are models of earlier struggles to come to terms with the social and economic programing of affordable housing. These projects, now largely forgotten, remind us that the need for affordable housing for all Americans is not a new problem, nor are the design problems and political questions that housing raises novel ones.

Very little of today's housing follows the Vanport City model of the home as a support for women in the industrial labor force; very little emulates the Baldwin Hills Village model of the home as a part of a well thought-out neighborhood. Most American housing is based on Levitt's model of the home as a haven for the male worker's family. Americans chose the Levittown model for housing in the late 1940s; we have mass-produced the home as haven and transformed our cities to fit this model and its particular social, economic, and environmental shortcomings. This choice is at the heart of the housing problem of the 1980s. Americans cannot solve their current housing problems without reexamining the ideal of the single-family house—that is, reexamining its history, and the ideals of family, gender, and society it embodies, as well as its design and financing.

Almost three-quarters of the total housing stock in the United States has been built since 1940. Out of 80.4 million occupied housing units counted in the 1980 census, nearly two-thirds, or 53.9 million housing units, are single-family detached homes. Owner-occupied units have been getting larger and larger in each decade since World War II: 84 percent consisted of five or more rooms in 1976. Yet households have been getting smaller, until nearly a quarter of all households in 1980 consisted of one person living alone, and close to a third consisted of two persons.[11]

During the last four decades bankers and builders have concentrated the bulk of capital resources for housing on the model of the single family detached house, despite the demographic shifts to new types of smaller households. As a result, many individuals and families are now experiencing serious difficulties in finding housing that meets their particular needs. The current American personal income tax structure favors homeowners (whose interest payments on mortgages are tax deductible) rather than renters, so no citizen who can help it wants to be a tenant for life.[12] Yet it appears that more and more households find homeownership beyond their reach, while many others cannot even locate affordable rental housing. Builders and would-be buyers speak of the end of the American dream of single-family homeownership.

The symptoms of this housing crisis begin with young couples, who even if they are both employed, often cannot qualify for a mortgage, since in 1982 the average price of existing single-family homes reached $87,600.[13] To lower their housing costs, they must commute long distances to remote suburbs where land is cheaper. At the same time, the elderly who live on fixed incomes alone or in couples—even those who own their houses outright—often find they cannot meet the property taxes, heating bills, and the demands for physical maintenance of single-family homes. The frail elderly often cannot drive, a necessity in most suburban locations.[14] Single-parent families often lack the support system of social services that such a family requires if the parent is holding a paid job. Infant care, day care, after school care, public transportation so that older children can move about independently, closeness to stores and health services, all are almost always lacking in neighborhoods where the housing was originally designed for households with a full-time housewife caring for husband and children.[15] Two-earner couples experience many of the same strains if the employed wife is also expected to carry the greater burden of family tasks.

Single people, male or female, old or young, straight or gay, often find that the housing options available to them lack flexibility, variety, and complexity. Coming home to an empty house or apartment every night can be dreary, but sharing traditional housing designed for the closeness of one family can be frustrating in its lack of privacy. More subtle options are hard to locate, and harder to finance.[16]

Couples undergoing divorce or separation experience additional frustration. If two incomes are needed to support one mortgage, neither partner may be able to afford to buy the other's share of a jointly owned house. At the same time, it may not be feasible to relinquish one low interest mortgage in favor of two high rentals. Furthermore, couples with children will find that the majority of urban landlords simply will not rent to families with children.[17] As families struggle to cope with these dilemmas, rigid zoning laws and financing arrangements that make "granny flats" or "daughter-in-law apartments" illegal only compound the problem.[18] It becomes clear that very few neighborhoods or towns have planned for a variety of housing types at affordable prices so that single parent families, singles, and the elderly can live in close proximity to more traditional families.

Serious unemployment and a dramatic rate of mortgage foreclosures also signal trouble for traditional families who are now homeowners.[19] Racial segregation is another major problem for minority households. Despite recent legislation, segregation in neighborhoods of single family detached houses has never been dealt with adequately because of the informal discriminatory practices of realtors, homeowners, and banks.[20] In poor inner-city neighborhoods, banks may refuse to grant loans, despite bans on "redlining." And public housing may create racial segregation based on poverty. Gated communities for the rich and second homes for the affluent contrast with burnt-out abandoned ghetto tenements and vandalized public housing projects to form the extreme ends of the American housing spectrum. At the very lowest end of the economic scale, an estimated half million to two and a half million homeless sleep out every night—on the heating vents of New York skyscrapers, under the freeway overpasses in Los Angeles, in the subway tunnels, doorways, and parks of numerous other cities and towns.[21]

The United States has a housing crisis of disturbing complexity, a crisis that, in different ways, affects rich and poor, male and female, young and old, white and minority Americans. We have not merely a housing shortage, but a broader set of unmet needs caused by the efforts of the entire society to fit itself into a housing pattern that reflects the dreams of the mid-nineteenth century better than the realities of the late twentieth century. Single-family suburban homes have become inseparable from the American dream of economic success and upward mobility. Their presence pervades every aspect of economic life, social life, and political life in the United States, because the mass production of these homes, beginning in the late 1940s, was an economic activity of overwhelming importance that has transformed the American landscape.

The purpose of this book is to support the search for more satisfactory patterns of housing, work, and family life in the United States, as well as in other countries where the employment of women in the paid labor force has created similar strains concerning outworn patterns of private and public life. The first part of the book looks at the evolution of American housing since colonial times and explores the the challenges to the suburban dream house posed by environmental groups, women's groups, and civil rights groups, as well as the threat to dream houses created by changing economic conditions.

The second part, "Rethinking Private Life," seeks to identify the deepest needs and desires associated with the ideal of home. What are the most basic human attachments to a home, and how are they expressed in modern, urban, industrial societies? Humans need nurturing, aesthetic pleasure, and economic security. Homes can contribute to the satisfaction of these desires, or their frustration. Three models of how to organize housing in industrial societies emerged in the last third of the nineteenth century. Those models each carried strong implications for nurturing, for aesthetic expression in architecture, and for economic development. The strengths and weaknesses of these three models are examined in the perspective of American experience and that of other nations (such as China, Cuba, Denmark, Sweden, and the USSR), to assess the state of the art of creating housing in world terms.

The third part, "Rethinking Public Life," probes for solutions in the planning and design of better housing, social services, and public space. These chapters deal with rehabilitation of the existing American fabric of homes and neighborhoods, as well as with suggestions for new construction. These possible solutions are supported by many examples of projects—good and bad—undertaken by individuals, small groups, local governments, and national governments.

Finding an egalitarian approach to affordable housing must involve individuals, families, neighbors' groups, citizens' groups, local officials, national policymakers, and practitioners in the planning and design professions. Especially, it must involve employed women who are concerned about their own and their children's futures in a society that has chosen a housing model antithetical to their needs.

Employed women and the members of their families now constitute an absolute majority of American citizens, but a majority whose voices have not yet been heard in the national arena. For this new majority, and the numerous housewives who support them fully, the time for change will come, and that change will involve nothing less than redesigning the American dream.

2

FROM IDEAL CITY TO DREAM HOUSE

Open the real estate section of a major Sunday newspaper in any American city and you will still find dream houses as well as dream apartments, dream lofts and dream condominiums by the hundreds. Developers often claim they are "planned with women in mind." They argue that women like elaborate stairways and formal entrances where they can greet their guests in style. They believe women favor romantic "master" bedrooms, where they can enjoy large closets, expansive dressing rooms, and extensive bathroom areas.[1] They advertise gourmet kitchens, where women can practice cooking as an art or as a science. Dream houses also have special marketing features for men, such as paneled dens, home workshops, and large garages. One can describe suburban housing as an architecture of gender, since houses provide settings for women and girls to be effective social status achievers, desirable sex objects, and skillful domestic servants, and for men and boys to be executive breadwinners, successful home handy men, and adept car mechanics.

Couples may accept or resist the real estate developers' definitions of their gender roles, but most of all, couples are likely to justify the dream house as a place where they can give their children "all the things we didn't have." While "all the things we didn't have" may include a large back yard, a gas-fired barbecue, swings and slides, shiny bicycles, a big family room, and spacious individual bedrooms, this phrase usually means something more than material acquisitions. It may mean a chance to surmount one's class and ethnic background. In this sense, single-family suburban domestic architecture is an architecture of Americanization in a nation of immigrants, and it implies a complete social planning strategy. "The things we didn't have" is also a euphemism for a private life without urban problems such as unemployment, poverty, hunger, racial prejudice, pollution, and violent crime. As a solution to these problems, this housing type offers short-term incentives to a particular kind of economic consumption. It has encouraged Americans to turn their backs on their cities, and to pretend they don't exist.

The dream house is a uniquely American form, because for the first time in history, a civilization has created a utopian ideal based on the house rather than the city or the nation. For hundreds of years, when individuals thought about putting an end to social problems, they designed model towns to express these desires, not model homes. In fact the ideal of a good town was once as important to American life as the ideal of a good house. To analyze how and when Americans gave up the model town in favor of the individual dream house is to begin to understand the fears, hopes, and miscalculations that have generated the current housing crisis.

The City on a Hill

In the seventeenth and eighteenth centuries, farmers, laborers, shopkeepers, landowners, soldiers, and housewives all came to the North American continent seeking a better way of life. The Puritans believed they were creating a "city upon a hill," a model for the rest of the world. The Quakers called their settlement a "city of brotherly love." The public spaces they established, such as the town commons of the Puritan villages in New England or the ordered squares of William Penn's Philadelphia, gave form to their collective ideals. Despite a strict, hierarchical organization of society, which they took for granted, these settlers sought a balance between personal space and social space. Their plans expressed a desire for more personal autonomy in terms of land ownership than English society had permitted, more lenient treatment of debtors and the poor, and more tolerance of religious dissidents. Their plans also expressed the settlers' mutual economic and social dependence.[2] While settlers usually tended separate fields at the edge of the settlements, they chose to live side by side. It would have been inconceivable to these first settlers to strive for the good life in America by building model houses rather than working for a model community.

The town commons or village greens created by the New England covenant communities remain some of the most beautiful, memorable, American public spaces. Originally town commons were used for cattle grazing. They formed a verdant heart for every settlement, bordered by the meeting house, the minister's house, and the houses of other settlers.[3] Because they represent American citizens' earliest covenants to provide and maintain public space, the village greens are an important part of our political heritage as well as our landscape heritage; they are our first and best planning tradition.

Each Farmer on His Own Farm

By the end of the eighteenth century the New England pattern of town building was challenged by an alternate approach. Thomas Jefferson, the first mainstream American political theorist to attempt a schematic spatial representation of a national ideal of democracy, favored the model family farm over the model village. The Declaration of Independence and the National Survey that Jefferson produced are the crucial statements of the rights of all men to life, liberty, and the pursuit of happiness in a landscape divided into small farms, where every man can own the means of agricultural production. As Jefferson's survey grid appeared on the American landscape west of the Alleghenies, in the late 1780s, this powerful theoretical statement of agrarian life became the framework for a national ideal of land ownership. However most of the early land sales resulted in the acquisition of large areas by speculators, not by small farmers.

Throughout the nineteenth and early twentieth centuries, the ideal of the model town was still debated, but the spatially and socially coherent settlements of the earliest settlers started to give way to distance between city and country, between capital and labor. Communitarian socialists—including the Owenites, Associationists,

Shakers, and Amana Inspirationists—did continue to argue that the good life could only be achieved through collective economic effort and the shared spaces of cooperatively owned housing in model towns.[4] From Maine to California, they built hundreds of experimental socialist towns. Although tens of thousands of Americans joined their communities, more rural Americans lived on the Jeffersonian grid.

The American Woman's Home

When the national economy shifted its emphasis from agriculture to industry, housing patterns changed. Between 1840 and 1920, the sprawling industrial city was on the rise. Millions of poor farmers and immigrants arrived in New York, Boston, Chicago, and other cities, eager to take any jobs they could find. They had few trade unions. Men, women, and children labored in factories under conditions that included unsafe machinery, foul air, corrosive wastes, and poor sanitation. When a man was crippled for life by a machine, or a woman's jaw rotted from phosphorous in a match factory, or a child lost several fingers in a press, the factory simply replaced the worker. There were no disability benefits, death benefits, or social security schemes—only charity or the workhouse. While these facts are often recounted, few historians convey the desperation and rage that such conditions generated.

The urban living conditions of this era were as bad as the working conditions. Tenement apartments often lacked windows, heating, running water, indoor plumbing, and proper sewers. In nineteenth-century cities, one urban family in five took in boarders, despite the crowding. The homeless slept in doorways or alleys. Food sold in slum neighborhoods was often adulterated or spoiled—water in the milk, powder in the flour, maggots in the meat. Tuberculosis, cholera, diphtheria, and influenza claimed as many lives as did industrial hazards. There were no public housing schemes or medical services, merely a few charitable associations struggling to cope with the needs of millions.

The dangers and discomforts of this urban setting eventually encouraged newly affluent urban businessmen to remove their families from urban centers. There were new forms of transportation, and businessmen began to commute by railroad and then by streetcar from the outskirts of the city to their downtown offices, stores, or factories. The earliest American suburban homes were designed

2.1　Street scene with market and tenements: a Jewish quarter of the lower East Side, New York City, 1900. (Library of Congress)

2.2 Tenement interior, Jersey Street, New York City, photographed by Jacob Riis about 1890. The mother holds her swaddled baby and looks resigned to her squalid home. (Library of Congress)

by Catharine Beecher and Andrew Jackson Downing, and promoted by small builders and the editors of women's magazines. Both Downing and Beecher started to popularize such suburban prototypes in the 1840s. These houses were designed to recall the values of the Puritan convenant community but to suit families whose lives centered around the profitable dealings of the new cities.

Downing's contribution was picturesque landscaping for the suburban retreat. Beecher named her 1869 prototype "The American Woman's Home," and her house was above all a space for woman's domestic labor in service of men and children. Essentially Beecher attempted to update Jefferson's ideal of equal male access to the means of agricultural production. Her ultimate objective was to give women control over the domestic space of the household to match male involvement in agricultural or industrial production. She ignored race and attempted to play off gender against class as a way of mitigating urban economic and spatial conflict, by stating that all women, rich or poor, could find a common identity in housework. She acknowledged conflict between men and women within the American family but was over-optimistic about her power to resolve it. Her suburban house was designed to put the American woman, newly described as a "minister of home" and a "true professional," in charge of a well-organized private domestic workplace in a democratic society where public life was run by men.

According to Beecher, a woman, nurturing her spouse and children, could create a "model family commonwealth" in her suburban home.[5] Beecher believed that women's exclusion from the paid labor force would mute class conflict, and that women's consumption of commodities would stimulate the economy. She argued that in this home a woman could perfect her capacity for self-sacrifice and thus gain rewards in heaven for what she gave up on earth. Her calculations about the model home did not include the social costs to women or the economic costs to the city.

Whether or not heaven could provide an ideal city for some women at some future time, as Beecher claimed, her strategy required more patience than many women possessed, and more wages than most skilled workers earned. Beecher's model houses were built for a small proportion of affluent citizens. Millions of workers, concentrated in the vast slums, could only dream about the small, clean middle-class suburbs of houses surrounded by grass and trees and advertised by one builder as "the workingman's reward." At the

2.3 "The Workingman's Reward, a Home at $10 a Month," as pointed out by an angel with a sword of justice and built by S. E. Gross, Chicago, 1891.

end of the nineteenth century, two-thirds of American urban residents were still tenants, most of them in the tenements.

"The City of the Faithfulest Friends"

Some of the greatest American writers, activists, and designers hoped for changes in the industrial city rather than an escape to model houses. Against the background of Jefferson's idealized family farm and Beecher's pious suburban house, several remarkable alternative visions of urban public space appeared. Between the late 1840s and the 1870s, the activists of the abolitionist movement and the woman's movement gathered the strength to make demands for political and spatial rights that were to inspire generations of reformers, and they saw the ideal city as the spatial expression of these rights, not the dream house.

One of the clearest statements of this urban vision came from Walt Whitman. Whitman, an editor, printer, and building contractor who became a great poet, defined the ideal American city in 1856 in his "Song of the Broad-Axe." The great city, for Whitman, was not "the place of the tallest and costliest buildings or shops selling goods from the rest of the earth." "A great city," he proclaimed, "is that which has the greatest men and women. . . ." A great city is "where the slave ceases and the master of slaves ceases." It is the city

> Where the citizen is always the head and ideal,
>   . . .
> Where children are taught to be laws to themselves,
>   and to depend upon themselves,
> Where women walk in public processions
>   in the streets the same as the men,
> Where they enter the public assembly and
>   take places the same as the men;
> Where the city of the faithfulest friends stands
>   . . .
> There the great city stands.[6]

The "city of the faithfulest friends" was a city of equal political participation, without regard to gender, race, class, or sexual preference, a city offering all adults access to public space and to public office. It was an urban place diametrically opposed to the sentimental, gender-stereotyped private domestic spaces that Jefferson and Beecher promoted.

Whitman wanted the new American city to reflect "Shapes of Democracy total, result of centuries." He believed that in the great city, where "fierce men and women pour forth," the public domain, accessible to all, would inspire a new, uniquely American architecture. "The shapes arise!" he exulted.[7]

While Whitman always admired happily married couples and parents with their children, there were three other constituencies he was particularly eager to describe. He instructed his readers, in "Poem of Remembrance for a Girl or Boy of These States," to foresee the end of slavery, to "Anticipate when the thirty or fifty millions are to become the hundred or two hundred millions, of equal freeman and freewoman, amicably joined." With regard to female citizens he said: "Anticipate the best women; / I say an unnumbered new race of hardy and well-defined women are to spread through all These States; / I say a girl fit for These States must be free, capable, dauntless, just the same as a boy."[8] When "In the New Garden, in All the Parts," Whitman imagined himself walking through modern cities, he was most interested in finding this type: "with determined will, I seek—the woman of the future, / You, born years, centuries after me, I seek."[9] In addition, as a single man who was given to wandering the streets, seeking lovers both male and female, Whitman celebrated a public domain open to "the dear love of comrades":

I dream'd in a dream I saw a city invincible to the attacks of the whole of
    the rest of the earth,
I dream'd that was the new city of Friends,
Nothing was greater there than the quality of robust love, it led the rest,
It was seen every hour in the actions of the men of that city,
And in all their looks and words.[10]

Although Whitman's aesthetic of urban space provided him with a "continued exaltation and absolute fulfillment,"[11] not every aspect of the American city could satisfy his critical sense of the dangers of bigotry, commercialism, and exploitation. At the very time that he was writing, many men were ridiculing women's desire for access to public space, racial segregation was practiced everywhere, and gay liberation was not even discussed, while the Jeffersonian family farm was still much romanticized.

2.4 Nostalgia for the patriarchal, rural household and the architecture of gender: Currier and Ives, "American Country Life: Summer's Evening," detail. This idyllic, romantic view was juxtaposed with harsh humor attacking advocates of change.

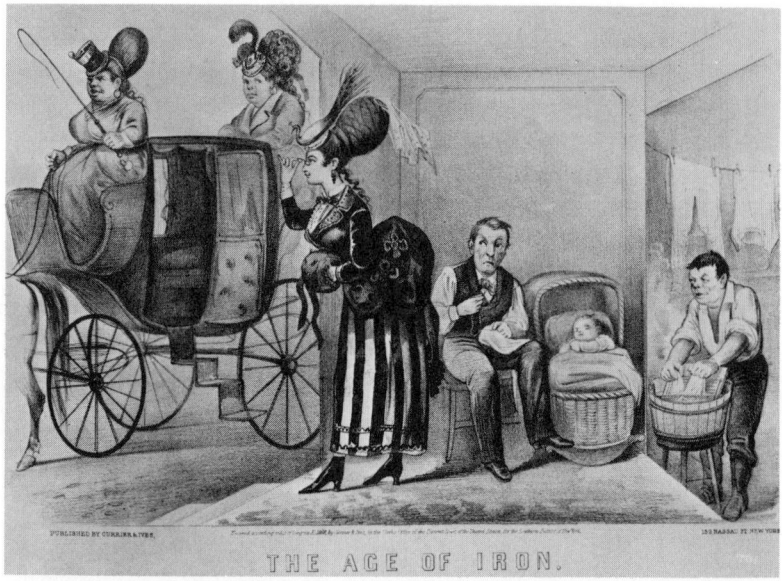

2.5 "The Age of Iron," by Currier and Ives, 1868, a satire about the impossibly extravagant demands of women's rights advocates, ridiculing women who forget their place. Women prepare to go out into urban space while men remain indoors sewing, washing, and minding the baby. Both class and gender are depicted: the coachwomen and the laundryman are working class, while the woman with the bustle and the man with the waistcoat seem to be their employers, and the main tension is in the glance he gives her departing back. This was not a response to female demands for male sharing of domestic work, but a joke about the silly things that would happen if women entered public life. (Library of Congress)

Evolution of the Public Landscape

Whitman's zeal to create a democratic public life in the American city was matched by Frederick Law Olmsted, founder of the profession of landscape architecture. On February 25, 1870, Olmsted traveled to Boston to address the American Social Science Association on the subject of "Public Parks and the Improvement of Towns." Already well known for his work in creating Central Park, in New York City, Olmsted gave a bold lecture contending that the American city should be replanned to foster friendly associations among its citizens, rich and poor, female and male, young and old, whether socialites from the salons or immigrants from the steerage.[12] The impetus for this urban spatial ideal was not democracy as an abstraction but specific demands for the equality of women and the assimilation of immigrants, mid-nineteenth-century political events that challenged all earlier definitions of public and private life.

In his address Olmsted defined a backward society as a nonurban society where the "men counted their women with their horses." Olmsted argued that in a modern society, women would seek their liberation in the city: "We all recognize that the tastes and dispositions of women are more and more potent in shaping the course of civilized progress, and we may see that women are even more susceptible to . . . [the] townward drift than men." Like Whitman, he valued the traditional family but also recognized the independent needs of women and children. Olmsted confessed himself "impatient of the common cant which assumes that the strong tendency of women to town life, even though it involves great privations and dangers, is a purely senseless, giddy, vain, frivolous, and degrading one." Instead, he claimed that the city would attract single, employed women because of its social life and would attract married women because publicly owned urban infrastructure and socialized labor would relieve them from the isolation and drudgery of the private, patriarchal household. He speculated about the possibility of providing municipal hot-air heat to every home and suggested that public laundries, bakeries, and kitchens would promote "the economy which comes by systematizing and concentrating, by the application of a large apparatus, processes which are otherwise conducted in a desultory way, wasteful of human strength."[13]

It is extremely revealing that Olmsted made little distinction between public sidewalks, public central heating for every home, and public kitchens. He and other social science idealists saw the era of industrial capitalism, when public space and urban infrastructure were created, as a time of urban evolution toward a more equal way of life. (He believed that model suburbs with common land, such as Riverside, Illinois, could be linked to the city and could also contribute to such goals, although he abhorred suburban sprawl.) Olmsted adopted his belief in evolution as a disciple of Charles Fourier, but many other socialists and feminists, including Edward Bellamy, August Bebel, Charlotte Perkins Gilman, Karl Marx, and Friedrich Engels, substituted other theories of human evolution and came to similar conclusions. All these American and European theorists saw the industrial capitalist city as the product of an economic system that would give way to a completely industrialized, urban, socialist society utilizing modern technology and socialized labor to handle not only industrial production but also housework and social services.

In this light, it is important to see that Olmsted's view of the public landscape as an expression of human social evolution was linked to housing and social service programs. These programs were the cooperative residential neighborhoods advocated by Melusina Fay Peirce (beginning in 1869), the municipal housekeeping campaigns launched in the temperance movement by Frances Willard (beginning in the 1870s), and the Social Settlement houses developed by Jane Addams (in the late 1880s). Olmsted with his public parks, Peirce with her ideal of model neighborhoods, and Willard and Addams with their plans for model urban social services together envisaged an ideal American city where landscape architecture, housing, and urban physical and social planning were intertwined. These activists did not divide private life from public life, domestic programs from public programs, economic initiatives from social initiatives, factual knowledge from ethical stances about that knowledge. Their confident wholeness of purpose was their great strength, and the understanding that existed between environmental reformers, reformers in the women's movement, and social scientists contributed in no small way to the appeal this urban vision had for great numbers of American women and men alike.

Domestic Evolution and the Homelike World

Peirce and her followers concerned themselves with developing a woman's perspective on the relationship between housing and household work.[14] For six decades these women, the material feminists, defined their movement with one powerful idea: that women must create new kinds of homes with socialized housework and child care before they could become truly equal members of society. They raised fundamental questions about what was called "woman's sphere" and "woman's work." They challenged two characteristics of industrial capitalism: the physical separation of household space from public space, and the economic separation of the domestic economy from the political economy. They experimented with new forms of neighborhood organizations, including housewives' cooperatives, as well as new building types, including the kitchenless house, the day care center, the public kitchen, and the community dining club. By redefining housework and the housing needs of women and their families, they pushed architects and urban planners to consider housing design as the spatial context for family life. The material feminists thought that domestic space in apartment hotels and new cooperative suburbs[15] promoted domestic evolution in the same way that Olmsted believed public space in parks and parkways promoted urban evolution.

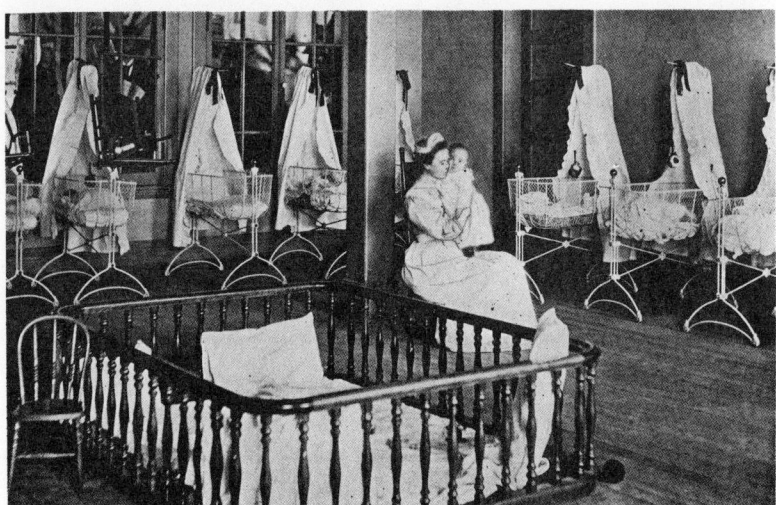

2.6 Nursery and day-care center, The Children's Building, World's Columbian Exhibition, Chicago, 1893.

During this period, Frances Willard, Jane Addams, and other leaders of the temperance and settlement movements were demanding women's active presence in urban public space and developing a theory of municipal housekeeping as their contribution to the "city of the faithfulest friends." They believed thay were bringing domestic virtues to public life, and they justified women's urban activism as an extension of their work in the home. This activism began in the winter of 1873, a depression year, when temperance women of southern Ohio launched the passionate speeches and startling public marches that Willard later compared to a western prairie fire: ". . . like the fires we used to kindle on the Western prairies, a match and a wisp of grass were all that was needed, and behold the spectacle of a prairie on fire . . . no more to be captured than a hurricane."[16] The Crusades, or the Women's Whiskey Wars as popular journalism referred to them, eventually mobilized tens of thousands of American women to demonstrate in the streets of their towns and cities, to claim public space and political power in new ways, while closing down saloons. This militance flared among women who had never prayed aloud in public, never presided at public meetings, never demonstrated in the streets, and, of course, were not allowed to vote.[17] They were not merely prim, severe anti-booze eccentrics, but political women with a complex purpose and a logical spatial target who used the rhetoric of domesticity in new ways.

The year after the Crusades began, Frances Willard founded the Women's Christian Temperance Union, a national organization based on the crusading spirit of the Whiskey Wars.[18] With the WCTU, Willard attacked the separation of private life and public life on behalf of women. The WCTU ultimately became the most powerful women's organization in the United States, with two hundred thousand members here and two million affilliates world wide, dedicated to temperance, women's suffrage, and urban reform. Willard defined women's urban work as an essential extension of the "home protection" demanded in the earlier temperance crusades. Her slogan "municipal housekeeping" joined women's presence in urban space and women's traditional work in a metaphor of political cleanup. Willard's acid comment that "men have made a dead failure of municipal government, just as they would of housekeeping" led to her argument that good government was only good housekeeping on a large scale.[19] Her municipal housekeeping campaigns attacked

the corruption and filth of the American city in an era when many
justified urban horrors as the "survival of the fittest." When WCTU
women came out of their homes and into the city, they aimed at
regulating industry, ending political corruption, improving housing,
education and health, and organizing trade unions for women workers. "Make the whole world homelike," said Willard. "Do everything."[20]

In this nurturant, political effort settlement workers such as Jane
Addams and members of trade unions, suffrage groups, and wom-
en's clubs joined WCTU women. Over several decades, the settlement workers built complex urban institutions to bring together
individuals of different economic and ethnic backgrounds to reform
the American economy and restore a sense of home and community
to the American city. As a homelike public place in the heart of the
slums, Jane Addams's Hull-House inspired over a hundred similar
settlement house projects. Its activities spanned a broad range of
interests but reformers stressed that they could extend the spirit of
home to all new immigrants by "settling" in poor neighborhoods.
At Hull-House groups of city gardners cultivated vacant lots; the
residents built the first urban playground in Chicago; they created a
child care center for children of employed mothers. They ran education classes on all kinds of subjects for children and adults, cultural to practical, from symphonies to shoemaking. *Hull-House Maps
and Papers,* a survey of the physical and economic conditions of
the slums of Chicago published in 1895, was a major American
research effort on the need for urban physical planning and social
services.[21] Various residents collaborated on this book and ultimately held many influential policymaking positions in city, state,
and national government to implement its conclusions. Like Olmsted,
the social settlement planners stressed equal access to public space
as a healing and strengthening force in a democratic American society. The advocate approach to urban physical and social planning
was certainly nourished right in the Hull-House dining room; when
settlement residents such as Florence Kelley and Mary Simkovitch
called the first national urban planning conference in 1909, their
leadership had long been acknowledged.

The settlement workers and the temperance workers formed the
coalitions that led to the reforms of the Progressive movement and
changed the standards of American urban politics. Unfortunately as
these women gained a popular audience, they and their organiza-

tions were pushed aside by ministers, politicians, planners, and social workers, men who began to take over leadership. Women had created a direct political challenge to their seclusion in the home by demanding a homelike city. Yet many men preferred to promote better government by *men* as defenders of women and children in the home rather than to accept direct female power. The Progressive Era thus was a time when women's activism and rage forced change but did not control the shape of change. The right to vote, won in 1920, implied that women would have the political power to make the "homelike world" a reality, but the same period unleashed the Red Scare, and red-baiting of politically active women.

"Good Homes Make Contented Workers"

In the early twentieth century, many battles for parks, housing, and better planning were lost, and the distinctive parts of the urban spatial ideal developed by Whitman, Olmsted, Peirce, Willard, and Addams were fragmented and misunderstood. The dense urban centers of industrial capitalism were succeeded by the suburbanized cities of modern capitalism.[22]

This change occurred over several decades. Conservative Americans had called on the social Darwinist argument of the "survival of the fittest" to excuse the sordid living and working conditions of the nineteenth-century city slums, but social reformers in the 1880s and 1890s eventually began to express aspirations for a nation of healthy Americans. Workers' anger also hastened change. Between the 1880s and 1920s, reformers began to fear that the American city would be torn apart by angry, propertyless people. The Haymarket Riots of 1886, the Pullman Strike of 1893, the New York garment strike of 1909, the Paterson mill strike of 1911, and the Lawrence strike of 1912 publicized workers' grievances and employers' lack of concern. Then in 1919, at the conclusion of World War I, four million people were on strike and the future of the American city seemed very uncertain. Not only were workers angry, veterans were upset that Blacks and women had taken over the jobs of white males during the war.[23]

Between the 1890s and the 1920s the National Civic Federation had brought together manufacturers and some labor leaders to discuss industrial policies and long-term planning. By 1919, many manufacturers began to concede that not only better wages but also better housing were essential underpinings for urban social order. Urban planners and housing reformers such as Lawrence Veiller and John Nolan had long been campaigning for better dwellings to help foster "a conservative point of view in the working man." In the post World War I era, many union leaders and corporate leaders finally agreed on this tactic. Trade unionists, who had concentrated their organizing on skilled male workers, wanted what they called a "family wage." This meant a wage for male workers high enough to assure that wives and children would not work in industry, a tactic that would, at the same time, lower the threat of wage competition by decreasing the available labor force. Industrialists, who had concentrated their money making around production rather than consumption, wanted to expand their domestic markets for manufactured goods. They saw the better-paid workers' families as potential consumers of items such as furniture, appliances, and automobiles. Both union leaders and manufacturers agreed that a more spacious, mass-produced form of housing was essential to enable workers and their families to consume. A growing number of employers decided that it would be a good idea to miniaturize and mass-produce the Victorian patriarchal, suburban businessman's dwelling for the majority of white, male, skilled workers.

As one corporate official described his attitude toward workers: "Get them to invest their savings in homes and own them. Then they won't leave and they won't strike. It ties them down so they have a stake in our prosperity." Or as a housing expert put it, "Happy workers invariably mean bigger profits, while unhappy workers are never a good investment." He advocated long home mortgages, because purchases of homes rather than rentals would promote steady employment: "Good homes make contented workers." Or as another sloganeer put it, showing the capitalist and the worker shaking hands: "After work, the happy home."[24] One political analyst has argued that the promotion of suburban home ownership of this kind effectively split the territorial base of the Socialist party, because it was aimed at native-born skilled workers, who moved out of the tenements, leaving the more recent immigrants in the inner-city.[25]

What did this strategy mean for the wives of working men? Garbed in rhetoric about a woman's place in the home, it reinforced the pressures on women to get out of the wartime labor force in 1919 in order to give their jobs to veterans. As men were to become homeowners responsible for regular mortgage payments, their wives were to become home managers taking care of the spouse and children. The male worker would return from his day in the factory to a private domestic world. In his house, he would find a retreat from the tense world of work, and his physical and emotional maintenance would be the duty of his wife. Thus the private suburban house was a stage set for the effective gender division of labor. It made gender appear a more important self-definition than class, race, or ethnicity; it made consumption seem to be as crucial as production.

Selling Mrs. Consumer

Corporations moving from World War I defense industries into peacetime production of domestic appliances and automobiles also found private homes and housewives' consumption of their products a key to success. Herbert Hoover, as Secretary of Commerce, served as president of Better Homes in America, an organization founded in 1922, designed to boost home ownership and consumption. There were several thousand local chapters composed of manufacturers, realtors, builders, and bankers. The rapid development of the advertising industry in the 1920s was also influential because advertisers promoted the private suburban dwelling as a setting for all other purchases.[26] The occupants of the suburban dwelling took on more than the house itself; they also had to have a car, a stove, a refrigerator, a vacuum cleaner, a washer, and carpets. Christine Frederick explained it all in 1929 in *Selling Mrs. Consumer,* a book dedicated to Hoover that promoted home ownership and easier consumer credit and advised advertising executives and marketing managers about manipulating American women. Frederick was particularly insistent that young married couples furnishing their first homes should be seen as prime consumers: "There is a direct and vital business interest in the subject of young love and marriage."[27]

By 1931 Hoover was President and his Commission on Home Building and Home Ownership established the private, single family home as a national goal to promote long term economic growth and recovery from the depression.[28] Eulogizing the rural ideal of "Home Sweet Home," Hoover noted that "Americans would never sing songs about a pile of rent receipts." Elementary schools taught students to make models of ideal houses. General Electric ran a design competition for a dream house for "Mr. and Mrs. Bliss" in 1935. In 1939 the personal income tax deduction for mortgage interest was introduced.[29] Still, this was brave talk with little action. Housing construction had peaked in the mid-1920s, and home ownership for the majority of urban workers remained a distant goal during the foreclosures of the Depression years and the housing shortages of the war years.

2.7 Selling Mrs. Consumer: the groom offers his bride the Domestic Sewing Machine, a ritual gesture equating consumption with love, 1882.

2.8 The realtor offers the housewife a Kitchen Aid dishwasher, *House and Home,* October 1956. This ritual gesture resembles the previous one, but the advertisement suggests that this brand of appliance helps builders sell more homes by persuading "Mrs. Consumer."

I'll Buy That Dream

After World War II, the strategy of homeownership for white male workers articulated more than twenty years earlier became reality. As in the years following World War I, many defense corporations wanted to give women's jobs to veterans and convert some defense industries to production of consumer goods. And this time national mortgage insurance programs were in place, the American banking system was ready, highway systems were organized, and the speculative builders took over.

Veterans, with their World War II savings, were encouraged by a national policy promoting home ownership in suburban areas to

2.9 William Garnett, four views of a California tract under construction: after bulldozing; after house and garage foundations were poured; during framing; and as salable space. (Copyright, William Garnett, 1955)

participate in the transformation of the American city and the American economy. The central city was abandoned by many younger workers and their families in favor of the suburban ring. Young people left their parents and kin in the ethnic neighborhoods of the old central cities and, whistling the hit tune, "I'll Buy That Dream," bought new cars and went to live in new tract houses, with nothing down and low FHA monthly payments. Just as the native-born

workers had left the more recent immigrants behind in the suburbanization of the 1920s, so the white workers left minority workers behind in the inner cities in the 1950s.[30] By the late 1970s, three-quarters of all AFL-CIO members were purchasing their homes on long mortgages.[31] Most of these families, headed by working men, identified themselves as "middle class."

The United States housing stock increased from 34.9 million

occupied units in 1940 to 80.4 million occupied units in 1980, as tracts of small houses, usually without day care centers or community facilities, spread over the countryside.[32] Housing starts by month and year became an important indicator of economic growth. In the forties, 9.8 million new units were constructed. In the fifties, this rose to 14.9 million. In the sixties, it climbed to 16.8 million. In the seventies, it totaled 22.4 million, despite a severe recession. Eventually only a quarter of the national housing stock consisted of pre–World War II structures.[33] Housing Americans was, as Hoover had predicted, a big, big business, and American banking, real estate, and transportation interests were intimately involved.

For both the huge merchant builders who emerged in the late 1940s and the small developers who built a few houses at a time, the heart of the housing business was the single-family detached house, accounting for 53.9 million units.[34] In the years between 1945 and 1980, suburban sprawl became a common phrase in Americans vocabularies; Malvina Reynolds sang "Little Boxes." Year by year, from 1950 to 1980, the dream houses got bigger and bigger until Americans enjoyed the largest amount of private housing space per person ever created in the history of urban civilization. Over 91 percent of U.S. households had one person per room or fewer in 1970; over 29.4 percent of U.S. households had seven or more rooms in their home in 1976.[35] The construction industry felt confident enough to announce that what was good for housing was good for the country.[36]

The dream house replaced the ideal city as the spatial representation of American hopes for the good life. It not only triumphed over the model town, the dream house also prevailed over two other models of housing, one based on an ideal of efficient collective consumption of scarce resources, the other based on an ideal of the model neighborhood. Yet the dream house had its critics, and by the late 1970s their accounting of its environmental, social, and economic costs could not be ignored.

What is the use of a house if you haven't got a tolerable planet
to put it on?

Henry David Thoreau

She felt bought and paid for, and it was all of a piece; the
house, the furniture, she, all were his, it said so on some
piece of paper.

Marilyn French

3

AWAKENING FROM THE DREAM

The personal happiness and economic potential of many Americans have been thwarted by the design of housing and public space, yet few of us employ the language of real estate development, architecture, or urban planning to trace the contours of loneliness, boredom, weariness, discrimination, or financial worry in our lives. It is much more common to complain about time or money than to fume about housing and urban space. In part this is because we think of our miseries as being caused by personal problems rather than social problems. Americans often say, "There aren't enough hours in the day," rather than "I'm frantic because the distance between my home and my work place is too great." Americans also say, "I can't afford the down payment to live in Newton," or in Marin County, or in Beverly Hills, rather than "I'm furious because only the affluent can live in a safe and pleasant neighborhood." Together, space, time, and money intersect to establish the physical settings where all the events of life will be staged. Whether they are harmonious or discordant, residential neighborhoods reverberate with meaning, and disappointments about them affect women and men of varied ages, income levels, ethnic groups, and racial groups.

The house is an image of the body, of the household, and of the household's relation to society; it is a physical space designed to mediate between nature and culture, between the landscape and the larger urban built environment. In this sense the dwelling is the basis of both architectural design (as archetypal shelter) and physical planning (as the replicable unit used to form neighborhoods, cities, and regions). Because the form of housing carries so many aesthetic, social, and economic messages, a serious misfit between a society and its housing stock can create profound unrest and disorientation. As we have seen, the squalid tenements of the nineteenth and early twentieth centuries reflected class oppression that at times became a threat to the urban social order. Today the problems of a housing strategy based on suburban dream houses underscore the conflicts of class, gender, and race that characterize our society.

Outgrowing Our Prescriptive Architecture

The United States is a society of diverse cultures and diverse household types, yet for the last four decades most American space has been shaped around a simplistic prescription for satisfaction. American cities and American housing have been designed to satisfy a nation of predominantly white, young, nuclear families, with father as breadwinner, mother as housewife, and children reared to emulate these same limited roles. While prescriptive literature in the form of sermons, housekeeping guides, and etiquette manuals has always been available to describe and define the ideal middle-class Christian family in our society, our post–World War II cities mark the triumph of a prescriptive architecture of gender on a national scale.

Today only a small percentage of American families include a male breadwinner, a nonemployed housewife, and two or more children under eighteen. The valiant World War II heroes and their blushing brides have now retired. Their children have grown up. The predominant family type is the two-earner family. The fastest growing family type is the single-parent family, and nine out of ten single parents are women. Almost a quarter of all households consist of one person living alone, be they young singles or the elderly. Yet Americans have not acknowledged that the cities and the housing built for the war heroes are no longer appropriate today.

Space is the problem rather than time or money. And this problem is inextricably tied to an architecture of home and neighborhood that celebrates a mid-nineteenth century ideal of separate spheres for women and men. This was an artificial environment that the most fanatical Victorian moralists only dreamed about, a utopia of male-female segregation they never expected the twentieth century to build. While maxims about true womanhood and manly dominance were the staple of Christian, bourgeois Victorian culture in the United States, England, and many other countries, only in the United States in the twentieth century were so many material resources committed to reinforcing these ideas by spatial design.

The veteran, his young wife, and their prospective children appeared as the model family of 1945. Millions of them confronted a serious housing shortage. In the aftermath of war, employing the veterans and removing women from the paid labor force was a national priority. So was building more housing, but the two ideals were conflated. Developers argued that a particular kind of house would help the veteran change from an aggressive air ace to a com-

3.1 Prospective buyers standing in line to view a furnished model home, by Kaiser, California, 1950s. Spending Sunday afternoons visiting model homes became a new family pastime.

muting salesman who loved to mow the lawn. He would also assist his wife to forget her skills as Rosie the Riveter and begin to enjoy furnishing her dream house in suburbia. As we have seen, Better Homes in America had tried to house the post–World War I family in segregated suburban residential communities, and this attempt, thwarted by the Great Depression, only intensified commitment to the same prescription for family bliss after World War II. The problem is that the spatial rules could have been written by Catharine Beecher in 1870; by 1920 they were anachronistic; by 1950, preposterous.

The outdated ideal of a particular kind of family life, however, had a function. Exaggerated, socially created male and female roles defined not only the labor market and housing design but also the parameters of urban planning. Postwar propaganda told women that their place was in the home, as nurturers; men were told that their place was in the public realm, as earners and decision makers. This ideal, gender-based division of labor described women's and men's economic, social, and political relationships to the private and public realms as distinctly different. Segregation of roles by gender was so pervasive and acceptable that it was used to justify housing schemes characterized by segregation by age, race, and class that couldn't be so easily advertised. In the richest nation in the world, economic deprivation, ethnic differences, age segregation, and racial segregation were hidden by a spatial prescription for married suburban bliss that emphasized gender as the most salient feature of every citizen's experience and aspirations.

Creating the Critique

One could define the essence of any utopian design as the desire to create a society where no one counts costs, and no one even understands the concept of costs or the human inability to make everything perfect for everyone. A cartoon in the New York *Times* in 1977, showing a dream house devouring a family, expressed a growing panic about our national housing strategy as a utopian design on which the long deferred costs had finally come due. Dream houses got out of control economically, environmentally, and socially because they carried unacknowledged costs: they required large amounts of energy consumption; they demanded a great deal of unpaid female labor; they were often unavailable to minorities; and eventually, they overwhelmed the institutions that had traditionally financed them. The *Times'* cartoonist forged two and a half decades of partial, tentative criticism from architects, planners, environmentalists, women, minorities, and economists into one powerful image of American life in decline.

The earliest critics of the dream house came from the professions of architecture and urban planning. They were angry because the basic building activity had bypassed both professions. Contractors received funding from federal housing agencies, bought farm land in a remote part of a metropolitan area—preferably a place without a planning board—and started "raising houses instead of potatoes" (as they said in Long Island). Many architects were appalled by the banal designs the builders threw up. William J. Levitt, for example, was considered one of the best developers of solidly constructed houses. He became a popular hero for the speed with which he built homes for veterans, but he simply built one design over and over in his first development.[1] Praised for his skill in reorganizing the logistics of traditional home construction, he responded to aesthetic critiques by developing three or four "models" that could be alternated on every street, a practice still followed by many builders today. Levitt's peace offering was to sponsor interior design contests for Levittown residents and invite well-known designers and architects to be the judges of the interior schemes created by the residents, whether modern, Early American, or country French.[2]

The predictable banality of it all was enforced by the federal agency responsible for funding: FHA design guidelines actually penalized any builder who hired a sophisticated architect by lowering the mortgagable values of houses that did not conform to their norms of design.[3] Flat roofs were particularly suspect at the FHA. (Curiously, Nazi policy had also decreed that only peaked-roof houses suited the Aryan race.)[4] But flat roofs had characterized many of the best multi-family housing designs in the twentieth century, including those of Irving Gill, Henry Wright, Clarence Stein, Rudolph Schindler, and other American and European architects who had worked on low cost housing but managed to make it harmonious and often elegant.

Architects gnashed their teeth, but their social and aesthetic critiques failed to address the basic gender division of labor. While they proposed the advantages of hiring skilled designers or of providing more community facilities and more shared spaces, they did not attack the Victorian programing at the heart of dream-house culture. Some American architects working with the material feminists had led the world in the development of innovative, nonsexist[5] housing prototypes between 1870 and 1940, but the practitioners of the 1950s could only deal with suburbia by asking for a bigger share of the individual commissions. In truth, most architects loved to design large single-family houses, one at a time, and this predilection shaped the profession's acquiescence.[6]

Urban planners, like architects, were early critics of the dream-house strategy, but their concerns, while tied to larger issues of private and public space, still lacked a thorough social foundation. Planners perceived that hasty, uncontrolled suburban developments for veterans' families would produce houses without adequate schools, parks, or other community facilities. They saw that suburban residents would then be taxed to pay for these improvements. while the speculative developers used their profits to build yet another subdivision. They predicted that new suburbs would drain the social and economic activities of the center city, and that urban blight and suburban sprawl would work together to wear away the best pedestrian districts of inner-city areas.[7] Some of them recognized the racism of all-white tracts, and worried about the consequences of "white flight" from inner cities.

All of these events came to pass, and yet, while planners decried haste, shoddy building, and greed, while they deplored racial segregation and lack of public transportation, few spoke about the outworn gender stereotypes embodied in the basic definition of the household. Indeed, planners themselves relied on the Victorian template of patriarchal family life when they exhorted Americans to pay more attention to community facilities to strengthen that same idealized family. Even Lewis Mumford, the most trenchant of all urban critics, rhapsodized: ". . . who can doubt that Victorian domesticity, among the upper half of the middle classes, was encouraged by all the comforts and conveniences, the sense of internal space and peace, that brought the Victorian father back nightly to his snug household." He ardently supported providing "a young couple with a dwelling house and a garden" to continue this model, while adding that the city planner must also "invent public ways of performing economically what the old, three-generation bourgeois family once privately encompassed"[8]—care for the elderly.

Planners also used the same outworn family model to study residential choices and to measure needs for new services. The "head of household" and his "journey to work" framed their locational concerns, instead of detailed analysis of the different needs and different experiences of men, women, and children.[9] Even when caucuses of Marxist urban planners responded to the extreme urban fiscal crises of the late 1970s, they too based their statements about housing reform around an unexamined acceptance of the dream house and the gender division of labor underlying it.[10] They proposed a socialist banking policy to keep traditional housing afloat.

In the late 1960s and early 1970s, the activists of two major social movements generated enough anger about the single-family detached houses to spur broader cultural critiques. Ecologists and feminists took up where the designers and planners left off: the former stressing the dire consequences of environmental decline, the latter emphasizing the crippling effects of stereotyped roles for women and men. Both movements stressed that consciousness must be followed by active protest. They organized the disaffected to rally against some of the excesses of the post–World War II American life style. Both stressed democracy and emphasized that personal life represented political choices; neither put architecture in the foreground, but they generated enough debate to illuminate basic conceptual shortcomings of both architecture and urban design.

Environmental Awareness

Environmentalists and energy planners pointed out that American dream houses and their dispersed settlement pattern used more nonrenewable resources than any society had ever consumed before, because builders had assumed that energy would always be cheaper than materials or labor. Thus Americans, as about six percent of the world's population, account for about a third of the world's nonrenewable resource consumption every year.[11] A white child born to a dream-house family in the United States will consume many times more resources than a Third World child over its lifetime.

These activists showed that the imbalance was partly the result of deliberate but uninformed choices in housing design. When builders of the 1950s constructed millions of dream houses lined up on suburban tracts, they broke with traditional regional responses to climate (typical of the adobes of the Southwest or the saltbox houses of New England) in favor of using standardized plans and materials. Huge picture windows created patterns of heat gain and heat loss that had to be compensated for by year round air-conditioning or

3.2 "Win a houseful of beautiful furniture!" Utopia on the model of single-family bliss and over-consumption, Pledge Furniture Sweepstakes.

intensive heating, depending on whether the standardized house was in Arizona or Massachusetts. Traditional siting also broke down. Builders' bulldozers leveled hills and trees that might have provided shade; the same house was built facing north, south, east, and west because the builders didn't care about the position of the sun so much as the profitability of the tract.

The dream houses, because of their isolation from community facilities and from each other, also required numerous private purchases of appliances such as stoves, clothes washers, and refrigerators. These appliances were often designed to increase rather than minimize the use of energy: in some cases the same manufacturers sold both consumer appliances and municipal generating equipment,[12] as a reinforcement of corporate interests. In addition to the wasteful use of energy, some appliances and all plumbing fixtures intensified the use of water. Toilets, garbage disposals, clothes washers, and dishwashers created an enormous volume of water usage in arid regions as well as in more temperate climates, by continuing the American practice of using water as a medium of carrying waste away, rather than reserving water for needed human use and recycling garbage and human waste as compost.

As the suburbs grew, the infrastructure of municipal water, gas, and power lines and roads expanded, and expanded again. Once on the path to lower densities, many cities found it hard to justify public transit expenditures. The journey to work for Americans averaged nine miles one way in 1976, when Americans owned 41 percent of the world's passenger cars to connect home and paid work. Indeed, they had more cars per household than children.[13] To get to distant houses, thousands of miles of roads and freeways were needed. But very few people wanted their dream house next to a busy freeway or shrouded in smog. To provide gas and electricity for these same houses, storage tanks and generating plants were needed, but no one wanted to be near them either.

Ultimately American corporations had to resort to some desperate strategies to assure continued energy consumption. Oil leases in foreign countries brought the accompanying threat of foreign wars. Nuclear power plants and liquid natural gas (LNG) terminals at home were even riskier strategies because of their long-term vulnerability to accidents and because of the lack of safe disposal procedures for nuclear waste materials. In the late 1970s, *The Ladies' Home Journal* carried a pro-nuclear advertisement showing housewives holding up a variety of home appliances and thanking the utility for creating nuclear power to keep their appliances going. The phrase "dream house" began to acquire ironic overtones. Even those families who would have accepted nearby gas or electrical installations refused to be near a nuclear plant or an LNG terminal.

The political movement launched by environmentalists had one great success by 1982. Steady, sustained political pressure on both utilities and government regulatory agencies had made it clear that nuclear power plants were financially unprofitable to design, build, and operate. This citizen resistance to poor energy planning marked a significant achievement for Americans concerned about the safety of their neighborhoods and the social responsibility of major corporations. Victories were won in the face of massive expenditures by utilities for political contributions and extensive lobbying efforts by utility executives speaking to many different audiences. The environmentalists' common sense dominated the debates; revelations about nukes built on earthquake faults and nukes built from upside-down blueprints did the rest.

When it came to renewable energy sources, the environmentalists produced only partial reforms. Conservation education often stressed saving more than sharing. Retrofitting of existing buildings might

involve elaborate technical skills, but economic and social reprograming, essential to the better use of space, was often ignored.
Thus ecologists Helga and William Olkowski criticized the ecolog-
ical and economic parasitism of the suburban dwelling: "The typical home now largely wastes the solar income it daily receives and
the mineral resources that pass through it. It takes from the forest
for its structure, furnishings, reading materials, and fuel as well.
The typical home also takes from the often fragile ecosystems of
estuary, swamp, desert and prairie for its food and fiber. It also uses
the waterways and mineral riches for its power and the products of
the marketplace. The house shelters its occupants, but to the larger
community it gives 'wastes.' These latter emerge unappreciated and
consequently unsorted: the metals with the glass, organic, paper,
and plastic all jumbled together; the toxic mixed with the benign.
Because the home is such a total parasite, as are its neighboring
urban habitats, it is not surprising that the occupants experience
themselves as victims or, at best, ineffectual ciphers in a large,
impersonal, centralized system." But the Olkowskis' powerful
experiment, the Integral Urban House, a collective project established by six adults, did not stress rethinking family life so much as
the introduction of urban agriculture and ecosystems analysis.[14] Other
designers of solar homes who received wide publicity had far less
to offer; some designs were based on new environmental gadgets
for the old dream house but retained the model family in 2,500
square feet of space.

In the same way, discussion of new solar technologies, such as
photovoltaic cells, often stopped at a certain level of technological
innovation. Big corporations (utilities and defense contractors)
received most of the government research and development money
to study the profitable future production of these technologies.
Neighborhood applications and small-town applications were seldom given the same level of support.[15] Here a mix of economic,
social, and technical reforms could have resulted in more innovative
programing. Using photovoltaic cells to cover the roof of every
existing dream house would turn the United States into a nation of
fifty-four million private power plants. Scale is still the most misunderstood environmental issue in the so-called appropriate technology movement. Between the giant corporations and the tiny
houses, environmental alternatives require new social, economic,
and architectural innovations as well as new, energy-saving inventions. While environmentalists are still developing a very effective
accounting of the wasteful, destructive patterns of present resource

3.3 Sketch of "The Integral Urban House" established by environmental activists with composting toilet, greenhouse, fish pond, and solar energy, Berkeley, California. (From *The Integral Urban House: Self-Reliant Living in the City* by Helga Olkowski, Bill Olkowski, Tom Javits, and the Farallones Institute Staff. Copyright © 1979 by Sierra Club Books. Reprinted by permission.)

use, they have not yet come to terms with the reconceptualization of the private home as the key to the next set of public issues they must address.

Feminist Unrest

The problems of domestic life documented by the women's movement also revolve around the hidden costs of building millions of homes on the Victorian model. The connections between home ownership, family structure, and women's status are complex. During the last three decades, while the majority of white male workers have achieved the dream houses in suburbia where their fantasies of proprietorship, authority, and consumption could be acted out, the majority of their spouses have entered the world of paid employment. Today, handicapped by the least suitable housing imaginable for employed wives and mothers, more than one out of two married women is in the paid labor force. (In 1890, the figure was one out of twenty.) Employed women often find themselves with two jobs: one at home, one at work. Pulled between unpaid work and paid work, women race from office or factory to home and back again. They know they have no time for themselves. They have to spend an inordinate amount of time simply struggling to get husbands or children to do a little more housework instead of leaving it all for Mom.[16]

While this pattern creates logistical problems for the employed housewife, those who stay home also have serious difficulties. Michele Rosaldo, a cultural anthropologist, argued that women's status is lowest in societies where women are most separated from public life.[17] And in the United States the suburban home is the single most important way of separating women, and thus lowering an individual woman's status. But as Bonnie Loyd, a geographer, points out, much of women's work in the household is status-producing work for the family, connected with the maintenance of the house.[18] So by glorifying her home through executing household tasks, a woman can guarantee her family's social status at the expense of her own. As Loyd notes, such activity often creates psychological conflict. This conflict increases when women who try to create interiors as a focus for entertaining come up against levels of consumption which are in fact new to them because of upward mobility. Terrified housewives who know little about designer furniture or antiques, cabinet work or colors, may consult women's magazines, home and life-style magazines, decorators, and department stores. Loyd quotes one psychiatrist who remarked in the 1950s of his female patients: "There is no time at which a woman is more apt to go to pieces than when she is engaged in decorating her home."[19]

Feminists of the 1960s, beginning with Betty Friedan, examined the relationships among women, advertisers, and mass-produced goods.[20] They saw the home as a box to be filled with commodities. Rugs and carpets need vacuuming, curtains need laundering, upholstered goods need shampooing—all fill up the domestic spaces to form colonial, Mediterranean, French Provincial, or some other ersatz decor. Women also criticized kitchens full of single-purpose appliances requiring frequent attention. These machines are lined up in one room, the kitchen, which is often designed to be isolated from the rest of family life. As one appliance manufacturer put it in *Good Housekeeping* in 1965: "This kitchen has almost everything. Tappan built-in electric range and oven, Tappan dish-washer and Tappan disposal, Tappan refrigerator. Only one thing's really missing. *You.*"

3.4 Housewife posed with the products of a week's work, Rye, New York. Photograph by Nina Leen, LIFE Mazagine, © 1947 Time, Inc.)

One of the most effective explorations of housewives' frustrations was an exhibit created in 1971, "Womanhouse," which incorporated the combined talents of twenty-six artists to transform an abandoned Los Angeles mansion into a series of environments. At the top of the staircase a mannequin in a wedding dress posed, suggesting the young bride's fascination with the dream house. At the bottom of the stairs her muddy train and two disembodied feet vanished into the wall. In the linen closet, another mannequin was trapped among the sheets and towels. In the kitchen, everything was painted pink, that stereotypically feminine color: the sink, the refrigerator, the potato peeler, the pots and pans, the walls. Inside the kitchen drawers newspaper linings revealed stories about women in public life. The bathtub contained colored sand, in the shape of a woman's body. As visitors to the exhibit touched the sand, the figure receded. After two weeks the woman disappeared. There were also rooms dedicated to a woman's enjoyment of her dream house as a place for privacy, fantasy, and playfulness. One room had huge toys, and in another, a crocheted spider web suggested a woman's place to spin out ideas.

The exhibition included some performances, and in one favorite theater piece, the artist simply walked to an ironing board and ironed sheets for thirty minutes. While the women decided it was hilarious, men were perplexed. "Womanhouse" addressed the ways that Americans have mystified the necessary work done in the house by isolating the housewife who cooks, cleans, and irons in a dream house. The artists illuminated some of women's positive feelings and attachments to domestic spaces as nurturing, controllable places, while criticizing the loneliness and isolation which many housewives encounter. Most effectively, they turned domestic space into public space temporarily by the appropriation of a residential structure for the exhibit, and thousands of visitors toured the house.

In the same way that the artists of "Womanhouse" protested the single-family home as an enclosure for women's lives, so the poets Adrienne Rich and Bernice Johnson Reagon cried out for change. Rich's "A Primary Ground," of 1974, told of the suffocation of traditional family life:

> Sensuality dessicates in words—
> risks of the portage, risks of the glacier
> never taken
> Protection is the genius of your house
> the pressure of the steam iron
> flattens the linen cloth again
> chestnuts puréed with care are dutifully eaten
> in every room the furniture reflects you
> larger than life, or dwindling

Most of all, Rich underlined the waste of female talent in this old pattern of domesticity:

> your wife's twin sister, speechless
> is dying in the house

> You and your wife take turns
> carrying up the trays,
> understanding her case, trying to make her understand.[21]

The image of "understanding her case" resonated through Rich's writings, as well as the demand for new forms of habitation.

In "The Fourth Month of the Landscape Architect," Rich fused images of pregnancy and a demand for the creation of a new kind of social space, as a female designer reviews the historical experience of women in her spatial imagination:

> I start to imagine
> plans for a house, a park
> . . .
> A city waits at the back of my skull
> eating its heart out to be born:
> how design the first
> city of the moon? how shall I see it
> for all of us who are done
> with enclosed spaces, purdah, the salon, the sweatshop loft,
> the ingenuity of the cloister?[22]

To read Rich's poems was to be exhorted to transcend the architecture of gender that diminished so many lives, yet it was only an exhortation and not a plan.

Writer, composer, and scholar, Bernice Johnson Reagon, in "My Black Mothers and Sisters," told feminists what the leaders of that struggle would need to be like:

> She could make space where there was none
> And she could organize the space she had
> My mama
> My grandmama
> Ms. Daniels
> dreamers who believed in being materialists—
> . . .
> We must apply energy to the development of our potential
> as parents
> as creative producers
> as the new way-makers.
> There must not be a woman's place for us
> We must be everywhere our people are
> or might be . . .[23]

To seize and hold more space, to redesign space, to deliver the goods of survival was an adequate definition of the task in its material and cultural dimensions, but still an exhortation.

While these women developed a critique of the suburban house and created a new consciousness that inspired some housewives to leave the seclusion of their homes, the critique did not go far enough. Gender was the culprit; material culture was satirized and criticized, but the architecture of gender was not reworked. The material feminists' idea that the gender division of labor was reinforced by spatial design was a lost intellectual tradition for most feminist activists of the 1970s, just as it was for architects and planners.

Indeed, feminists often agitated for something very like the single-family house even as they proposed to put it under women's control. Articles and manifestos on the housing needs of single-parent mothers stressed their desire not to be stigmatized by special housing "projects," their quite natural desire for their children to feel that their homes were "just like everyone else's."[24] Emergency shelters for battered women and their children—which involved integrated housing, child care, and social service arrangements—were usually seen as temporary solutions to women's housing needs, and the stated goal of such groups was to return the woman and her children to "normal" housing as soon as possible. Not surprisingly, this "normal" housing created great stress when women left the community of the shelter to return to the dream-house world.[25] In the 1970s, campaigns on behalf of employed women that stressed gaining economic justice through increased access to home ownership also accepted the dream-house design. At HUD, Donna Shalala's "Women and Mortgage Credit" program promoted female ownership with the slogan, "If a woman's place is in the home, it might as well be her own."[26] While this pragmatic program met with quick success, HUD's sponsorship of in-depth research by architects and urban planners revealed that long-term problems about the nature of housing design would demand far more complex policy initiatives. Neither a single-family house filled with solar gadgets nor home ownership for single mothers addresses the largest political and spatial issues inherent in the dream-house culture. The need to unite architects, planners, environmentalists, and feminists is urgent. As material conditions change, the shock reverberates. The economic problems of this housing form are finally provoking the intensive public policy review that no previous protest movement was ever able to generate.

Race, Gender, and the Economic Crisis

When Americans discuss the good life, they still speak about their hopes or their fears in terms of buying houses. Home ownership has not only symbolized a family's social status, but also guaranteed its economic security. The homeowner has been an owner-speculator, an identity acknowledged by one Florida developer who advertises his homes with the slogan, "To her, it's a nest; to him, a nest egg."[27] The "nest egg" explains why Americans struggle to "climb the ladder of life from renter to owner."[28] After years of mortgage payments to the bank (and substantial income tax deductions), some older homeowners have needed a speculative profit from the sale of the house to provide adequate retirement income. "For years your house has made you happy. Now it's going to make you rich," claims Jon Douglas, a California real estate agent seeking couples to list their homes for sale with him.[29]

Because home ownership has been closely associated with an individual's tax position and retirement income, it has created a sense of progress through life for the two-thirds of American families who have managed to attain it. The process of entering the market has been a rite of passage for thirty-year-olds equipped with the savings, marriage, and children that make this choice seem logical. Ownership and intense participation in the culture of home have characterized the middle years of life. For the retirees who sell their houses, detachment from gender roles has come with age and the speculative bonus of leaving suburbia.

Of course, one-third of American families have never had a chance to participate in these rituals. The roots of this problem lie in the five groups of Americans that were excluded from home ownership in the late 1940s. First, white women of all classes were expected to gain access to housing through their husbands. Second, the white elderly working class and lower middle class, who were no longer wage earners in the prime of life, were left behind in the old inner-city neighborhoods. Third, minority men of all classes were excluded from suburban home ownership when suburban tracts specifically excluded minority families; the FHA actually had agents whose job it was to keep minorities out, and they pressured any builder or lender who didn't agree.[30] Minority men were expected to become tenants in old slums in the central cities or owners in other segregated neighborhoods vacated by the "white flight" to the suburbs.

The majority of housing units in these segregated areas were difficult to finance since banks usually refused to give home mortgages in "redlined" ghetto areas. Fourth, minority women of all classes were not to be homeowners. So minority women often became the domestic servants in other women's suburban houses to earn the money to keep their own families together. Fifth, the minority elderly of all classes were left in the central cities. Close to their offspring, they often remained in three-generation households, sometimes caring for their grandchildren while their daughters worked outside the home.

Home ownership did develop among approximately 40 percent of minority male workers and their families in the late 1960s and 1970s, encouraged by the Fair Housing Act of 1968. The Act outlawed segregation and made blockbusting less possible. Redlining of ghetto areas continued, however, and kept many minority families from buying. Eventually the Equal Credit Opportunity Act of 1973 also made home ownership possible for a small number of women by forbidding discrimination by mortgage lenders on the basis of sex. This meant that mortgage bankers could not apply the so-called rule of thumb (perhaps better described as the rule of uterus) to discount the income of any women of child-bearing age by at least 50 percent when determining mortgage eligibility.[31] Still, very few employed women of any age had the income to qualify as sole owners, so this law helped two earner couples more than female heads of households. In this latter group, a home ownership rate of about 40 percent is similar to the minority rate.

As these groups moved into potential home ownership in the 1970s, they encountered increasingly inflated prices. Between 1970 and 1982, average housing prices across the nation jumped from $28,700 to $87,600.[32] The inflation was exacerbated as thirty million baby-boom children of the post–World War II era came of home-buying age in the 1970s; an equivalent or greater number will reach their thirties in the 1980s.[33] As the price of houses turned into a steadily rising line on real estage agents' graphs, millions of these young Americans, most of them the product of the veterans' suburban tracts, found that they couldn't afford to buy homes. They heard economists predict that they would be tenants most of their lives unless they could inherit their parents' houses. They added their frustrations to those of people long excluded from home ownership, including minorities and women for whom the economic obstacles remained although the legal and institutional barriers to home ownership were decreasing. A frantic scramble ensued as all three groups struggled to get into the housing market with "starter" homes.

As a result of the scramble, a rising percentage of household income was spent on housing. Americans' indebtedness for residential mortgages mushroomed from $661 billion in 1976 to $1,172 billion in 1982.[34] Finally the housing market was declared problematic by all but the most optimistic builders. Some introduced tiny "studio houses" and 300-sq.-ft. condominiums at exorbitant prices, and then attempted to distract attention from the size of these units with minimal furniture.[35] Others introduced "mingles" designs or "double master bedroom" plans to help new kinds of households squeeze themselves into outmoded land use and financing patterns, essentially proposing that two households could share one dream house or one condo, since each one could only afford half the asking price. Makers of mobile homes saw their chance. Changing the name of their product to "manufactured housing," they argued that they, and only they, could make houses cheaply enough to "save the American dream."

Bankers tried to patch up the economic crisis in the housing market with new balloon mortgage plans which deferred some interest payments for certain highly educated young professionals (charging them large sums at age thirty-five rather than at age thirty), with variable rate mortgages, and "growing equity" mortgages. These "creative financing" devices didn't do much for the mass market; they helped affluent people become overextended. Bankers also demanded new government subsidies for home buyers, and federal

3.5   Mobile homes on a sales lot in Connecticut, 1982.

3.6 When average house prices in the United States reached the $80,000 range, mobile-home lobbyists began arguing that only their product was cheap enough to "save the American dream." These two ads, aimed at urban planners to make them change zoning so that mobile homes could be legal in districts forbidding their use, were published in *Planning*, December 1982 and January 1983. "$43,475?" suggests that an "all new, 3BR" is still available, provided that planners "allow it to be." "You mean you don't *want* your own adult children living in your community?" tries to persuade readers that only mobile homes can save the three-generation family.

bailouts for failing savings and loan institutions. Real estate agents who were suffering too (from lack of commissions) began to take full-page advertisements in metropolitan papers, criticizing defense appropriations and deficit spending as harmful to the economy. One advertisement showed a little house with a peaked roof sagging under the weight of a sack of dollars for the Pentagon.

By 1983, two things were clear: certain groups were unable to enter the housing market, and many Americans who had already bought houses discovered that they couldn't afford to move. Others found that they couldn't even afford to stay where they were. Unemployment was high, and some people, caught with mortgage payments they couldn't meet, lost their homes to foreclosures. Neither the anxious owners nor the foreclosing banks could sell out because of the sluggish market. Some pessimistic economists began predicting a housing crash similar to the stock market crash of 1929, which started the Great Depression. They predicted that as high rates caused demand to fall, the building construction industry would slump and even fail. At the same time, rising unemployment in all sectors of the economy would contribute to increasing mortgage defaults, weakening the banking system (housing represents half of all its transactions) and further undermining the real estate market and the construction industry. Just as these economic interdependencies had promoted paper profits and growth, so they could contribute to a downward spiral of decline and even collapse.

Although the crisis did not become a crash, now is the moment of opportunity. The inadequacies of dream-house architecture can no longer be ignored. To renew democratic, self-sufficient traditions and survive as an urbanized, modern society, Americans must search for an adequate way to organize and pay for the spaces we live in, a way more compatible with the human life cycle. As a rich nation, we need to examine these issues in world perspective, if we care at all about world peace or about our international influence as a democracy. As a nation that has pioneered self-awareness and personal growth, we must also examine these housing issues from the perspective of our most intimate psychological and sexual desires as women and men. It is not enough to face the loss of the dream house with nostalgia about the end of an era, or with despair that America's resources stretched just so far and no farther. We need to reconstruct the social, economic, and spatial bases of our beliefs about individual happiness, solid family life, and decent neighborhoods.

There is no private life which is not determined by a wider public life.

George Eliot

part II

Rethinking

Private Life

4

HOME, MOM, AND APPLE PIE

Home is where the heart is. Home, sweet home. Whoever speaks of housing must also speak of home; the word means both the physical space and the nurturing that takes place there. In American life, it is hard to separate the ideal of home from the ideals of mom and apple pie, of mother love and home cooking. Rethinking home life involves rethinking the spatial, technological, cultural, social, and economic dimensions of sheltering, nurturing, and feeding society, activities often discussed as if they had existed unchanged from the beginning of time, unsmirched by capitalist development, technological manipulation, or social pressures. Social scientists, despite an interest in careful historical and economic analysis of family life, have scarcely explored the realities of domestic work.[1] Yet among feminists, mother love and home cooking have been celebrated targets provoking witty slogans, and it is understood that "Home, sweet home, has never meant housework, sweet housework," as Charlotte Perkins Gilman put it in the 1890s. It has also been clear that mothering is political. Lily Braun, the German feminist wrote: "After the birth of my son, the problems of women's liberation were no longer mere theories. They cut into my own flesh." But there has been no clear contemporary agreement in the United States, much less in the rest of the world, about what constitutes a fully egalitarian political position on domestic life, since male participation in nurturing work is in some ways incompatible with full recognition of female skills.[2]

Nurturing men and children has traditionally been woman's work. A brief analysis of such work in this country reveals the many separate tasks involved. Home cooking requires meals prepared to suit the personal likes and dislikes of family members. It is also one of the most satisfying and creative aesthetic activities for many women and men. House-cleaning requires sweeping, vacuuming, washing, polishing, and tidying the living space. Laundry requires sorting, washing, drying, folding or ironing, and putting away clean clothes and linens. Health care begins at home, and home remedies and prescribed medicines are distributed there. Mental health also begins at home when homemakers smooth out worries and provide emotional support so that all family members make successful connections and adjustments to the larger society. This is crucial not only for the education of young, but also for adults, who must sustain the pressures of earning a living, and for the aged, who need emotional support in their declining years.

Equally important are those ties to kin and community that maintain the social status and ethnic identity of the household. Maintenance of these ties often includes cultural rituals—the preparation of Thanksgiving dinners, Seders, Cinco de Mayo celebrations—with all the food, clothing, and special objects associated with each event. Recreation is another home task: arranging for children's play, family vacations, team sports for the young, parties and socials for adolescents. In urban societies, recreation also means arranging family experiences of nature, such as visits to parks or camping trips.

A good home life for a family of four took about sixty hours of nurturing work per week in 1982.[3] That work may have been more physically arduous in the past, but never more complex than now. Beyond the house and the immediate neighborhood, home life in most urban industrial societies today includes the management of extensive relationships with stores, banks, and other commercial service facilities, and with public institutions such as schools, hospitals, clinics, and government offices. Part of homemaking involves seeing that each family member's myriad personal needs are fully met. The new dress must be the right size; the new fourth grade teacher must understand a child's history of learning difficulties. Sometimes relationships with stores or institutions turn into adversary ones. If the new car is a lemon; if the grade school isn't teach-

4.1 Doris Lee, "Thanksgiving," 1935. (Collection of The Art Institute of Chicago)

ing reading fast enough, if the hospital offers an incorrect diagnosis, if the social security benefit check is late, then the stressful nature of the homemaker's brokering work between home, market, and state is exacerbated.

Italian social theorist Laura Balbo has written brilliantly about the key roles women play in sustaining these three sectors of modern society. Not only do homemakers make the bridge between commercial services, government bureaucracies, and the family. They are also low-paid providers of service performing heroic feats of overtime in the commercial or state sectors.[4] Much of the nurturing work of women requires a high level of skill, understanding, judgment, and patience. Yet when this work is conducted in the private home, women's time and skills often go unrecognized. Traditionally, marriage has been a homemaker's labor agreement—and a rather vague one at that—to provide personal service and nurturing to a man and their children for the duration of the relationship in exchange for financial support. Homemakers, as the one group of workers for whom no legal limits on hours, pension benefits, health insurance, or paid vacations have ever applied, have often found that the only time their work of cooking, cleaning, and nurturing compelled attention was when it was *not* done.

While "man's home is his castle," a woman often lacks any private space in her home. Society defines the ideal home as a warm, supportive place for men and children, but for homemakers it has always been a workplace, where a "woman's work is never done." While women may have gourmet kitchens, sewing rooms, and so-called "master" bedrooms to inhabit, even in these spaces the homemaker's role is to service, not to claim autonomy and privacy. There has been little nurturing for homemakers themselves unless they break down. In crises, women have looked to other women for emotional support. This may be the informal help acknowledged by homemaker and author Erma Bombeck, who dedicated one of her books to the other homemakers in her car pool: the women who, "when I was drowning in a car pool threw me a line. . . . always a funny one."[5] Women's support may also come from mothers, sisters, female friends, and female kin, who traditionally rally in crises. It may come from the range of services provided by the feminist movement, such as discussion groups, crisis centers, health centers, and hostels. Or it may come from husbands and children who finally notice when their wives and mothers break down.

American urban design, social policy planning, and housing design have seldom taken the complexity of homemaking into account. To rethink private life, it is essential to be explicit about the range of needs that homes and homemakers fulfill. Home life is the source of great cultural richness and diversity in an immigrant nation. Home life is also the key to social services—education, health, mental health. And home life is the key to successful urban design, in the patterning of residential space, commercial space, and institutional space, so that the linkages between home, market, and state can be sustained without undue hardship.

Yet in the last thirty years, the cultural strength of home has been debated: the success of the family in providing socialization for children has been challenged; the failure of many residential neighborhoods has been noted.[6] In light of the extensive literature on such topics as divorce and family violence, it is surprising to see how few alternative models of home life are discussed in a serious, sustained way. Many critics fail to distinguish between the traditional patriarchal family and other models of family life. Others welcome new models but fail to record the struggles to transform the patriarchal family that feminists have waged for at least two hundred years.[7] Innovative, egalitarian housing strategies that lead to new forms of housing cannot be developed without a reformulation of the traditional family and its gender division of nurturing work. Americans experiencing demographic changes need to make ideological changes, but before considering these let us examine the history of three alternative models of home, mom, and apple pie.

Three Models of Home

In the years between 1870 and 1930, home life provoked a phenomenal amount of political debate. Because this topic linked the Woman Question to the Labor Question, it attracted the attention of housewives, feminist activists, domestic servants, inventors, economists, architects, urban planners, utopian novelists, visionaries, and efficiency experts. Housework, factory work, and home were all susceptible to restructuring in the industrial city. Women and men of all political persuasions generally agreed that household work, as it had been carried out in the pre-industrial houses of the first half of the nineteenth century, left most women little time to be good wives and mothers. Industrial development was transforming all other work and workplaces, and it was expected that domestic work, and residential environments would be transformed as well. Activists raised fundamental questions about the relationships between women and men, households and servants. They explored the economic and social definitions of ''woman's work.'' They also raised basic questions about household space, public space, and the relationship between economic policies and family life concretized in domestic architecture and residential neighborhoods.

Many proposed solutions drew, in one way or another, on the possibilities suggested by new aspects of urban and industrial life: new forms of specialization and division of labor, new technologies, new concentrations of dwelling units in urban apartment houses or suburban neighborhoods. But all of the domestic theorists also had to deal with a number of unwelcome consequences of these new developments: hierarchy in the workplace; replacement of hand craft skills by mechanization; erosion of privacy in crowded urban dwellings; development of conspicuous domestic consumption in bourgeois neighborhoods. Although life in the isolated household was burdensome, inefficient, and stifling, many reformers feared that the socialization of domestic work would deprive industrial society of its last vestige of uncapitalized, uncompetitive, skilled work: that is, of mother love and home cooking.

For the most part, the major domestic strategies of the time have been ignored or misunderstood by both historians and political theorists. William O'Neill, in his popular book *Everyone Was Brave*, scathingly condemned the leaders of the nineteenth-century woman's movement as "weak and evasive" activists completely unable to tackle the difficult ideological problem of the family. He called them frustrated women who never understood that a revolution in domestic life was needed to achieve feminist aims.[8] Betty Friedan, in her recent book *The Second Stage*, reiterates O'Neill's views approvingly, as support for her contention that modern feminists must be the first to introduce serious concern for domestic life into feminist organizing.[9] While Friedan calls the family the "new feminist frontier," some contemporary Marxists still dismiss any serious theoretical concern with housework as a waste of time; they look to wage work to liberate women, much as Bebel did in 1883 and Lenin in 1919.[10]

Almost all American women involved in politics between 1870 and 1930 saw domestic work and family life as important theoretical and practical issues; the material feminists, as we have seen, argued that no adequate theory of political economy could develop without full consideration of domestic work.[11] They contended against both businessmen and Marxists with an eloquence that has rarely been equaled. Since the years between 1870 and 1930 produced three major strategies for domestic reform—Catharine Beecher's haven strategy, a Marxist industrial strategy, and the material feminists' neighborhood strategy—finding a new approach requires that all of these strategies, and the experiences of trying to implement them, are clearly understood.

The leading exponent of the home as haven was the domestic advice giver Catharine Beecher. In *The American Woman's Home* (1869) and earlier books, she not only explained the technological and architectural basis of a refined suburban home. She also proposed to increase the effectiveness of the isolated housewife and to glorify woman's traditional sphere of work. Released from some of her former drudgery by better design, the housewife, always a maker of perfect pies, would be newly equipped with a better pastry counter and flour bin, and a better oven, so she could devote more of her labor to becoming an emotional support for her husband and an inspiring mother for her children. Self-sacrifice would be her leading virtue. The home, a spiritual and physical shelter from the competition and exploitation of industrial capitalist society, and a training ground for the young, would become a haven in a heartless world. Beecher believed this division of labor between men and women would blunt the negative effects of industrial society on male workers. She argued that both rich and poor women, removed from competition with men in paid work, would find gender a more engrossing identification than class.

For Beecher, it was extremely important that the housewife do all the work of nurturing with her own two hands. As she performed many different tasks each day, she was to be a sacred figure, above and beyond the cash nexus; her personal services as wife and mother were beyond price. Thus the biological mother was presented as the only focus for her children's needs; the virtuous wife was presented as the only one who could meet her husband's needs as well. The spatial envelope for all of this exclusive nurturing was the little cottage in a garden: nature surrounding the home reinforced the belief in woman's natural, biologically determined role within it.

4.2 The haven strategy was expressed in *The American Woman's Home,* 1869, frontispiece. Women are the key figures caring for men and children.

4.3 Title page, *The American Woman's Home.* The man who pays for all of this is shown as a very tiny figure admiring the facade.

The industrial strategy, as articulated by the German Marxist August Bebel in his classic book *Women Under Socialism* (1883), was to move most traditional household work into the factory, abolishing women's domestic sphere entirely. Bebel argued: "The small private kitchen is, just like the workshop of the small master mechanic, a transition stage, an arrangement by which time, power and material are senselessly squandered and wasted. . . . in the future the domestic kitchen is rendered wholly superfluous by all the central institutions for the preparation of food. . . ."[12] He also predicted that just as factory kitchens would prepare dinners, and large state bakeries would bake pies, so mechanical laundries would wash clothes and cities would provide central heating. Children would be trained in public institutions from their earliest years. Women would take up industrial employment outside the household, and the household would lose control of many private activities. The effects of industrialization would be general, and women would share in the gains and losses with men, although their new factory work would probably be occupationally segregated labor in the laundry or the pie factory. A life of dedication to greater industrial production and the socialist state would reward personal sacrifice in the Marxist version of the industrial strategy.

In Bebel's version of home life, both nature and biology disappear in favor of industrial efficiency. Bebel believed that nurturing work should be done by women, but he tended to see women as interchangeable service workers. The patriarchal demand that women nurture with a personal touch, so central to Beecher, was replaced by a sense that any day-care worker could offer a substitute for mother love and any canteen worker could serve up a substitute for home cooking. The spatial container for this interchangeable, industrial nurturing was to be the apartment house composed of industrial components and equipped with large mess halls, recreation clubs, child-care centers, and kitchenless apartments. Of course, service

4.4 The industrial strategy, as promoted by Bebel, is here illustrated by a view of women as paid workers making frozen dinners on an assembly line, 1945.

workers would need to be constantly on duty to keep these residential complexes running, but Bebel did not consider this service as labor of any particular value or skill; in fact, he underestimated the importance of the socialized home as workplace, even as he recognized the private home as workshop.

Midway between the haven strategy and the industrial strategy, there was a third strategy. The material feminists led by Melusina Fay Peirce wanted to socialize housework under women's control through neighborhood networks. In contrast to the advocates of the haven approach, who praised woman's traditional skills but denied women money, or the advocates of the industrial approach, who denied women's traditional skills but gave women wages, the material feminists argued that women should be paid for what they were already doing. As Jane Cunningham Croly put it in Stanton and Anthony's newspaper, *The Revolution:* "I demand for the wife who acts as cook, as nursery-maid, or seamstress, or all three, fair wages, or her rightful share in the net income. I demand that the bearing and rearing of children, the most exacting of employments, shall be the best paid work in the world. . . ."[13]

While material feminists agreed that women were already doing half the necessary labor in industrial society and should receive half the wages for this, they believed that women would have to reorganize their labor to gain these demands. The first reason for organizing was to present a united front; the second was to utilize the possibility of new technologies and the specialization and division of labor, to perfect their skills and to shorten their hours. Peirce, the most important material feminist theorist in the United States between 1868 and 1884, argued that "it is just as necessary, and just as honorable for a wife to earn money as it is for her husband," but she criticized the traditional arrangement of domestic work as forcing the housewife to become a "jack-of-all-trades."[14]

Peirce's proposed alternative was the producers' cooperative, including former housewives and former servants, all doing cooking, baking, laundry, and sewing in one technologically well-equipped neighborhood workplace. They would send the freshly baked pies, the clean laundry, or the mended garments home to their own husbands (or their former male employers) for cash on delivery. Peirce planned to overcome the isolation and economic dependency inherent in the haven approach, and the alienation inherent in the industrial approach. While revering woman's traditional nurturing skills and neighborhood networks, the material basis of wom-

4.5 The neighborhood strategy inspired this sketch by Thomas Nast, 1870, of a harried, servantless housewife confronting her labors. Some housewives felt the only solution was cooperation by neighbors working together and sharing tasks.

en's sphere, Peirce proposed to transform these skills and networks into a new kind of economic power for women by elevating nurturing to the scale of several dozen united households.

Peirce also overcame another great flaw in the haven approach: in the early 1870s, there were very few technological advances, aside from Beecher's own little inventions and architectural refinements, to help the housewife who worked alone. Almost all of the major advances such as clothes-washing machines, dishwashers, refrigerators, and new kinds of stoves were being developed for commercial laundries, breweries, hotels, hospitals, and apartment houses. They were designed to serve fifty to five hundred people, not one family. Peirce proposed, like Bebel, to use this technology, but to use it at the neighborhood scale, in a community workplace with a series of open courtyards set apart from kitchenless houses in a landscaped setting or integrated with kitchenless apartments. Peirce experimented with both as building types.

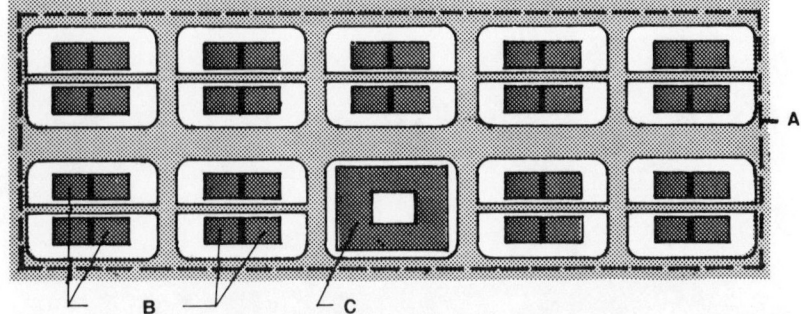

4.6 The neighborhood strategy, as introduced in Melusina Peirce's proposal for cooperative housekeeping: *A*, district of 36 families; *B*, kitchenless houses; *C*, work center for housewives' producers' cooperative, 1868–69.

Peirce understood economic activity as the activities of industrial production and human reproduction changing over time. She envisioned that her cooperative housekeeping strategies would lead to complete economic equality for women, because she argued that men could sustain farming and manufacturing while women ran the new and expanding areas of retail activity and service industries, in addition to their old standby—household production.[15] Thus she retained a gender division of labor but planned to revise national measures of productive economic activity. In this part of her analysis, Peirce anticipated Richard Ely, Helen Campbell, and Ellen Swallow Richards, who attempted, beginning in the 1880s and 1890s, to introduce home economics (or domestic economy) into academic debates and public policy as the "economics of consumption" on an equal plane with the economics of production.[16] Of course, all of the material feminists knew what many later Marxist and neo-classical economists alike have tended to forget: it is not the wage that defines work, it is the labor.

When Catharine Beecher, August Bebel, and Melusina Peirce framed their views of what the industrial revolution should mean to domestic life, they set up models of women's work and family life marked by all the hopes and fears of the mid-nineteenth century. In parricular, they accepted gender stereotypes so strong that not one of these models incorporated any substantial male responsibility for housework and child care. Yet Beecher's and Bebel's models of home continued to shape home life and public policy for over a century. The haven strategy and the industrial strategy became the ruling paradigms[17] for domestic life in capitalist and in state socialist societies where the paid employment of women was a fact, not a hope or a fear. Neither model of home life incorporated any substantial critique of male exclusion from the domestic scene; both models disconnected household space from other parts of the industrial city and its economy. Attempts to repair their conceptual difficulties accelerated in the years after World War I, but neither model has undergone the total revision that would enable planners of housing, jobs, and services to create the spatial settings for modern societies where the paid employment of women is essential.

As a result, women have become disadvantaged workers in both capitalist and state socialist societies. If we look at the evolution of these two models, we see that there have been many ingenious modifications and many ideological surprises as capitalists attempted to industrialize the haven while state socialists attempted to domesticate the industrial strategy. The neighborhood strategy of Peirce met a rather different fate. Its adherents advanced their arguments effectively in the United States and Europe, creating many interesting small experiments. As a result, this strategy provided an argument for justice and women's liberation that was never a policy framework for a government, but was often borrowed for rhetorical effect.

The evolution of all three models of home in different industrial societies during the twentieth century tells a great deal about political theory: capitalism and the role of the state in advanced capitalist societies; socialism and the role of the state in state socialist societies; feminism and the persistence of male economic control of female labor. It is a story far too complex to be told in full here, yet a brief review may help readers of many different political persuasions to make common cause. While the story does not deal at all with the fate of home life in economically developing nations, it may be read as a cautionary tale for any nation just beginning to make national policies about housing and the employment of women. In the American context, the history of the three models of home may help to illuminate the way to salvage the housing stock we now have while leaving the Victorian conventions of gender behind.

Modifying Beecher's Haven Strategy: Miniaturized Technology and Household Engineering

The first to modify the house as haven were manufacturers who introduced industrially produced appliances and products into the home. These were profitable extensions of the market economy justified as aids to the hardworking homemaker. What is astonishing is that these inventions eroded the autonomy of women at least as much as they contributed to saving women's labor. Eventually the haven strategy produced not a skilled housewife happy at home, supported by her husband's "family" wage, but a harried woman constantly struggling to keep up standards.

The years since 1900 have seen the production of privately owned clothes washers, clothes dryers, refrigerators, gas and electric stoves, freezers, dishwashers, toasters, blenders, electric ovens, food processors, vacuum cleaners, and electric brooms.[18] Many of these appliances were the result of an extended campaign to miniaturize earlier hotel technology in the post–World War I era, and their potential for lightening household labor was tremendous. Unfortunately manufacturers began their sales of all such appliances and home improvemtnts by advertising in women's magazines with themes of fear and guilt.[19] "For the health of your family . . . keep your foods sweet and pure, free from odors, impurities, and contamination," read the copy for McCray Sanitary Refrigerators. "Don't apologize for your toilet! Modernize it," said Pfau Manufacturing Company. Women were also told that liberation could be bought: "Electricity has brought to women a new freedom [represented by the figure of Liberty, wearing a crown and classical drapery] . . . the easy scientific method of cleaning with the Western Electric Vacuum cleaner."[20] The ideal of the "laboratory-clean home" was only part of the pseudo science the housewife had to achieve.

In the first three decades of the twentieth century, industrial engineers and home economists joined forces to show housewives how to apply Frederick Taylor's factory-oriented, time-and-motion studies to their tasks at home. Since there had been no division and specialization of labor in the home, the industrial paraphernalia of task analysis with stopwatches simply made housewives into split personalities: they were the managers supervising their own speedup. As Christine Frederick put it, "Today, the woman in the home is called upon to be an executive as well as a manual laborer."[21] Or as one woman complained, "The role of the housewife is, therefore, analogous to that of the president of a corporation who would not only determine policies and make overall plans but also spend the major part of his time and energy in such activities as sweeping the plant and oiling the machines. . . ."[22] Such pseudo efficiency and mock-industrial conditions matched the pseudo science of the kitchen as laboratory.

While household engineers made women guilty for not doing tasks fast enough, advertisers made both men and women guilty when they sold through the emotional blackmail of love. Men were told that if they loved their wives, they owed it to them to buy particular appliances. Women were told that if they bought certain items, men would love them more. "Man seeks no club, when the home has a Hub," wrote one stove manufacturer. The American response to such ad campaigns was extensive purchasing, but researchers who have studied time budgets find that conflicts within the home continued and the work of the "haven" housewives was still "never done." Jo Ann Vanek reported in her extensive survey in *Scientific American* that household standards have risen but women's time has not been saved.[23] To take just one example, Vanek shows that the full-time urban or rural housewife spent more hours doing laundry in the 1970s than in the 1920s, despite all the new washing machines, dryers, bleaches, and detergents, because her family had more clothes and wanted them cleaner. The familiar "ring around the collar" commercials dramatize the conflict: a husband and his five-year-old son jeer at a woman for using a detergent that can't remove the stains on their shirt collars. Her guilty response exemplifies the ways that conflict within a family can be exploited by advertisers.

The popularity of gourmet cooking, the expansion of the size of houses, and the increasing complexity of home furnishings have also contributed to an increasing demand for female labor hours in the home. Another development launched in the 1920s and continued through the 1980s was the creation of a culture of mothering which demanded intense attention to children at every stage of their development. Although the numbers of children were shrinking, mothers were expected to spend more time with each one. When American technology finally produced a baby-sitting machine (TV), many households used it over six hours per day. However, television created as many problems as it solved, since children listened to endless commercials for candy and toys.

Clearly, family values must be more carefully integrated with research, development, and marketing before new technological inventions can aid the homemaker and parent in a substantial, lasting way. Clothes washers, dishwashers, refrigerators, and reliable stoves are valuable inventions, but the context for their use can be improved, and their environmental efficiency can be improved. Other "inventions" are better eliminated from home life, or should be developed at the neighborhood scale. To measure the "standard of living," as the U.S. Census now does, in terms of the number of families owning a particular appliance is misleading.

Commercial Services

When increasing numbers of American housewives and mothers
entered the paid labor force in the 1960s and 1970s, and commercial
services became a fast-growing sector of the economy, there was a
second major modification of the haven strategy. By 1978 it was
estimated that Americans spent a third of their food budgets on meals
in restaurants and fast-food establishments.[24] The proportion of restaurant food eaten by two-earner couples was, as might be expected,
higher than for one-earner couples with a full-time housewife.
McDonald's slogan, "You deserve a break," captured the mood of
the customers for 40 billion burgers. "It's nice to feel so good about
a meal," sang Colonel Sanders' chorus. "We're cooking dinner in
your neighborhood," ran the folksy copy line for a California chain
of fast-food restaurants. In the 1980s happy family life and the consumption of industrially produced meals were rapidly colliding in
the minds of advertising copywriters, just as political liberation for
women and the purchase of electrical appliances had meshed as
themes in the 1920s.

Harland Sanders, the goateed Kentucky colonel dressed in a white
suit with a black string tie, smiles at motorists from the streetcorners
and roadsides of America. A man who started his career running a
small café behind a gas station in Corbin, Kentucky, in 1929, he
became the king of the take-out chicken business in three decades.
By 1971 Colonel Sanders Kentucky Fried Chicken franchised 3,500
businesses doing $700 million worth of business every year.[25] When
fast food came of age as one of many commercial services supported by working women and their families, Sanders became a
hero as an entrepreneur. When he died in 1980, his body lay in the
rotunda of the state capitol in Frankfort. In Louisville, his home
town, the flags on city buildings were flown at half-staff. But was
Sanders a hero to women? Hardly. His franchises employed thousands of non-union women at low wages to prepare and serve his
industrial food products. These commercial services and products
filled in for home cooking, but they drained a woman's salary. One
woman's precarious haven was sustained by the products of another
woman's small wages in this fast-growing sector of the market
economy. Those theorists who argued that such commercial services "liberated" women considered only the consumer and not the
producer. Of course, the quality and price of commercial fast food

varies greatly, as do the costs and conditions of production. The Silver Spoon in New York and A Movable Feast in Cambridge, Massachusetts, run by professional cooks, offer a range of carefully prepared soups, main courses, and desserts to affluent households whose members have no time to create elegant dinners. Colonel Sanders chicken is the inexpensive, mass-produced equivalent, and its workers are paid accordingly.

Almost as common as the fast-food place on the corner is the commercial child-care facility. Profit-making child care is also big business. Most are single operations run by licensed day-care providers. The fastest growing group, however, are more carefully calculated to run as franchises, such as the Kinder Care chain, with six hundred centers in thirty-five states, run by a millionaire from Montgomery, Alabama. Their education director is an ex–Air Force colonel who designed a program for the chain's standardized plastic schoolhouses.[26] While some expensive commercial day-care services may provide adequate developmental child care for the children of affluent families, many cheap day-care centers exist by paying low wages to their staffs.

Other types of profitable, personalized commercial services now offered to the home-as-haven include private cooks, nurses, maids, and baby sitters (long employed by the affluent), and also new rent-a-wife services by the hour. The *New York Times* Home section regularly lists eight or ten such services in New York. In Toronto, Duncan Edwards, the Rent-A-Shopper, charges $5.00 to $7.00 per hour to execute your shopping list.[27] In Vancouver, Jenifer Svendsen runs The Professional Wife. Her clients are generally male or female executives who can pay $8.00 to $10.00 per hour for entertaining out-of-town guests, food shopping, and canning.[28] (Canning? Yes, an executive woman, married to a man who believes in homemade preserves, hires Svendsen to do her home canning, and so far, her husband can't taste the difference!) The bargain end of the spectrum on personal service is the maid franchise operation. For families who cannot afford a Professional Wife or a maid on a regular basis, Rent-A-Maid of Los Angeles and similar services offer to deliver a maid to your door for $35.00 per full day. Such services may manage to make a profit by recruiting minority women and illegal immigrants from the barrio; the Los Angeles Rent-A-Wife charges $25.00 per hour to provide mother love and home cooking.[29]

State Services and Employer Services

A national day-care bill was passed by both houses of Congress in 1971, only to be vetoed by Richard Nixon, who argued that he was defending the American family. The need for developmental child care has been fought by conservatives, who fail to appreciate that while half of the mothers of children under six are in the paid labor force, there is subsidized day care for a small percent of the children of employed mothers.[30] When the topic turns to welfare mothers, the lack of day care becomes a clear example of inept policy. Welfare mothers often live in public housing, without day care services. If they are told they must get off welfare and find paid employment, usually there is no public day care and no adequate provision for commercial child care expenses, which may take a third or half of their pay, and leave the mothers with less income than the AFDC check they have forfeited by undertaking paid work.[31] So, reluctantly, some go back to AFDC.

Employers of women could solve the problem by providing day care but they usually refuse to recognize that sustaining home life is an economic activity benefiting the whole society. Historically, most employers have improved services for female employees only when they experienced a drastic shortage of female labor. The outstanding examples of American corporations' ability to try harder have occurred in wartime or boom time, when manufacturers in need of skilled female labor discovered that providing good day care will attract women workers. A Texas pacemaker firm called Intermedics, Inc., extends this benefit to women electronics workers and thereby cuts absenteeism.[32] Several Los Angeles hospitals view better day-care services as the key to recruiting and keeping trained registered nurses, who are in very short supply.[33] At the moment, however, most employed housewives and mothers can expect no special services from their employers. Experiments in Flex-time, or flexible work schedules,[34] have been heavily publicized as employers' initiatives to help employed women at no cost to themselves. Such arrangements do not eliminate the double day, however, they merely make it less logistically stressful. Employer sponsored day care and flexible work schedules are worth campaigning for, but trade unions and women's groups should recognize they are only part of a broader solution to women's double workload.

Male Participation

One last attempt to modify the round of tasks for the housewife has been the call for male participation by women themselves. Training boys for housework and child care, and insisting that adult men take part educates men to understand the levels of skill involved. Recent imaginative projects along these lines include grade-school courses for boys on how to take care of babies and YWHA play groups for fathers and children.[35] Both traditional consciousness-raising and these new courses reveal to men and boys the skills needed for nurturing, the time involved, and the role that space plays in isolating the nurturer. They find that kitchens are often designed for one worker, not two; that supermarkets are designed for the longest possible trip, not the shortest; and that men's rooms, like women's rooms, have no place where a diaper can be changed. Men who do housework and parenting then begin to see the patterns of private and public life in the divided American city. But how many men and boys ever achieve this level of consciousness?

In the United States we have had, most recently, ten years of active struggle for male participation in housework. Yet recent sociological studies show that American men now do only 10 percent to 15 percent of household work (a smaller percentage than children contribute) and women still bear the brunt of 70 percent to 90 percent, even when both members of a couple are in the paid labor force.[36] Indeed, economist Heidi Hartmann suggests that men actually demand 8 hours more service per week than they contribute.[37] A 1976 study found that the work week of American women is 21 hours longer than that of men.[38]

A closer look at male behavior in different classes reveals common gender stereotypes underlying the struggle over housework within the family. Men pretend to be incompetent; they call the jobs trivial.[39] They may also have very heavy overtime (whether at executive or blue-collar jobs) and argue that their time is always worth more than a woman's time. Men may also find that even if they do participate, a couple with young children still can't manage alone if both partners are employed full time. An even more insurmountable problem to male participation is the absence of men in many households.[40] Men's reluctance to take part in nurturing the next generation is only part of the problem. In many cases the ideal of male involvement has blinded many angry women to the severe logistical

problems presented by the house itself. By receiving male cooper-
ation, some time in the distant future, some women think their problems will be solved. This hope obscures the need for sweeping spatial
and economic reforms to change the underlying architecture of gender.

Modifying Bebel's Industrial Strategy:
Private Life and Home Cooking

In the same way that Beecher's haven strategy of keeping domestic
work out of the market economy was slowly eroded, so Bebel's
ideal strategy for the state socialist world has also been betrayed by
the retention of a second shift of private life and home cooking.
Bebel argued that only a comprehensive program of industrial
development for all women, including the design of new services
and new housing forms, could ameliorate rather than exploit wom-
en's position.[41] This has never been realized, because patriarchal
control of women's nurturing work continues in the home. Domestic drudgery accompanies industrial work for women; it has not
withered away under the "dictatorship of the proletariat," just as
the state has not.

One might expect good comprehensive planning of services in
state socialist countries such as Cuba, China, and the Soviet Union,
where the state owns the factories, runs the shops, runs the day care,
runs the transit, and owns the housing. At the state's discretion, day
care and other services can be located in the factory or in the residential neighborhood. Indeed, day care, other social services, and
even the factory itself can be placed in the residential neighborhood.
Despite this potential ability to meet employed women's needs, such
decisions are not usually made in ways which increase women's
autonomy.

The first opportunity for fulfilling Bebel's ideal occurred in the
Soviet Union, after the October Revolution of 1917. Lenin and
Alexandra Kollontai led Bolshevik support for housing and services
for employed women. They argued for the transformation of the
home by the state and experimented with these ideas as the basis of
national housing policy. Lenin, in *The Great Initiative*, wrote about
the need for housing with collective services in order to involve
women in industrial production: "Are we devoting enough attention
to the germs of communism that already exist in this area [of the

liberation of women]? No and again no. Public dining halls, creches, kindergartens—these are exemplary instances of these germs, these are those simple, everyday means, free of all bombast, grandiloquence and pompous solemnity, which, however, are *truly* such that they can *liberate women*, truly such that they can decrease and do away with her inequality vis-à-vis man in regard to her role in social production and public life. These means are not new, they have (like all the material prerequisites of socialism) been created by large-scale capitalism, but under capitalism they have firstly remained a rarity, secondly—and particularly important—they were either *hucksterish* enterprises, with all the bad sides of speculation, of profit-making, of deception, of falsification or else they were a 'trapeze act' of bourgeois charity, rightly hated and disclaimed by the best workers.''[42] Following Lenin's encouragement, the new regime developed a program of building multi-family housing with collective services, beginning with competitions by architects to generate new designs for the "House for the New Way of Life."

While the competition designs had a strong intellectual impact on designers of mass housing all over the world, ultimately few of them were built as intended. The USSR lacked the technology and the funds to follow through on its commitment to urban housing under Lenin. Under Stalin, the commitment itself dissolved. Stalin's ascendancy in the 1930s ended the official policy of women's liberation. Divorce and abortion were made difficult; "Soviet motherhood'' was exalted, and experiments in collective living and new kinds of housing ended. Only the most minimal support for women's paid labor-force participation was provided: day care in large, bureaucratic centers stressing obedience, discipline, and propaganda.

As a result, women in the USSR were encouraged to join the paid labor force without recognition of their first job in the home. A specialist in Soviet housing concludes that "Soviet society today has but little connection with the fraternal, egalitarian, and self-managing society dreamed of by a few during the short period of cultural explosion which followed the Revolution.'' Workers live in small private apartments in dreary, mass housing projects, where miles and miles of identical buildings have been constructed with industrialized building systems, but individual units are cramped and inconvenient. Appliances are minimal. Laundry is done in the sink; cooking on a two-burner countertop unit without oven. Refrigerators are rare status symbols for the favored elite. "Soviet architecture today—in particular in the field of housing—well reflects daily life in the USSR. . . . It reflects the real condition of women in the Soviet Union—a far cry from the idyllic pictures once painted by Alexandra Kollontai.''[43]

Recent research on the time budgets of women and men in the Soviet Union shows the extent of inequality: 90 percent of all Soviet women between the ages of twenty and forty-nine are in the paid labor force. While women's housework time decreased somewhat between 1923 and 1966, men's time spent in housework has not increased. As a result, women's total work week is still seventeen hours longer than men's.[44] Moscow is one of the few cities in the world to provide enough day-care services for the children of all employed mothers, but while this day care permits women to function as full-time paid workers (51 percent of the Soviet Union's labor force), their housing has not been designed to include either Bebel's industrialized housekeeping services or American kitchen appliances.[45] So, one can compare women's work in the United States and the Soviet Union. The USSR has emphasized state subsidized day care and women's involvement in industrial production. The U.S. has emphasized commercial day care and women's consumption of appliances and commercial services. In both cultures, the majority of married women have two jobs, work 17–21 hours per week more than men, and earn about 60 percent of what men earn. The "new way of life" in the USSR has been as elusive as the "new woman" in the USA.

The situation for employed women is quite similar in other state socialist countries whose economic development has been influenced by the Soviet Union. Given that standing in long lines to purchase scarce food supplies and consumer goods has long been a problem for housewives in state socialist societies, Cuba developed the Plan Jaba or Shopping Bag Plan in the early 1970s to permit employed women to go to the head of lines in crowded stores. However pragmatic the Plan Jaba was, as a solution to the woman's double day as paid worker and mother, and as a solution to the hours of queuing, one could hardly call it a major theoretical innovation. The publicity given to it as a fine example of socialist liberation for women was quite overdone. In much the same vein, Cuba has also offered employed women special access to rationed goods and factory laundry services.[46] So far so good, but such services cannot correct basic problems in both home and factory. The location of factories in neighborhoods is not a service to women but a disservice when the well-located factories offer only low-paid work for women. In Cuba, a textile factory staffed primarily by low-paid women was located in the Alamar housing project outside Havana; a shoe factory staffed by low-paid women was placed in the Jose Marti neighborhood in Santiago. In addition, the large and well-designed day-care centers in housing projects employed only women as day-care workers, at low salaries, because child care was considered a woman's job.

Chinese examples of residential quarter planning for employed women are similar. During the Great Leap Forward, so-called housewives factories were located in residential neighborhoods; the female workers received low wages and worked in relatively primitive industrial conditions. All this was justified for some time as a transitional stage of national economic development. However in 1980, the Chinese were planning an entire new town, which included new housewives' factories, to accompany a large new steel plant for male workers who would earn much higher wages.[47] Chinese residential neighborhoods, like the Cuban ones, have also employed women as day-care workers and community-health workers at very low wages. So while the socialization of traditional women's work is proceeding at a rapid rate to support women's involvement in industrial production, both the industrial workers and the service workers are still in female ghettos, and female responsibility for nurturing work remains the norm.

During the last decade women in state socialist countries have raised the issue of male participation, as have their counterparts in the United States. Cuban women developed a strong critique of what they call the "second shift," or their responsibility for housework once the paid shift is over. A cartoon shows an agricultural worker with a mound of sugar cane she has just cut, saying "Finished! Now to cook, wash, and iron!" As a result of such campaigns the Cuban Family Code of 1974 was made law. In principle it aimed at having men share what was formerly "women's work." In practice, the law depended upon private struggle between husband and wife for day-to-day enforcement. Men feigned incompetence, especially in the area of cooking and cleaning. The gender stereotyping of low-paid jobs for women outside the home, in day-care centers for example, only reinforced the problem at home. Some Cuban men tried, but many argued that domestic sharing could wait for the next generation. While Community Party policy has urged male cadres to assume half the domestic chores, Heidi Steffens, a writer for

Cuba Review, recounted a popular mid-1970s anecdote. A well-known member of the Central Committee of the party took over the job of doing the daily laundry, but he insisted that his wife hang it out and bring it in from the line, since he didn't want the neighbors to see his loss of *machismo.*[48] The power of *machismo* can also be understood in terms of men who cite pressure to do "woman's work" as one of their reasons for emigration.[49]

Finished! Now to cook, wash, and iron!

4.7   Unfulfilled promises of the industrial strategy are satirized in this cartoon from Cuba showing a woman who has cut mounds of sugar cane: "Finished!" she says, "Now to cook, wash, and iron."

In China, where there have also been general political policies that housework should be shared, the ambience is even less supportive. Sometimes the elderly—more often a grandmother than a grandfather—will fill in. The history of party pronouncements on housework can be correlated with the need to move women into or out of the paid labor force. A recent party directive instructed male members not to let themselves be henpecked into too much domestic activity at the expense of their very important political work,[50] so full male participation in housework continues to be a distant goal rather than a reality. In state socialist countries, as in capitalist ones, the hope of male participation hides the inadequacy of the basic model concerning work and home. It encourages both women and men to think that the next generation might negotiate a better solution in terms of time, rather than to consider the overall inadequacies of spatial and economic planning.

Modifying Peirce's Neighborhood Strategy:
Cash without Community

While the haven strategy and the industrial strategy suffered slow disintegration into the double day, Melusina Peirce's neighborhood strategy never became mainstream. Like Bebel and Beecher, she failed to incorporate male participation in housework and child care, but at least she had a strong economic reason for the exclusion. Peirce wanted to overcome the isolation of housewives, the lack of specialization of tasks, the lack of labor-saving technology, and the lack of financial security for any woman who had spent a lifetime in domestic labor. She saw men as a threat to women's traditional economic activities and wanted women to defend and expand their household activities on their own terms, rather than have them be taken over by men's commercial enterprises.

Peirce herself organized a bakery, laundry, grocery, and sewing service in Cambridge, Massachusetts, in 1868.[51] In the next half century, dozens of other experiments were conducted, including a family dining club in Warren, Ohio, from 1903 to 1923 and a Cleaning Club in Northbrook, Illinois, in the late 1940s. In Massachusetts, between 1926 and 1931 Ethel Puffer Howes made an even more ambitious experiment, providing models of community-run services: a cooperative dinner kitchen for the home delivery of hot food, a cooperative nursery school, a home helpers' bureau, and a job placement advisory service for college graduates. As the head of the Institute for the Coordination of Women's Interests at Smith College, Howes believed that her model institutions could be recreated throughout the nation by housewives who also wished to enter paid employment. Unfortunately during the Depression prejudice against women's employment combined with the Smith College faculty's suspicions that Howes' ideas were unacademic, ending this project after its five years of successful operation.

A consistent problem for all of these neighborhood strategy experiments was recruiting adequate capital to initiate change. Some housewives' experiments failed because husbands found their wives' demands for pay for collective labor too expensive—they believed that these housewives' isolated, unpaid labor was actually free. Other experiments—including some which lasted the longest—relied on ties between neighbors and kin but involved little money changing hands. This tradition of housewives' neighborly sharing of tasks

Cleaning Club Meets Today

Here is an idea, originated by four friends, that could be emulated in almost any community

By RUTH W. LEE

LAMENTING THE FACT they were so completely tied to their household tasks and to their homes, due to the scarcity of regular help or even sitters, four friends and neighbors in the village of Northbrook, Illinois, jointly hit upon an idea which has solved many of their problems.

It's a Cleaning Club, the members of which combine forces once a week to help each other with household tasks. They meet from about nine-thirty in the morning until five, bring the children with them, and make a social occasion out of any major task which the hostess wants done. In return for their joint efforts, which have included window washing, mending, painting, housecleaning and dressmaking, the hostess cooks and serves lunch, and keeps her eye on all the children. The dividends have been far greater than merely accomplishing some household task. Not only have the members had the pleasure of being together weekly, and the keen satisfaction of getting things done, but the children have become good friends, have learned to get along well together, and have thrived on their day-long visits to the members' homes. Even the husbands have shared the fun by occasionally joining in for potluck suppers.

At the beginning, the mothers drew lots for the first meeting, which was won by Mrs. L. D. Gordon. Her planned job for the day was having the windows washed. The mothers arrived shortly after the older children had gone off to school. Mrs. Carroll Daley brought three-year-old Susie to play with Mrs. Carl J. Nelson's two-year-old Meredith. Kay, aged six, daughter of Mrs. Peter Brown, had companionship in Jim Gordon, who is the same age. The children were enchanted to play with new toys in a new room, and proved to be on their best behavior. They happily took naps in strange beds and, after the older ones came home from school in the afternoon, all played together outside while the mothers continued their work.

At the second meeting of the club, Mrs. Nelson (Turn to page 93)

4.8 The neighborhood strategy, as developed by members of a housewives' mutual aid Cleaning Club, Northbrook, Illinois, *Parents' Magazine*, January 1945. This was based on bartered labor.

moved too slowly for many nineteenth-century feminists who attempted to move the neighborhood strategy in the direction of more businesslike enterprises run by professional women for professional women. They believed that the increasing involvement of women in the paid labor force could provide the new economic resources—women's salaries—for transforming traditional domesticity. Yet while more cash was a resource, the ideal of neighborhood organization of women suffered as a result.

In the 1890s the idea of neighborhood domestic reform as "good business" became quite popular when the American feminist Charlotte Perkins Gilman proposed the construction of special apartment houses for employed women and their families. In *Women and Economics,* she noted that employed women required day care and cooked-food service to enjoy home life after a day of paid work, and argued that if any astute business woman were to construct an apartment hotel with these facilities for professional women and their families, it would be filled at once. She believed that female entrepreneurs would find this "one of the biggest businesses on earth."[52]

Service Houses, Collective Houses, "One-Kitchen Houses," and Family Hotels

Gilman's work was translated into several European languages, and her argument was taken up by many European as well as American feminist women and men looking for a better approach to housing. The builder Otto Fick constructed the first "service house" in Copenhagen in 1903, a small apartment house occupied by tenants who enjoyed food service, cleaning, and laundry service. The building was explicitly designed for married women in the paid labor force, but Fick thought career and motherhood incompatible and prohibited children.[53] A second fault can be seen in Fick's claim that he was the "inventor of a new mode of living which simultaneously has all the features of a profitable business venture."[54] (His claim depended upon residents' paying the service personnel low wages and making a profit on the market price of shares in the residents' association when they sold out.) Nevertheless, Fick achieved a level of social and technological innovation which Gilman had only proposed, and his project operated until 1942.[55]

A Stockholm resident who became involved with the combination of housing and services was the builder Olle Enkvist, who built the collective houses Marieberg (1944), Nockebyhove (1951), Blackeberg (1952), and Hasselby (1955–56).[56] All had restaurants and full child care.[57] Unlike Fick, who believed in joint stock ownership by a residents' association, Enkvist owned these buildings as benign landlord. His success was measured in long waiting lists of prospective tenants, but after his death there were numerous tenant confrontations with the new management, especially when, in the

1970s, the new management wished to close the collective dining rooms because they didn't generate as much profit as the rental apartments. This probably would have seemed most ironic to Enkvist, who decided against delivery systems for cooked food (such as the elevators Fick had used for food) on the grounds that a large dining room with private family tables was more conducive to social contacts. Hasselby tenants did prove they could cater for themselves without losing money (serving about one hundred people daily for three years), but management found this level of participation cumbersome and called the police to eject the tenants. The turmoil of de-collectivization then led to the impression that these projects were social or financial failures,[58] although many functioned smoothly and successfully for thirty years. Their main failure was that the landlord did not turn a high profit.

In England, Gilman's arguments were taken up by Ebenezer Howard, founder of the Garden Cities movement, who proposed the "cooperative quadrangle" as the basis of new town planning in 1898.[59] Howard's cooperative quadrangles were to be composed of garden apartments served by a collective kitchen, dining room, and open space. They were designed to release women from household drudgery in the private home, and between 1911 and 1930 several of these projects were built for various constituencies, including single female professionals and the elderly as well as two-earner couples. Howard himself lived in Homesgarth, Letchworth. The quadrangles never became the standard housing available in the garden cities, but they did provide some very successful alternative projects within these new towns. In time their dining rooms also seemed expensive compared with local restaurants.

In the years after World War I, Clementina Black of London argued for the postwar adoption of "Domestic Federations" similar to Howard's designs.[60] In the years after World War II, Sir Charles Reilly, member of Parliament and head of the School of Architecture at Liverpool University, proposed a plan for reconstruction which incorporated many of the features of Howard's cooperative quadrangles.[61] He organized neighborhoods of duplex houses around nurseries, community kitchens, and open spaces.

In the United States, the implementation of Gilman's ideas was most closely approximated with the apartment hotels built between 1898 and 1930 in major cities and a few other experimental projects. Mary Beard, the well-known historian, lived in one such apartment hotel with her husband and children; they were located on the bus line to the New York Public Library. Knowing that three meals a day would be served to her family, she was able to hop on the bus and tend to her research. Georgia O'Keefe lived in a similar hotel with good light for painting. For less affluent women, Finnish and Jewish workers' housing cooperatives provided child-care services, bed-sitting rooms for the elderly, and tea rooms adjacent to family apartments.[62] The Workers Cooperative Colony in the Bronx, organized and owned by needle trades workers, was an early example of this kind of project in the mid-1920s. Again, the cost of providing services with well-paid unionized service workers made competition with commercial groceries, restaurants, and laundries difficult.

All these attempts to define supportive residential communities for employed women and their families ran into two related economic difficulties. First, the economic value of housework was never adequately understood. Second, the economic value of the new services was unclear, in relation both to the old-fashioned system of hiring personal servants and the new commercial services and industrial products developed for haven housewives. Such services, when produced by low-paid female workers, were cheaper, if less intimate and desirable, than community-generated alternatives. Economies of scale worked in favor of the nationally distributed products and services, even if they were impersonal. Once the substitution of cash for personal participation by residents had been arranged, the difference between industrial and neighborhood services might be difficult to discern. So professional women, if they attempted to buy a form of the neighborhood strategy, wound up closer to Colonel Sanders, year by year.

In much the same way, housewives struggling for economic independence through the neighborhood strategy would find themselves close to the haven strategy if they focused on wages and omitted the ideal of reshaping household work in community form. Eleanor Rathbone, an economist, feminist, and Member of Parliament in England, formed a club to lobby for wages for wives as early as 1918.[63] Some Americans also supported this cause in the 1940s.[64] Rathbone started by seeking a decent wage for housework; in the late 1940s, she won for mothers the Family Allowance: a small subsidy for a second child and any additional ones. Inspired by the concept of Family Allowances, and the potential of organizing to increase them, some British feminists revived the idea of larger payments for housework in the early 1970s. Led by Selma James, they demanded the state pay wages to all women for their housework. To attract supporters, the organizers ran skits about women's work in urban neighborhoods on market days. They passed out free potholders with their slogan to remind women of the campaign for wages every time they picked up a hot pot. They used union techniques of insisting on wages, wages, wages. "Just give us the money. All we want is the money," James incanted at one meeting.

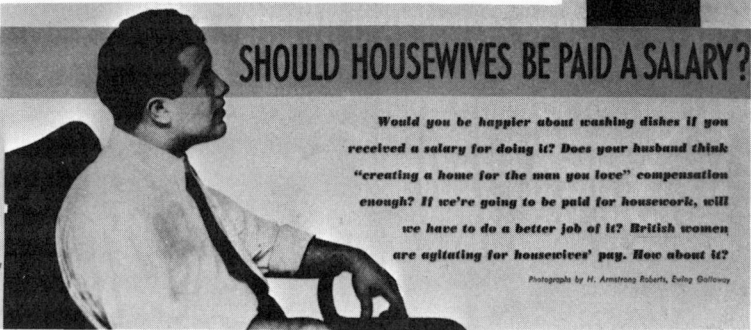

SHOULD HOUSEWIVES BE PAID A SALARY?

Would you be happier about washing dishes if you received a salary for doing it? Does your husband think "creating a home for the man you love" compensation enough? If we're going to be paid for housework, will we have to do a better job of it? British women are agitating for housewives' pay. How about it?

Photographs by H. Armstrong Roberts, Ewing Galloway

4.9 The neighborhood strategy, as developed by advocates of cash for housework: "Should Housewives Be Paid a Salary?" The article on the economics of the neighborhood strategy was inspired by Rathbone's successful "family allowance" campaigns in England, and published in *American Home*, February 1947.

Wages for Housework organized effectively among welfare recipients and single-parent mothers. They created special sub-organizations: Lesbians for Wages for Housework, and Black Women for Wages for Housework. The campaign developed successful recruiting tactics, but there was no mass movement. Organizers demonstrated the value of a housewife's day but could not change it, because their emphasis was on cash, not community. Their campaigns had some of the weaknesses of American welfare-rights organizing of the 1960s in that Wages for Housework did not confront the isolated home as haven, the setting for housework. They accepted females as domestic workers and identified the welfare state (rather than employers or husbands) as the primary target of their activities. Furthermore, they defined sexual services as "all in a day's work" for the housewife in a way which made it easy to organize angry women who felt sexually exploited, but difficult to articulate a more sophisticated position on male-female relationships.

Wages for Housework never lacked vitality, even if it lacked subtlety. A china bank in the shape of a rolling pin, made in the 1940s, carried the message of the earlier British feminists, "If women were paid for all they do, there'd be a lot of wages due."[65] But just as Rathbone had found a wage for haven housewives politically impossible in the 1940s, so it was in the 1970s. Even if they had won, financial recognition from the state for the work of homemaking would not have been enough to transform the haven housewife's situation.

Gary Trudeau's *Doonesbury* cartoon on "Trade-a-Maid" schemes, where American haven housewives swap chores, points up this problem as well. As Nichole, the "Alternate Life Stylist" explains it, "Housewife *A* and her best friend, Housewife *B,* spend weekdays cleaning each other's home. Their respective husbands pay for their services, just as they would for those of a first-class maid."[66] The employed wives then become eligible for Social Security, and for tax deductions on cleaning equipment. They receive cash but neither husband suffers loss of family income since the swap means both wives are paid equally. However, they still work in isolation, since receiving a wage for housework (whether paid by individual husbands or by the state) does not transform the home as haven, nor does it utilize the full range of technologies available in twentieth-century society. "It's illegal, though, right?" worries the interviewer. "Not yet," says Nichole.

Another American proposal captures the essence of the neighbor-hood strategy and avoids the question of industrial technologies by stressing the value of women offering social services to each other in the neighborhood. In 1977 Nona Glazer, Linda Mjaka, Joan Acker, and Christine Bose suggested institutionalizing housewives' cooperative services by establishing government funding for Neigh-bors in Community Helping Environments (NICHE).[67] In *Women in a Full Employment Economy,* they explained how to start Neigh-borhood Service Houses, where women would supervise children's play, care for sick children, facilitate repair service to homes, encourage bartering, distribute hot meals, and work with battered women, abused children, and rape victims. In return for providing these family and community services, women would receive at least a minimum wage. This proposal recognized that women's cooper-ation to socialize homemaking tasks could transform women's experience. NICHE also saw economic recognition of domestic labor as essential, but it did not involve proposals for male participation. Since NICHE was relying on the state to provide the wages, they had selected almost as difficult a program as the Wages for House-work campaigns. In a Democratic administration concerned about full employment the proposal looked possible; when Republicans took office and slashed all social services, the proposal looked even more relevant, but funding appeared impossible.

All of these campaigns to bring models of home life up to date point to the need for complex innovations—socially, economically, and environmentally. Truly successful solutions would reward housework and parenting as essential to society, incorporate male responsibility for nurturing, build on existing networks of neigh-bors, kin, and friends to ensure that personal preferences and ethnic customs in nurturing work are respected, and incorporate new tech-nologies, in order to promote equality for women within a more caring society. Yet before any specific policy changes can be pro-posed, it is essential to recognize the consistent economic and spa-tial failures that marred previous attempts. Beecher's and Bebel's models were too simplistic. If Beecher's glorification of the home-maker was a fantasy about recovering the pre-industrial past, Bebel's rejection of the homemaker was a fantasy about embracing the totally industrial future. As public policy, these strategies led to ironies compounded upon ironies; after a century, women had gotten the worst of both worlds, having been economically disadvantaged by the double day and spatially manipulated by the refusal of designers and planners to treat the home as a workplace.

Yet the most humiliating aspect of women's experience as nurturers was not their economic or spatial frustration, but the suppression of the third approach to home life, in order that the first two strategies could be presented as modern. The advocates of neighborhood networks were attacked as socialist sympathizers in the United States in the 1920s, and as bourgeois deviationists who should be expelled from the Communist Party in Germany and the USSR. Women have had warmed-over Beecher presented to them as women's liberation through Western Electric vacuum cleaners and Colonel Sanders; warmed-over Bebel presented as women's liberation through the Plan Jaba and the housewives' factories. Full recognition of what women actually contribute to society in the twentieth century is essential to recover nurturing from the domain of corporate or bureaucratic planning. No one has put the problem of nurturing more succinctly than Melusina Peirce: "Two things women must do somehow, as the conditions not only of the future happiness, progress, and elevation of their sex, but of its bare respectability and morality. 1st. They *must* earn their own living. 2nd. They *must* be organized among themselves."[68] If this is still the best advice to women about how to deal with their traditional work, two large areas of concern remain, the architectural aesthetics of home life and the economics of getting and spending. The three models of home life that have characterized nurturing have also had strong implications for housing design and for economic productivity, as house forms and systems of national accounting have reflected underlying ideas about the nature of home, mom, and apple pie.

Morals reformed—health preserved—industry invigorated
. . . all by a simple idea in architecture!

Jeremy Bentham

Huts, huts are safe.

Henry David Thoreau

A new life demands new forms.
Prospectus for the House of the New Way of Life

5

ROOF, FIRE, AND CENTER

The house forms of tribal societies dazzle the world traveler with ingenious responses to the challenge of building for various sites, climates, and household types. The jungle houses on stilts near the upper Amazon, the neat igloos of Eskimos, the three-story adobe apartment complexes of the pueblos in New Mexico, the white-rimmed cave dwellings of the fishermen of Southern Morocco, the tall wind-scoop houses of Hyderabad in India, the dark, arching spaces of Bedouin tents, the turf-insulated circles of Mongolian yurts, all speak of skillful builders. Here are women and men exploiting the potential of sun and wind, making the maximum use of reeds, ice, mud, rock, clay, goat hair, or grass. House forms also reveal the varied marriage and kinship patterns of pre-industrial societies: the long houses of the Iroquois accommodate many firesides consisting of a woman and her children; the circular dwellings of the Hakka shelter an Asian communal tradition; the painted tipis of the Kiowa communicate hierarchies in a nomadic culture; the compounds of the Yoruba define the status of each wife; the courtyards with high thresholds of the Han keep evil spirits and strangers from joining the extended family; the high-walled houses and carved doors of Muslim Lamu enforce purdah. Each of these designs encompasses a web of economic arrangements concerning men, women, and children: through the organization of space they reinforce people's relationships to land, tools, rooms, animals, fire, food, and each other.

Vernacular house forms are economic diagrams of the reproduction of the human race; they are also aesthetic essays on the meaning of life within a particular culture, its joys and rituals, its superstitions and stigmas. House forms cannot be separated from their physical and social contexts. One cannot imagine a pueblo in Alaska or an igloo in the Amazon Basin any more than one can conceive of an Iroquois woman living in a house designed for purdah. These climatic and cultural connections are all the stronger because in the pre-industrial world, house and household goods are a unity. The cooking vessels, the rugs, the doors, the beds, all cling to the dwelling, reflecting the inhabitants' fears and desires, rituals and taboos, entwined with the experiences of heat, cold, hunger, feasting, marriage, war, birth, and death.

In industrial societies, humans retain a strong desire to own a piece of land, a house, and meaningful household objects in order to communicate, to themselves and to others, just who they are and how they wish to be treated. Unfortunately, ordering the domestic sphere in industrial society is no longer always so direct an expression of personality or culture. The processes of making pots, weaving rugs, praying for rain, or dancing for good harvests have given way to the act of purchasing art as a commodity in an art gallery, and the process of dwelling has given way to purchasing residential space from a realtor. The production of most residential space in the United States is handled by speculative developers, although sometimes developers hire architects to help them make aesthetic decisions. As a result of treating housing space as a commodity, residents' uncertainty about the meaning of roof, fire, and center is profound—as profound as the ambivalance about home, mom, and apple pie. The transition from vernacular house forms to modern housing has left everyone, architects included, confused about styles, periods, places, and cultural symbols. The aesthetic confusion and the familial confusion compound each other, and neither can be unraveled without the other.

Three Models of Home Translated into Built Form

When nineteenth-century theorists generated three schematic models of how home life might be developed in industrial society, they also generated three schematic building programs for housing, strongly related to three architectural styles. The haven strategy produced the program for the detached, single-family suburban house treated aesthetically as a primitive, sacred hut; the industrial strategy produced the program for high-rise mass housing treated aesthetically as an efficient machine for collective consumption; and the neighborhood strategy produced the program for low-rise, multi-family housing treated aesthetically as a village with shared commons, courtyards, arcades, and kitchens. We have seen how the earliest formulations of the haven strategy and the industrial strategy required constant revision in the twentieth century, and how they evolved as models of family life, with many borrowings from each other and from the neighborhood strategy to shore them up. In the same way, basic programmatic and aesthetic deficienties in the sacred hut model or the efficient machine model for housing were soon apparent. Architects, urban planners, and builders began to borrow each other's aesthetic approaches: primitive hut buildings were realized with machine-aesthetic materials; mass-consumption buildings were trimmed with primitive half-timbering; the designers of both kinds of projects also borrowed the rhetoric of the neighborhood strategy to declare that they "freed women for modern life" or that they offered "an unsurpassed sense of community," although this rarely meant that they included significant, shared social services or social space.

A building program is the implicit or explicit statement of spatial requirements to be fulfilled within the constraints of available sites, budgets, and technologies; it can be simple or detailed, but it will usually define the building type (such as detached one-family house, or thirty-unit apartment house) and the intended activities such as eating, sleeping, or parking the car. A program will also usually specify what kinds of spaces are to be provided for these activities, such as kitchen, dining room, bedroom, or garage; how large these spaces must be; and what sorts of daylight, mechanical systems, and other equipment are necessary. At the same time that the building program conveys the economic, social, and technical requirements for built space, the architectural style chosen for a building conveys the cultural requirements. The choice of style may be made by the client or by the designer; it can be as enduring as any religious dogma or as fleeting as high fashion.

The one thing that architectural style cannot do is transform the building program. So if the basic social model of home is outdated, or the basic economic model of home is not appropriate, then architectural design cannot save the situation. Architects cannot make outmoded family etiquette modern; they cannot make false economic definitions of private and public work equitable. Because architectural style and building program represent form and content (or, if you will, cultural superstructure and material base), architectural styles and building programs often conflict in industrial societies. The architectural fashions of this world fail to convince when the program is inappropriate.

Few housing experts acknowledge this. Urban planners and social scientists have tended to divide the content and form of housing by focusing almost exclusively on programmatic analysis and treating aesthetics as irrelevant. Architects and art historians have tended to conflate content and form by focusing on the aesthetic analysis of design and subsuming the program under this formal discussion. Because program and style have often been seen as unrelated parts of a shelter planning problem, or as identical aspects of a housing design solution, confusion about housing lies at the heart of the identity crisis of the modern professions of architecture and urban planning.

The architectural historian Kenneth Frampton has written that modern architects, since the Enlightenment, have wavered between rationalism and piety, between the geometric utopias of a designer such as Ledoux and the piety of a Gothic revivalist such as Pugin: ". . . in its efforts to transcend the division of labor and the harsh realities of industrial production and urbanization, bourgeois culture has oscillated between the extremes of totally planned and industrialized utopias on the one hand, and, on the other, a denial of the actual historical reality of machine production."[1] But Ledoux, after all, had temples to both virgins and prostitutes in his ideal city; for all their aesthetic differences Pugin and Ledoux shared a nineteenth-century commitment to separate spheres for men and women, and to a male double standard of sexual conduct. Such romantic views of gender underlie the designers' predicament: most modern practitioners have been unable to develop more subtle definitions of private and public domains. Thus housing is the great missed opportunity for the design professions in the last century. Under every modern economic and political system, most architects have failed to understand the social programing and the aesthetic complexities essential to the production of space for modern family life. They have, instead, tended to follow Beecher or Bebel, seeing women as pre-industrial hearth tenders, or as industrial wage workers identical to men. As architectural critic Ada Louise Huxtable has put it, "Housing remains architecture's and society's chief unsolved problem."[2]

The Aesthetics of the Haven Strategy: The Single-Family House as Primitive Sacred Hut

For many Europeans, and for many settlers in North America who came from Europe, the archetypal house is a hut with a peaked roof, a strong door, and small windows to resist snow, wind, and rain. The house may be constructed of wood, if it is near a forest; or stone, if it is near a quarry. One large hearth provides a warm, bright place, the center of nurturing activity. The archetype can be elaborated in its English, French, German, Scandinavian, and American versions. As *ham, domus, bauen,* or log cabin, the image has been analyzed, romanticized, sanctified, psychoanalyzed, celebrated, and copied, a process traced with great wit and insight by geographer Kathleen Ann Mackie. In her intellectual history of the ideal of home, she notes that home distinguishes "familiarity from strangeness, security from insecurity, certainty from doubt, order from chaos, comfort from adventure, settlement from wandering, here from away."[3]

Clare Cooper and Carl Jung see the house as a symbol of self.[4] Lord Raglan, Martin Heidegger, Mircea Eliade, and Francesco Dal Co, all contend that building a dwelling involves the construction of a temple and a world view.[5] Joseph Rykwert showed that Adam and Eve's house in paradise provided an archetype for many architects' endeavors.[6] John Brinckerhoff Jackson brought to life the "westward-moving house" as an image of the expansion of the United States.[7] For Adrienne Rich, "protection is the genius of your house," and many of her best poems explore the archetype.[8]

When any culture clings to a rural house type—the sacred hut—rather than devising a successful urban house type, it remains a culture of people trying to be farmers and rejecting city life. The

United States is particularly vulnerable to this charge, underlined by the predominance of the isolated farm on the Jeffersonian grid, as opposed to the New England Puritan farm village. This country, where many inhabitants still earned a living on the family farm as late as 1900, has struggled to keep the sacred hut alive: in mass suburbia, in the affluent classes' search for colonial farmhouses as second homes, and in the hippie fondness for building primitive shelters. However pervasive the nostaligic attachment to rural house types, this is not a fully conscious, politically informed, aesthetic choice. The aesthetic disjunction between the pre-industrial ideal of sacred hut and the reality of housing in the United States is very poorly understood, and therefore Americans still crave aesthetic and emotional gratifications from single-family dwellings that no architect or builder can possibly provide.

Early settlers lived in wigwams, sod houses, dugouts, log cabins, and a variety of crude structures they generally were eager to replace. *The Bark Covered House* is one American's account of upward mobility achieved in Michigan through clearing the land, building a log cabin, and then building, over time, two more substantial frame dwellings.[9] Settlers didn't cherish the memory of the crude shelters, at least not until they were ensconced in something more comfortable. By the early nineteenth century, when the Greek Revival became a popular style for farmhouses as well as public buildings, the builders of New England and the midwest created some of the most austere and beautiful structures in America, with roof lines defining a pediment, carrying associations of Greek temples, and delicate, wooden, geometric ornament displaying their skill and taste. Sketches of such farmhouses often appeared in atlases of various counties, testaments to their owners' success and the builders' sensitivities.

By the 1840s, suburban development around Eastern cities leaned to Gothic Revival, guided by Downing's and Beecher's books, because this curious aesthetic was thought to enhance the sacredness of home. Downing sought spiritual connectedness in picturesque suburban landscaping and provided Gothic cottages to suit any budget; Beecher put three crosses on the roof line of her house, as well as numerous altarlike spaces inside, just so that no one could miss her point about woman's role as "minister" in the "home church of Jesus Christ."[10] In the last third of the nineteenth century, a series of other styles became popular. French Mansard, Italianate, Queen Anne, Romanesque Revival, and even Egyptian Revival

5.1 House as primitive shelter: John Curry and wife in front of their sod house, near West Union, Custer County, Nebraska, 1886, the agricultural precedent for the suburban architecture of gender. (Nebraska State Historical Society)

5.2 Home as primitive sacred hut, from *Suburbia,* by Bill Owens. Boat and camper replace the team of horses and sewing machine as symbols of mobility and modernity.

competed with Gothic; eventually Colonial Revival created the greatest enthusiasm in the early twentieth century. In this eclectic scene, only the housewife and her housework remained constant to sanctify the home church, the mother close to the hearth performing the sacred rites of cooking and cleaning.

In the twentieth century architects began to challenge these eclectic, ornamented styles and attempted to produce modern architecture, but they kept the old rituals intact and, in some cases, even tried to add to them. Frank Lloyd Wright, designer of prairie houses and author of manifestos on organic architecture, represents modern design to many. He explored horizontal lines, flowing spaces, and functional interests such as sliding partitions and single surface workspaces in kitchens (earlier developer by Beecher). Yet Wright's Affleck House of 1938 returns to the forms of the German peasant's cottage of 1750. Wright reproduced the "Lord's Corner," or Herrgottswinkel, almost exactly as the superstitious peasant patriarchs would have built it: a cult corner next to the dining table where the householder sits as head, with his sons and male servants on the high-backed bench next to the wall, and his wife, daughters, and female servants on the backless bench next to the kitchen (nearer to the stove and better able to serve the food).[11] While Wright described the Affleck House as an uncluttered, informal area for modern living, the pre-industrial religious orientation helped the businessman preside at home.

In her scathing, witty book, *The Home,* published in 1902, Charlotte Perkins Gilman asked, "By what art, what charm, what miracle has the twentieth century preserved, alive, the prehistoric squaw?"[12] The answer was, by taking attention away from program and focusing on style. Home economists and household engineers soon attempted to provide a more modern answer, to sweep the sacred hut into the twentieth century with the magical power of technology. Cooking with electricity, first illustrated as harnessing the force of lightning bolts in an alchemist's laboratory in the late ninteenth century, was tamed into an aesthetic of single-purpose appliance consumption by the 1930s. The architectural competition for "The House of Modern Living," or the house for Mr. and Mrs. Bliss, sponsored by *Architectural Forum* and General Electric in the Depression Era, celebrated the traditional nuclear family—the father an engineer, the mother a college graduate in home economics, two children, one boy, and one girl—and showed how electricity could transform their domestic lives. The winner incorporated thirty-two different electrical appliances in his design, every one made by General Electric, including radio, electric iron, mixer, waffle iron, coffee maker, stove, refrigerator, dishwasher, air-conditioner, sun lamp, razor blade sharpener, and curling iron.[13] The aesthetic for modern living with electricity was, in the first-prize winner, streamlined moderne with a flat roof, but the judges had by then no single strong position about architectural style or the cultural meanings attached to it. In the second-prize house the force of modern technology inhabited a Cape Cod colonial with dormers.

Whatever the façade, electricity gave modern man a way out of household chores: Mrs. Bliss does all her own housework, the architectural program stated. ''She actually enjoys the work.'' While the unfortunate ''actually'' almost gave the lie to this assertion, the competition organizers quickly followed up with a most effective advertising slogan: ''Electricity is her servant.'' Housewife as home minister had the divine power working for her.

By the time the Levitts grappled with the aesthetics of the sacred hut in Levittown in the late 1940s, almost all of the serious aesthetic and spiritual dilemmas about the suburban tract house had been resolved for them by the formulas of architects, household engineers, and corporate marketing experts. The Levitts had only to deliver the cultural and architectural package more effectively than the competition, which they did, and then to contend with the gasps of horror that ensued because of the awesome, urban scale of their mass production of rural, sacred huts. The lessons of GE were not lost on the Levitts: with each identical house in the first Levittown a washing machine was provided as part of the standard equipment. And the modified Cape Cod houses sat on sacred ground fenced with white pickets, true to Downing's view of suburban landscaping as an essentially religious process.[14] One more refinement of the precinct of home was achieved when, in a later development, Levitt not only managed to supply television as a standard item, but also to build it into the living room wall so that it qualified as an item of household equipment that could be financed on the mortgage.[15] Next to the hearth, the bright, beady eye of the baby-sitting machine reassured both children and adults that the scant physical community of the mass-produced sacred huts was redeemed by the magical electronic community created by national television.

Following Levitt's example, the tracts grew and the tract builders prospered for thirty-odd years before the current crisis. Choice for consumers was a superficial stylistic one of eclectic façades on close-to-identical houses with close-to-identical appliances. Fads came and went. The boxes doubled in size between 1950 and 1975. Many critics got tired of berating suburbia for its stylistic blandness; it became acceptable to praise it as "popular culture," or at least to let it pass as good enough for the blue-collar inhabitant. A professor of architecture reported that homeowners in two American subdivisions near Buffalo, New York, preferred tract houses in nostalgic styles, such as Midwestern farmhouse with porch, English Tudor house with half-timbering, Western Ranch house with fieldstone chimney, Mediterranean house with archways, or colonial American with brick front and end chimneys. This research, funded by the National Endowment for the Arts, was not much more far reaching than most tract developers' marketing surveys, since the researcher concluded that "builders are providing a viable range of home styles."[16]

A more critical assessment of the suburban aesthetic was offered by Tom Wolfe in *From Bauhaus to Our House,* but like many other high-culture critics, he sneered at both the blue-collar residents, for their kitschy taste, and the white-collar architects who had failed to enlighten them about greater aesthetic joys. The architects, he claimed, were fools twice over: once for accepting European definitions of a "nonbourgeois" modern machine aesthetic, and twice for trying to apply it in competition with speculative private-home builders in the United States context. As Wolfe put it, there was no need for anyone to get interested in low-cost housing, especially multi-family housing, since there was no constituency for it: "The workers . . . bought houses with pitched roofs and shingles and clapboard siding, with no structure expressed if there was any way around it, with gaslight-style front-porch lamps and mailboxes set up on lengths of stiffened chain that seemed to defy gravity—the more cute and antiquey touches, the better—and they loaded these houses with 'drapes' such as baffled all description and wall-to-wall carpet you could lose a shoe in, and they put barbecue pits and fishponds with concrete cherubs urinating into them on the lawn out back, and they parked the Buick Electras out front and had Evinrude cruisers up on two trailers in the carport just beyond the breezeway."[17]

This is the image that Bill Owens' documentary photographs in *Suburbia* give us, too, but with irony to replace Wolfe's disdain. Owens shows the failure of suburban spaces to reflect cultural diversity—black and Asian families and white ethnic families struggle with the same ersatz "Colonial" styles and furnishings.[18] Owens and Wolfe both observe that American women and men have to assemble their interior home decor from a range of machine-made products. What is most disconcerting is that these are all advertised as luxury goods but designed for obsolescence. In earlier times American women made handsome quilts and painted stencil decorations on their walls and floors, but today's American housewife faces synthetic materials, all simulating something more expensive: wallpaper resembling bamboo, linoleum resembling ceramic tile, plastic paneling resembling wood. It is her job to confront the interior of the badly designed suburban home (or urban apartment) and make it homelike. Her husband's job is usually to maintain the exterior of the house and the car under similar stresses, also caused by poor design: shoddy building and unrealistic automotive styling. Only the yard will respond well to care; it often becomes the focus of one or both partners' attention, the essential connection to nature, the green justification for the design failures around it.

Denise Scott Brown and Robert Venturi were kinder to suburbia in their aesthetic appraisal, *Signs of Life,* a Renwick exhibit. They took gaslights and cherubs, Sears' Chippendale and Caldor's Colonial Revival seriously, and dissected them semiotically as meaningful objects, carrying archetypal messages.[19] Yet, like Wolfe, they missed the point: consumer choices of mass-produced, machine-made goods cannot carry the same aesthetic meanings as the houses and household objects made by the inhabitants of a pre-industrial folk culture who have not experienced the commodification of land, house, and household goods.

The Sacred Hut Moving Down the Highway

If electricity was used to give the sacred hut a new magic and acceptability in the 1920s and 1930s, the current development likely to prolong the program for the single-family dwelling is the industrially produced mobile home, or as it is now being renamed by makers, "manufactured housing." These boxes do begin to make suburbia look warm, personal, generous, and human in comparison. Mobile homes derive from Conestoga Wagons and gypsy wagons; the idea of living on the road was first popularized with the development of the automobile and survives in recreation vehicles and the many institutions they have spawned, from trailer parks and CB networks to Good Samaritan Clubs on the road. Yet most mobile homes now move only once. Many manufacturers saw in the mobile home the legal and economic possibilities for cheap shelter, financed on the installment plan like an automobile, and designed to standards lower than local building or zoning codes might have permitted for regular tract housing. The vagaries of the construction trades could be bypassed in the factory; so could the decision making by planning boards and mortgage bankers. As the industry grew, until in 1981 an astonishing 36 percent of new single-family dwellings were mobile homes, choice of styles expanded.[20]

Companies began to offer pop-up roof lines, pop-out bay windows, decorative door treatments, double-wide units made by joining two mobile homes, and similar modifications to make the basic metal box look less like a freight car and more like a sacred hut. Today manufactured housing comes in Colonial, Tudor, Mediterranean, and every other style, just like tract houses. While the walls are thin, a full line of appliances can be installed. Manufactured housing represents a final attempt to miniaturize the Victorian gentleman's suburban villa, with dimensions far more cramped than Levittown. Increasingly, local planning authorities are pressured by some residents to permit more mobile home parks and also to accept mobile homes as second units on existing sites. The elderly may want to live next to their children's houses; the mobile home (in one case soberly renamed "The Elder Cottage") offers quick ways to increase suburban densities at lower costs.[21] But cheap shelter doesn't have to be shoddy or kitschy: the manufactured box exploits the assembly line to prolong the problems of inadequate architectural programing and inadequate neighborhood planning that the housing crisis should force us to solve.

High-Priced, High-Tech, and High-Culture Huts

While mobile homes are often purchased by the working class, even the wealthy can make themselves uncomfortable, given the confusion about the aesthetics of housing. Those who buy large tracts of land and hire architects to design 5,000-square-foot houses may suit their personal tastes in ways that mass production cannot. But rather than achieving the elegant Savile Row tailoring of personal space, many have paid for the emperor's new clothes. This is not an entirely new phenomenon. Henry James commented on the conspicuous consumption of the owners of "ample villas" in eclectic styles in the New Jersey suburbs in *The American Scene* in 1904: "It would have rested on the cold-blooded critic, doubtless, to explain why the crudity of wealth did strike him with so direct a force . . . nothing but the scale of the houses and their candid look of having cost as much as they knew how. Unmistakably they all proclaimed it— they would have cost still more had the way but been shown them; and, meanwhile, they added as with one voice, they would take a fresh start as soon as ever it should be. 'We are only installments, symbols, stopgaps,' they practically admitted, and with no shade of embarrassment; 'expensive as we are, we having nothing to do with continuity, responsibility, transmission, and don't in the least care what becomes of us after we have served our present purpose.' "[22] James concluded that large new houses for newly rich clients, looming in bright green grassy lots next to the road, symbolized business success at the expense of both privacy and community: ". . . in such conditions there couldn't *be* any manners to speak of; . . . the basis of privacy was somehow wanting for them. . . ."[23]

Thorstein Veblen also condemned the trappings of eclectic late-nineteenth century domestic display: "The canon of beauty requires expression of the generic. The 'novelty' due to the demands of conspicuous waste traverses this canon of beauty, in that it results in making the physiognomy of our objects of taste a congeries of idiosyncracies. . . . It would be extremely difficult to find a modern civilized residence or public building which can claim anything better than relative inoffensiveness in the eyes of anyone who will dissociate the elements of beauty from those of honorific waste."[24] Yet Robert Woods Kennedy in his influential book of the 1950s, *The House and the Art of Its Design,* recommended that designers promote the "honorific waste" that James and Veblen so deplored. Kennedy argued that, as an architect, it was his job to provide houses that helped his clients to indulge in status-conscious consumption, and he showed how to display the housewife "as a sexual being" as well as how to display the family's possessions "as proper symbols of socio-economic class," claiming that both forms of expression were essential to modern family life.[25] He thereby evaded the problem the architectural profession needs to solve, a problem Veblen was aware of. Then, as now, while architects are not responsible for the overwhelming majority of housing units constructed by builders, they are responsible for accepting or rejecting the basic program for housing presented to them by those clients they do have. And they are responsible for the values they express when speaking about the goals of good design to each other and to their students, as well as to their clients and the general public.

In our own decade, single-family houses designed by many fashionable architects reflect a rather academic approach to the question of how to dwell. Rather than attempting to expand the sacred-hut program or alter the context, many architects have strained to enhance the experience of dwelling with images of the sacred, the arcane, the difficult.[26] Other designers have embraced the engineering tradition. Buckminster Fuller's Dymaxion house of 1927, suspended on a mast off the ground (and his Wichita house, of 1944), were for decades the definitive statement of the machine aesthetic applied to the sacred-hut program,[27] but in recent years Stanley Tigerman of Chicago has outdone Bucky. His futuristic "house that thinks for itself" incorporates home computers and robotized carts to execute many household functions.[28] Here the Victorian dwelling's spatial program is sustained in the late-twentieth century by micro-chip technology. Shopping, bill paying, and taxes can be done on the computer; the robotized cart can fetch laundry from a bedroom hamper and take it to the washing machine and dryer; the computer provides children's games to add a second, more engaging babysitting machine to the television, one that can accommodate children's participation. Surveillance systems of various kinds are integrated into the computer, so that when anyone intrudes into the private haven of this suburban home, the violation is noted and reported to the local police. (One no longer needs the chilling little signs that adorn the lawns of Los Angeles' wealthy suburbs, saying that intrusions will be met by "armed response.")

Tigerman's house—patriarchal, isolated, and nostalgic in its traditional plan but science-fiction-like in its use of electronic equipment—hints at the aesthetic choices for the twenty-first century. Assuming that factory-produced mobile homes are the ultimate cheap miniaturization of the suburban tract house, one can conceive of a future when millions of such manufactured boxes are equipped with the latest home computers to persuade the consumer that the manufactured box offers a new, modern aesthetic experience. This might even be advertised as an experience that liberates the housewife, since not only will electricity be her servant, but also the robot. Everything in our American cultural tradition suggests that manufacturers and advertisers will use these claims if they think they will be effective.

While Tigerman didn't explore this, another recent development, noted in *The Electronic Cottage,* by Joseph Deken, is paid work at home through the use of home computers.[29] One can see this as a potential support for freelancers and for flexible schedules, or as the end of unionization drives and the beginning of cottage industries handling all white-collar work as piecework. These are complex economic and spatial choices that citizens in this society should be planning for, but it is more likely that they will be presented by manufacturers of home computers as consumer options to purchasers of computer systems. The differences between citizens' discussing new computer technologies and shoppers' contemplating them are profound. The computer programer or secretary who winds up with a terminal or a word processor at home could become more like a pre-industrial weaver on the putting-out system than like a worker of the modern world. The historical isolation of the housewife as an invisible worker in the sacred hut could be the model for the manipulation of more and more paid workers back into piecework, non-union jobs, and the isolation of the private sphere. In contrast, a strategy of utilizing collectively owned computers in a neighborhood workplace could offer a social setting for work, and the possibility for sustained union organization by workers using these new machines, as well as the benefits of less commuting and more flexible hours.

Do the two alternative models of home offer any stronger, more coherent solutions? Certainly the industrial strategy has an aesthetic history no less complicated than the haven strategy in its evolution over the past century.

The Aesthetics of the Industrial Strategy: Mass Housing As Efficient Machine for Collective Consumption

With the Industrial Revolution, many European designers thought the peasant farmer's single-family home as a sacred hut was outmoded, but the housing that replaced these rural cottages was frightening. The sordid tenements spawned by industrial production were about as far from the sacred properties of roof and hearth as one could get. Because of their inadequate sanitary design and overcrowding, they were the first human dwellings that actually killed people who tried to shelter in them. To take the place of both huts and tenements, designers proposed to create new multi-family buildings for sheltering and feeding the workers relocated from country to city. Perhaps the most extreme example of this aesthetic, and one of the earliest and most influential, was Jeremy Bentham's Panopticon. Bentham, associated with the philosophy of Utilitarianism and slogans such as "the greatest good for the greatest number," developed his architectural scheme to show how the urban poor might be kept from starving at a minimum expense to the British taxpayers of the 1780s. In the Panopticon, Bentham arranged people in tiers in a multi-sided building with a single all-seeing person supervising from the center. The building had folding beds ranging in size from cradles for babies to bunks for adult males— reflecting the preoccupation with body measurements first developed by slave-ship owners and ultimately a staple of *existenzminimum* (minimum existence) housing. The basic design, Bentham thought, could be used as a poorhouse, an orphanage, a penitentiary, a hospital, a mental asylum, or a school. In other words, the poor, the deviant, and the wards of society could be housed there. Only prison officials literally adopted this architectural program, but the attitude of architectural determinism that Bentham launched became quite pervasive. Bentham chortled, "Morals reformed— health preserved—industry invigorated. . . . all by a simple idea in architecture!"[30] Many architects and politicians took up his belief in the power of space alone to change society, ignoring the necessity for more basic economic reforms.

The Machine Aesthetic, Reform, and Revolution

The Panopticon was a poorhouse justified as an efficient collective architectural machine. The model-housing schemes of Robert Owen and Charles Fourier, called the parallelogram and the phalanstery, were "social palaces" scaled to suit new groups of male and female workers and justified for their economies as part of model settlements. Owen's plans resembled the grand squares of town houses built by the English aristocracy; Fourier was inspired by both Versailles and the Palais Royale. Their conceptions relied on the isolated, experimental community as an alternative to the city but were far more generous in the dimensions of private housing space and collective services than Bentham's design—and less rigidly deterministic. Both Owen and Fourier hoped to unite social, economic, and aesthetic improvements in their new communities for one to two thousand people. In the United States some of the most influenced intellectuals of the 1840s, such as Margaret Fuller and Nathaniel Hawthorne, adopted Fourier's ideas as residents of Brook Farm. When they built themselves a phalanstery to house an experimental community of both workers and intellectuals, their friend Thoreau came over from Concord to West Roxbury to have a look at the imported new design for collective housing, childcare, and dining. Fresh from the woods around Walden Pond, Thoreau shook his head and muttered, "Huts, huts are safe."[31] Of course, he went to dine with his mother or sister whenever his hut lost its appeal.

As the ideas about collective housing tried out in the model communities of the 1840s began to lead to the urban apartment houses of the 1850s, 1860s, and 1870s, many new urban experiments were tried for all classes, including worker's model tenements, apartment hotels, and neighborhood public kitchens. In the 1880s Bebel drew from this tradition when he predicted a future of industrial equality and collective living, based on mass housing and state control. The continuing construction of urban philanthropic and public housing for workers was given a great push during the reconstruction following World War I. The American housing expert, Catherine Bauer, brilliantly chronicled the European excitement with housing for a social purpose in her excellent *Modern Housing* of 1934, covering Holland, Germany, Belgium, France, and England.[32] Socialist architects such as Ernest May and Bruno Taut were particularly influential in exploring the social and physical issues involved in designing multi-family dwellings.[33] Most unconventional of all were the Bolsheviks in the Soviet Union, who promoted the "House of the New Way of Life," the collective-house designed for the family with both adults employed.

In the prospectus for the 1926 Competition for a Communal Dwelling, the Moscow City Society instructed architects to reorganize the traditional home:

> It is the duty of technological innovation, the duty of the architect, to place new demands on housing and to design in so far as possible a house that will transform the so-called family hearth from a boring, confining cell that at present burdens down women in particular into a place of pleasant and carefree relaxation.
>
> A new life demands new forms.
>
> The worker does not desire his mother, wife or sisters to be a nursery maid, washerwoman or cook with unlimited hours; he does not desire

children to rob him and particularly their mother of the possibility of employing their free time for social labor, mental and physical pleasures. . . .[34]

As a result of this competition and others, programs for apartment houses including day-care facilities, dining rooms, and recreation rooms were adopted by numerous well-known Soviet architects.

Today, many of these projects seem to be designed by individuals intoxicated with the machine aesthetic as a statement about modernity. Some of the Soviet architects subscribed to the spirit of the Italian Futurists, without understanding the anti-humanist, anti-feminist bias behind their sketches. Filippo Marinetti had exulted in his 1909 manifesto of Futurism: "Time and space died yesterday. Already we live in the absolute, since we have already created speed, eternal and ever present. . . . We wish to glorify war—the only healthy giver of the world—militarism, patriotism, the destructive arm of the anarchist, the beautiful ideas that kill, the contempt of women. We wish to destroy museums, the libraries, and to fight against moralism, feminism, and all opportunist and utilitarian meanness."[35]

When Soviet architects attempted to join Bebel's program for women's paid work and collective services run by the state with the anti-hearth, anti-culture, pro-industry machine aesthetic of Marinetti, a conflict between the housing program and its architectural expression occurred. The architects of the collective dwellings began, following Bebel, Zetkin, and Kollontai, to strip away traditional patriarchal definitions of family activities and space. But they proposed to replace family houses with minimum one-person private spaces, including folding beds, tables, and chairs placed in rooms often calculated by size more than quality. They removed traditional symbolic family spaces like the hearth, and social functions like dining, from the private dwelling unit in order to make cooking and eating collective activities—one designer actually drew an assembly line to speed the distribution of food down the center of the collective table. Another development was the use of industrial components such as metal frame windows and metal stairs in housing design, especially in large community spaces. The results were stark. In contrast, the Soviet graphics, paintings, set designs, and costume designs of the same era were often more intriguing than the architecture, largely because the smaller scale of experimentation encouraged humor and seriousness without self-consciousness, qualities the architects and planners often lacked.

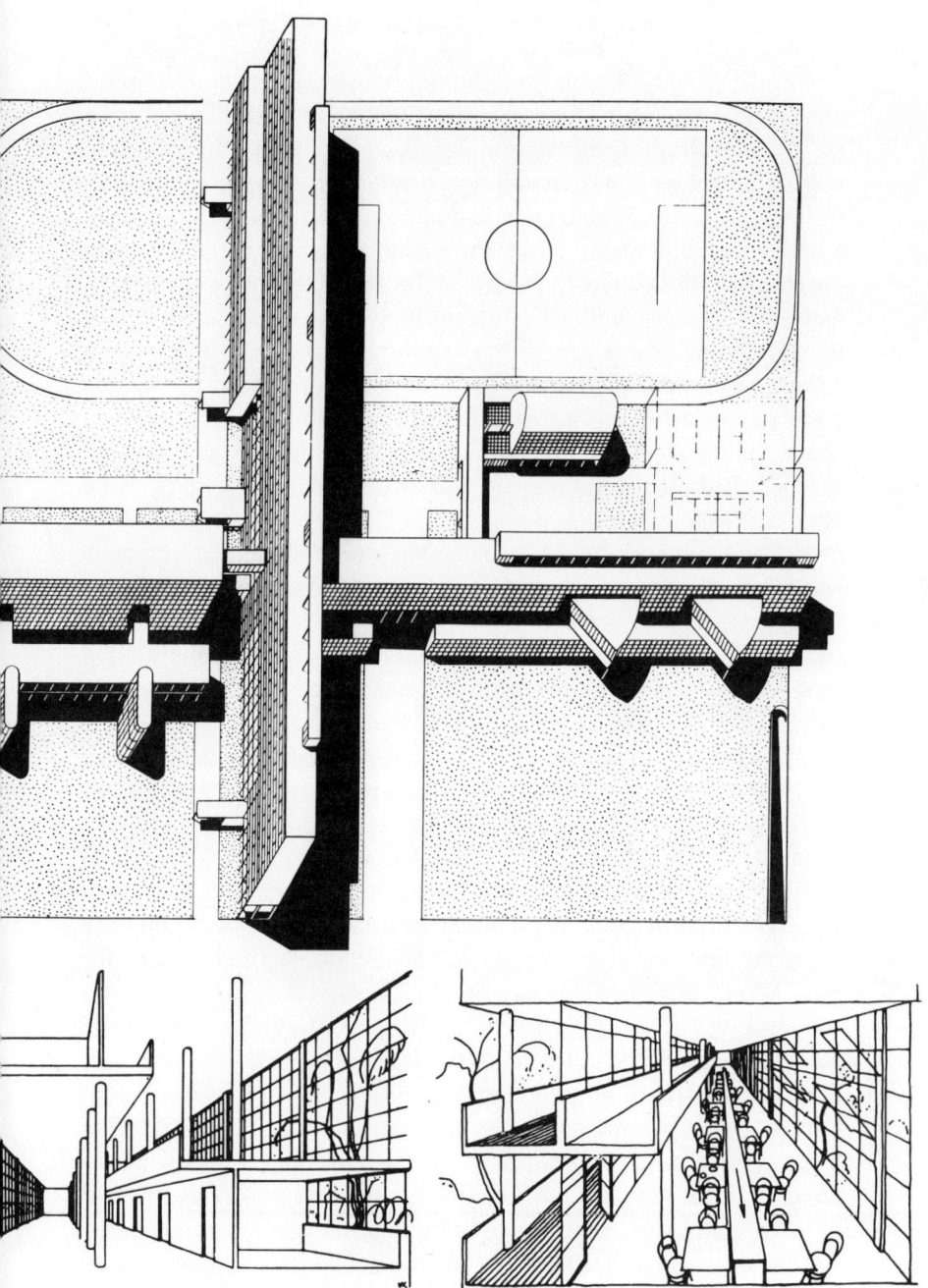

5.3 Home as efficient machine for collective consumption, Barsch and Vladimirov design for a communal house, USSR, 1929. 5.4 Interior view of the communal house. 5.5 Dining room with assembly line for food.

Ultimately very few of these Soviet housing projects were built, and construction problems made some that were realized not merely cold but chilling. There were shortages of building materials and technical problems with detailing. A national housing shortage in the 1920s caused extreme crowding of more than one family in many existing and new units, hardly the social context in which any new program for collective living could be promoted as revolutionary and desirable. Alexandra Kollontai did attempt to evaluate the aesthetic and practical results of the experiments in her book *Women's Labor in Economic Development:* ". . . where previously the women were particularly anxious to have a household of their own, . . . today, on the contrary, it is the husband who suggests that it would not be a bad idea to take a flat, have dinner at home and the wife always about—while the women, especially the growing numbers of women workers who are being drawn into the Republic's creative activities, will not even hear of a 'household of one's own.' 'Better to separate than to agree to a family life with a household and the petty family worries; now I am free to work for the Revolution, but then—then I would be fettered. No, separation would be preferable.' And the husbands have to make the best of it.''[36] There were great attitudinal changes among some Soviet women (not all), but they did not receive adequate material support.

The Soviet housing problem was further complicated by the devastation of World War II, so that as late as 1957, a slogan used to cheer on Soviet builders was ''A separate apartment for each family.'' Historian Anatole Kopp notes that this ''allows us to imagine what the real housing situation in the USSR was like.''[37] In the post–World War II era, an extreme focus on quantity and a push for prefabricated systems obscured many issues of variety and quality, from the scale of the unit plan to the scale of the site plan.

Of all the housing designers influenced by the Soviet experiments, the most influential was Le Corbusier, who admired their plans more than their politics. He made a lasting impact when he suggested that the choice for the twentieth century was architecture or revolution, and announced, ''Revolution can be avoided.''[38] Corbusier worked in Paris, and his plan for a Contemporary City showed machine-aesthetic housing in an urban context, towers in a park, connected by freeways, an image of the 1920s that remained influential through mid-century. Drawing on the ideas of Charles Fourier, and believing that women would remain in paid work, Corbusier also designed the Unité d'Habitation, an apartment building with services. Several of these were built after World War II in various locations. The most famous one in Marseilles included a roof-top day-care center and an internal street of small shops and services within the apartment complex. Sculptural concrete gave these buildings a rough, dynamic quality enhanced by Corbusier's lively sense of color. They became powerful aesthetic models for architects interested in high-rise housing in the United States, Western Europe, Eastern Europe, and the Soviet Union for the next two or three decades, although the programs of Fourier and the Soviets underlying this design were not always well understood by those who copied the form.

Unfortunately, as prefabrication techniques improved and government supports for housing increased, it became possible to put up large groups of high rises with crude industrialized building systems. Not 1,620 residents (Fourier's ideal number, retained by Le Corbusier), but 16,000 or 60,000 might be accommodated; not sculptural concrete but factory-made panels, all identical, could be used. While talented designers, such as Shadrach Woods, managed to build successful housing projects that overcame the disadvantages of precast systems and even reflected the cultural identities of different groups of tenants in significant ways, most housing architects failed to cope. The 20,000-person, postwar housing project, divorced from any context of social idealism, was the perfect job for an egomaniac—or a hack. Just as Americans of the 1950s gasped at the urban scale of Levittown's sacred huts, so Europeans gasped at the urban scale of the new industrialized housing estates, "machines for living." Since a home is neither a sacred hut nor a machine, these popular aesthetic responses in both Europe and the United States made sense, but often cultural critics and designers idealized the opposing tradition. Some Americans thought high-rise housing more elegant than eclectic suburbia; some Europeans preferred the variety of the single-family suburban houses to the towers of identical units they deplored. There was never enough effort to explore a middle ground between the supercongestion of one and the isolation of the other, although some designers did take up this task.

The Machine Aesthetic Modified

The inventive Dutch designer N. J. Habraken attempted to soften and personalize mass housing, beginning with his book *Supports: An Alternative to Mass Housing* in 1964.[39] Habraken rightly criticized the totalitarian, soulless, sameness of mass housing estates produced for the post–World War II reconstruction of Europe. He proposed instead to limit industrialized building systems to the structural frameworks for new housing, and then to establish a more personalized tradition of the insertion of wall panels, doors, windows, and interior partitions and equipment according to the tenants' own purchases from a wide range of available manufactured products. Habraken saw tenant participation in design as desirable, and he believed community-oriented local architects could work with tenants to help them complete their apartments. He allowed for various types of households and for changes in the household over the life cycle by specifying that apartments should expand and contract through attachable capsules and movable exterior and interior walls. Several such projects were built through the energy and dedication of Habraken's disciples, who conducted heroic campaigns to educate public housing agencies, private developers, and tenants to the benefits of such user participation.

However, in housing, flexibility wasn't the only issue. Social services and community spaces serving diverse households had to be part of a larger program. In order to keep the efficient collective consumption of space from becoming too privatized, the special social needs of families headed by women, the elderly, and single people had to be highlighted. One of the most innovative support structures in the early 1970s did include the provision of services for the larger community as well as for tenants. In Rolf Spille's Steilshoop Project in Hamburg, Germany, a group of parents and single people modified public housing by keeping the structural framework but building interior dwelling units of varying sizes, along with shared dining and child care spaces, private work spaces, and social services.[40] The project also included a number of former mental patients as residents and served as a half-way house for them. Steilshoop suggests the extent to which residential stereotypes can be broken down; the sick, the aged, the unmarried were integrated into new types of households and housing complexes, rather than segregated in separate housing projects. Every group of six or seven households became a little neighborhood in itself.

In the United States, the technical side of Habraken's approach was adopted, without much understanding of its social and economic bases, by James Wines and the architectural firm SITE.[41] Their "Highrise of Homes" proposal showed suburban sacred huts with trees and grass filling the floors of a nine- to eleven-story support structure. Component catalogues offered choices of doors, windows, and wall treatments, but no social space was emphasized. In fact, this drawing smashed the sacred huts and the machine for living together quite dramatically, but did not attempt to overcome the programmatic problems of either model, nor did it explain why the speculators' sacred huts were worth the trouble of such intensive engineering efforts.

Cuban designers made another kind of attack on the machine-aesthetic and prefabrication. In the 1970s, they received the industrialized building systems exported to them by the Soviet Union as part of their foreign aid package. The Cubans redesigned these systems; they organized an unusual microbrigade strategy to get more housing built by unskilled workers; and in addition, they had a lively indigenous tradition of graphic design. They simply spent time, money, and energy painting the gray concrete four story walk-ups in every possible wonderful color combination—red and yellow, white and orange, green and blue, until they had produced results not unlike the sculptures of De Stijl or Purism, but with a less academic, more Latin flavor. Lush tropical landscaping was added, greenery and sun took over, and the results are a great improvement on the mass housing designed by Soviet engineers and architects. They reconciled the need for mass production with varied collective—rather than individual—expression.

The Machine Aesthetic and Social Engineering

By the mid-twentieth century there also developed a large corps of behavioral experts who professed to be able to help designers of mass housing match tenants' life styles with appropriate spatial responses, thus ensuring more pleasant aesthetic and social experiences. Women might have expected that the involvement of sociologists, social geographers, and environmental psychologists would give to housing design a sense of scrutinizing individual needs a bit more precisely. Some behavioral scientists who began to work on architectural programming and postconstruction evaluation did claim to research "needs." However, the researchers attracted to housing design were often not the most sophisticated social scientists, but those most limited in their political interests and methodological approaches. While some exceptional researchers such as Florence Ladd, Sandra Howell, and Clare Cooper were skillful in illuminating the spatial needs of teenagers, the elderly, and families, others presented tired stereotypes as good practice, "social science," or "self-awareness." The clients likely to employ them were often the largest bureaucracies with the strongest interest in standardizing human behavior—housing agencies at the flexible end of the spectrum, big corporations in the middle, social welfare groups and departments of correction, heirs of the Benthamite tradition, at the rigid end. The result was the programing of space in mass housing to suit highly normative schemes of human values.

The evolution of Parker Morris housing standards, originated in England but disseminated in "Homes For Today and Tomorrow" throughout the rest of the English speaking world, provides a case in point. First-year design students still study these sketches of residential life accompanied by little scenarios of home activities, complete with standard dimensions for housing space. There is nothing wrong with the dimensions, but the scenarios, even in the 1972 edition, are what Octavia Hill, the Victorian housing manager so influenced by Ruskin, might have drawn up in the 1890s had she the option of programing new buildings instead of managing old ones. The characters are respectable, clean, tidy parents, heavy TV-watchers and appliance-users, never rowdy, drunk, lustful, sick, or careless. Most of all, they move through life in a rigidly frozen division of labor. At noon, for instance, "When the children play indoors Mother needs to be able to see them from the kitchen, but they should be away from the kitchen equipment and not under her feet." Or at 7 P.M., "When Father repairs something, he needs to be out of Mother's way in the kitchen and where he will not disturb sleeping children." He washes the car, she gets out of the kitchen occasionally to vacuum the floor and dress the baby. As a supposed concession to changing roles, the designer is now instructed to plan the interior and exterior carefully, "to give working wives a better chance of doing both jobs [housework and paid employment] without too much strain."[42]

The next generation of researchers claimed even more authority to help people work through, verbalize, and enjoy their experience of housing. Like their Parker Morris predecessors, they were normative. Their great norm was not respectability but "do your own thing." An example of one very flawed work of this genre is Glenn Robert Lym's *A Psychology of Building: How We Shape and Experience Our Structured Space*. He offers a chapter on "Spatial Orders," and another on "The Spatial Order of the Home" in which he analyzes two couples, their apartments in multi-family housing complexes, and the life choices they are supposed to represent. In each example the man and woman are fighting over territory in a two-bedroom apartment. In each couple, the male attempts to seize the second bedroom and make it into a personal, inviolable work space his wife cannot enter. In the first example the male seizes the second bedroom for his private study, while his wife does her work on the dining-room table. The male also appropriates the couple's only oriental rug for his study. Lym quotes the wife, who declares: "When my husband is not home, I open the study door, even though I know the cat will go in and pull up on the rug. I just leave it open and that way the study becomes a part of the apartment." Lym decides that this woman has achieved emotional growth because she has developed a personal, door-opening ritual to get a look at the jointly owned rug and "to make herself feel whole again."[43] The question of where she works and when is never addressed.

In Lym's second example, the male wants to use the second bedroom as a work space for ceramics, his hobby, and his wife wants it to be a clean, unchaotic, dining room, since there is no other place for their dining table. The husband protests: "We should each have a place that is all our own, that we can just do whatever we feel like, make all kinds of mess or noise. I'd have my pots all over. And when I would get done potting, I wouldn't clean up." Lym's analysis is confined to cheering this husband for resisting the role of "son to a manipulatory wife-mother." Lym does not ask who does the cooking and serving of food, nor does he consider the dining room a work space. He also fails to ask how the wife is to get comparable space of her own, since there is no other room available. Lym claims that the male in this case "evolved a spatial order of the home as a single personal space amid collective space." He praised him and others who have "entered into a responsive dialogue with their physical environments" and "used housing to reflect upon and to help come to terms with themselves."[44]

On the subject of male-female territory, Virginia Woolf, in *A Room of One's Own* in 1928, had more perceptive things to say: "I thought how unpleasant it is to be locked out; and I thought how it is worse to be locked in. . . ." Woolf saw "the safety and prosperity of one sex and . . . the poverty and insecurity of the other,"[45] but for many social scientists concerned about housing her essay seems never to have become required reading. The failure of territorial analysis to deal with gender and aesthetics, at a theoretical as well as an empirical level,[46] suggests that there is a great need of new research to look at spatial cognition in the context of gender socialization.[47]

Dynamite

The social scientists claimed to be able to help people adjust to mass housing and the industrial aesthetic. If Corbusier said "Architecture or Revolution. Revolution can be avoided," the social workers and social scientists said, "We can help manage the architecture." In the United States, Corbusier's ideas about the ideal city as a collection of residential towers in a park influenced public housing agencies, who after the 1949 Housing Act were empowered to build for the poor and minority groups who could not afford suburban tract houses. Subsidies were greatest for the FHA / VA homeowner (suburban mortgage supports, tax deductions, and highways, rather than direct housing construction and public transportation subsidies), while the public housing that was built was often cheap, nasty, and badly thought-out. Pioneers of housing reform such as Edith Elmer Wood and Catherine Bauer who had drafted, lobbied, and nursed the Wagner Act through Congress in 1937 were dismayed at many of the resulting programs—Bauer herself repudiated "the dreary deadlock of public housing" in the 1950s, having shown how to do much better in the Mackley Houses of 1935 in Philadelphia,[48] when she helped members of a textile union get good housing and services. Conventional construction, rather than industrialized building systems, was generally used for public housing in the United States, but this was a testament to the power of the building trades unions and of construction materials suppliers more than any resistance to the machine aesthetic of Europe. The buildings were similar in scale and uniformity of units.

Public housing projects in New York, Chicago, Boston, and smaller places were, in the 1950s and early 1960s, usually grim, brick structures badly sited in islands of asphalt, whether three stories high or thirty. Although the mid-1960s introduced more varied, low-rise designs, on scattered sites, the earlier "projects" continue to house the poorest people with no other housing choices. In 1981 the 1.2 million Public Housing Authority tenants averaged 28 percent of median U.S. family income. Almost 60 percent were minority households; 25 percent elderly.[49] Female-headed families predominated. The projects became sites of crime, none more so than the Pruitt-Igoe complex in Saint Louis, designed in the mid-1950s by Minoru Yamasaki and demolished in 1972—as an unliveable place—by the agency that built it.

Pruitt-Igoe came to stand for the confrontation between the public housing bureaucracies and ghetto residents who objected to the building program as much as to the aesthetic. Ignoring the subtle social and architectural analyses of Pruitt-Igoe by sociologist Lee Rainwater, architectural critic Charles Jencks pushed aside all of the complexities of female-headed families and ghetto residents' lives to identify the dynamiting of Pruitt-Igoe as the start of an era when architects would stop trying to resolve social issues and return to an "art for art's sake" approach to design. For Jencks, mass housing was so identified with the modern movement in architecture that when mass housing was challenged as an architectural program, he felt able to denounce any worth in the machine aesthetic as an architectural style. Thus he wrote that the end of the modern movement in architecture, as a style, occurred at exactly the hour when the public housing complex by Yamasaki was demolished: July 15, 1972, 3:32 P.M., "Boom, boom, boom."[50]

Jencks became famous when he announced the arrival of post-Modern architecture as an aesthetic alternative, with a collection of examples by practitioners known for their stylistic eclecticism. Architects long frustrated by the overall conditions of work in the profession rushed to follow these new aesthetic adventures and abandon their sense of guilt and frustration about the larger problems of patronage for housing. In the ensuing stampede, many modest examples of good multi-family housing with careful social and aesthetic planning, such as the Mackley Houses or some of the projects done by Lynda Simmons of Phipps Houses, a nonprofit housing developer in New York, were overlooked as uninteresting, "built sociology."

Just as the single-family, sacred hut architects had borrowed more and more heavily on the machine aesthetic so Jencks encouraged

machine aesthetic designers to return to the sacred hut and its archetypal significance. He himself began to work on a single-family
house with murals of the four seasons and 52 steps, one for each
week of the year, claiming that cosmological symbolism (what he
called "programming") reached the heart of architectural meaning.[51] One can contrast Jencks' response to Pruitt-Igoe to that of Jan
Wampler, a more socially concerned housing architect and critic,
who used the same moment of reconsideration to begin an ambitious
design project to modernize a large public housing complex,
Columbia Point, in Dorchester, Massachusetts.[52] Wampler tried to
reprogram the buildings to suit the Black and Hispanic single-parent
families who lived there. He combined small units to make larger
ones, introduced extensive spaces for day-care and community
facilities, redesigned windows and added landscaping. Unfortunately, just after this project won a major award, Wampler chose an
inopportune moment to testify against corruption in public works
and public housing in Massachusetts, and his project was never
implemented.

While Wampler reprogramed his housing to deal with poverty
and women's needs, he was much less influential than Jencks, who
did try to write about the social and economic puzzles of corporate
and government patronage, but was unable to analyze the programmatic faults of either sacred-hut or machine-aesthetic housing.
Instead, Jencks developed a series of oppositional categories such
as warm / cold and female / male to try to sort out aesthetic issues.
He opposed warm, female, organic, complex, and ornamented
qualities, against cold, male, synthetic, straightforward, high-tech
qualities, but his confusion between program and style was
obvious.[53] In his book, *The Language of Post-Modern Architecture,* he couldn't resist including an interior perspective of "A
Brothel for Oil Men in the Desert" (complete with scantily clad
prostitutes) as an example of warm, complex, pneumatic architecture, although it distracted from his larger argument. Jencks'
"female / male" stylistic dichotomy represented the same old program for gender: earth mother and organization man, prehistoric
squaw and racing-car driver, prostitute and petroleum engineer.

Just as the advocates of the haven strategy had secluded women
in the home to keep the human race partly protected from the market
economy (and then asked women to undertake wage work to help
pay for the seclusion), so the advocates of the industrial strategy
had demanded the full integration of women into the socialized labor

of industrial society (and then asked women to keep the hearth fires burning too). Neither model of home life led to an acceptable building program for housing in the twentieth century. Ingenious community participation and behavioral engineering can't correct the wrong program, any more than new technologies can fix the tracts of sacred huts. Modern family patterns and housing needs are too complex for either caricature. The housing bureaucracy's dynamite didn't help, nor did any use of this incident to date the end of an era, when, in fact, hundreds of millions of urban residents all over the world live in high-rise mass housing and will continue to do so. Several million Americans in high-rise public housing may find their future aesthetic satisfaction depends on learning how best to modify these structures in social, economic, and aesthetic terms. If the tracts of suburbia fail to offer solutions, perhaps the history of the neighborhood strategy and its aesthetic offers some clues.

The Aesthetics of the Neighborhood Strategy: Shared Greens, Courtyards, and Arcades in the Village and the Cloister

The aesthetic models for the neighborhood strategy were the village and the cloister. The designers who favored this approach believed that in terms of housing, the whole must be more than the sum of its parts. For private space to become a home, it must be joined to a range of semi-private, semi-public, and public spaces, and linked to appropriate social and economic institutions assuring the continuity of human activity in these spaces. The neighborhood strategy not only involved thinking about the reorganization of home in industrial society, it also involved defining "home" at every spatial level—from the house, to the neighborhood, the town, the homeland, and the planet. If the haven strategy stressed privacy, and the industrial strategy stressed efficiency; the neighborhood strategy highlighted accountability.

Just as Bentham's Panopticon prefigured later interest in the home as machine, so Thomas Jefferson's "academical village" at the University of Virginia prefigured later interest in the home as part of a neighborhood. Although Jefferson had also promoted the isolated family farm, his University of Virginia commission offered him the chance to build housing for students and faculty beginning in 1817. He organized the students' rooms along an arcaded walk

5.6 Home as a neighborhood modeled on the pre-industrial village. Raymond Unwin, sketch of a cooperative quadrangle, 1902.

5.7 Barry Parker, sketch of a cooperative quadrangle, 1912. This is very similar to examples built at Welwyn, Letchworth, and Hampstead in England; it recalls the cloisters of Oxford and Cambridge colleges.

5.8 Precedent for the neighborhood strategy: Thomas Jefferson, the "academical village" of the University of Virginia, view. Pavilions housing professors are linked by arcades lined with rooms for students.

punctuated by pavilions serving as faculty residences and lecture halls. A domed library culminated the scheme. Among the precedents for this project were the French hospital designs of the late eighteenth century, but Jefferson also cherished the Carthusian monastery of Pavia, near Milan, as a model of collective living and he visited it before commencing his design work at Charlottesville.

An archetypal expression of the relationship between privacy and community, Pavia consisted of private cells for each monk, connected by a generous arcade to a communal dining room, church, and large estate (where produce was grown to support not only the praying monks but each of the lay brothers and agricultural workers necessary to provide the economic base for the spiritual activity). The cells looked like sacred huts. They were peaked-roof houses with walled gardens, heavy doors, small windows, well-defined chimneys. The monks devised ingenious, flexible, minimal furnishings for each hut that still look modern. At the same time, the monastery was a collective; the broad arcade gathered the meditating monks into the common dining room. When Jefferson translated the spatial program at Pavia into the University of Virginia, in the early nineteenth century, the monks' huts become the professors' pavilions. (There, too, hierarchies of labor were required: just as the monks had lay brothers, the young men had personal servants and the professors had household slaves.) Using this monastic model, Jefferson's design of the academical village still stands as one of the most important American architectural statements about how to link individuals, households, and work spaces.

5.9 Precedent for the neighborhood strategy, Certosa di Pavia, view of the main cloister showing arcade linking each monk's cell and garden to the common dining room, chapel, and other facilities.

5.10 Certosa di Pavia, private garden at the monk's cell.

5.11 Certosa di Pavia, folding table with shelves

Throughout the second half of the nineteenth century, as American women began to experiment with the neighborhood strategy and its implications for housing design, plans for courtyards and arcades appeared. Following the work of Caroline Howard Gilman, Jane Sophia Appleton, and Amelia Bloomer, Melusina Peirce began to develop a more thorough analysis of the architectural implications of cooperative housekeeping.[54] When she proposed a housewives' producers cooperative in 1868, she also introduced the idea of a model neighborhood of thirty-six houses with a single work center, a building with a central courtyard and arcades. Marie Stevens Howland tried to develop this idea.[55] In the 1890s, Mary Coleman Stuckert of Denver reiterated Peirce's and Howland's ideas when she exhibited a model for an urban row house development with a central open space, central kitchen and shared child-care facilities. In 1915 Alice Constance Austin tried to develop a new Californian city with the same centralized services.[56] While they built relatively little themselves, the influence of these material feminists on architects and planners in both the United States and Europe was considerable. They must be credited with the concept of modern family life crucial to the programing of modern housing.

Finally the designers of the Garden Cities movement, including Ebenezer Howard, Raymond Unwin, and M. H. Baillie Scott, translated the material feminists' ideas into built form. Their overall objectives included ending the split between town and country, easing the conflict between capital and labor through cooperative production, and ending the servant problem and the exploitation of women through cooperative cooking and dining.[57] The physical framework for this activity was the new town of 30,000 people, designed around "cooperative quadrangles," or living groups of about thirty households with a common dining room. Unwin's sketch of the earliest cooperative quadrangle suggests an Oxford or Cambridge college, or a medieval village, which was the inspiration many designers, such as M. H. Baillie Scott, also adopted.

The cooperative quadrangle looked like home—albeit an institutional one. The inglenooks, half-timbering, stucco, peaked roofs, massive hearths, numerous chimneys, and the interior detailing with wood and handmade ceramic tile, all recalled the Arts and Crafts movement led by Charles Ashbee and William Morris, and their polemics against the machine. The cozy feeling of these cloistered housing quadrangles was enhanced by flower gardens and vegetable gardens, shaded arcades and benches. Unlike the sacred hut houses of the early twentieth century that shared some of these materials and details, the quadrangles of the Garden City designers attempted to recreate the scale of larger social institutions, recognizing that the rural subsistence farmstead could no longer be the unit of urban organization or of aesthetic expression.

While the Garden Cities influenced planners all over the world, and one of Howard's favorite architectural styles—Tudor revival—became popular with architects all over the United States, the program for the cooperative quadrangle was not part of the set of ideas fully realized in England or widely exported. In the United States, between 1910 and 1940, several housing developments were influenced by the Garden Cities approach. The concepts of neighborhood planning at Forest Hills, New York, developed by Grosvenor Atterbury in 1911, included the provision of an apartment hotel structure for singles and the elderly in a town square at the railroad station, as well as clusters of attached houses. Clarence Stein and Henry Wright, the designers of several major projects, began developing their idea, called the superblock, in 1924 at Sunnyside, Long Island, where they created a small park at the heart of a moderate income housing development. In 1929 at Radburn, New Jersey, Stein and Wright designed a garden city "for the motor age," restricting the domain of the automobile by developing pedestrian courtyards leading to a larger park system running through the project.

Finally, one project synthesized the influence of Jefferson's academical village, the feminist experiments, and the Garden Cities. As we have seen, the Baldwin Hills Village in Los Angeles, where Clarence Stein served as consultant to Robert Alexander and the other local architects, opened in 1942.[58] A leisurely walk through the three parks of this project today reveals mature trees, tended flowers, an expansion and contraction of landscaped spaces that is in striking contradiction to awareness that one is in the heart of a major city, in the center of a low-cost housing complex.[59] Each housing unit, small or large, also has a private garden. Serpentine walls enclosing the gardens recall Jefferson's influence. Like Markelius in Stockholm and Howard at Homesgarth, some of the designers moved into this project themselves, as a statement of their convictions, to reiterate the connections between personal life style and political beliefs so lacking in many other housing designers' work.

Another brilliant designer in the American tradition who found

low-cost housing with shared courtyards the most interesting architectural problem he undertook was Irving Gill. Gill, educated in the
office of Louis Sullivan, was the son of a building contractor from
Syracuse, New York. American to the core, he tried to find a way
to develop a vernacular style suited to Los Angeles and San Diego.
He admired the adobe structures, arcades and courtyards of the
Spanish colonial style, but redefined these traditions with a pure
geometry of cubes and circles, and with an innovative technological
approach using concrete walls poured in place in the ground and
raised into position in the manner of traditional barn raising. If ever
a designer was prepared to resolve the aesthetic and technical ambi-
guities of the twentieth century, it was Gill.

His Horatio West Court in Santa Monica and his Lewis Courts in
Sierra Madre both display his genius for manipulating shared spaces.
(The Lewis Courts are especially successful, so much so that the
client decided that middle-class rents could be charged for what
started as a low-income housing project.) In each case Gill also

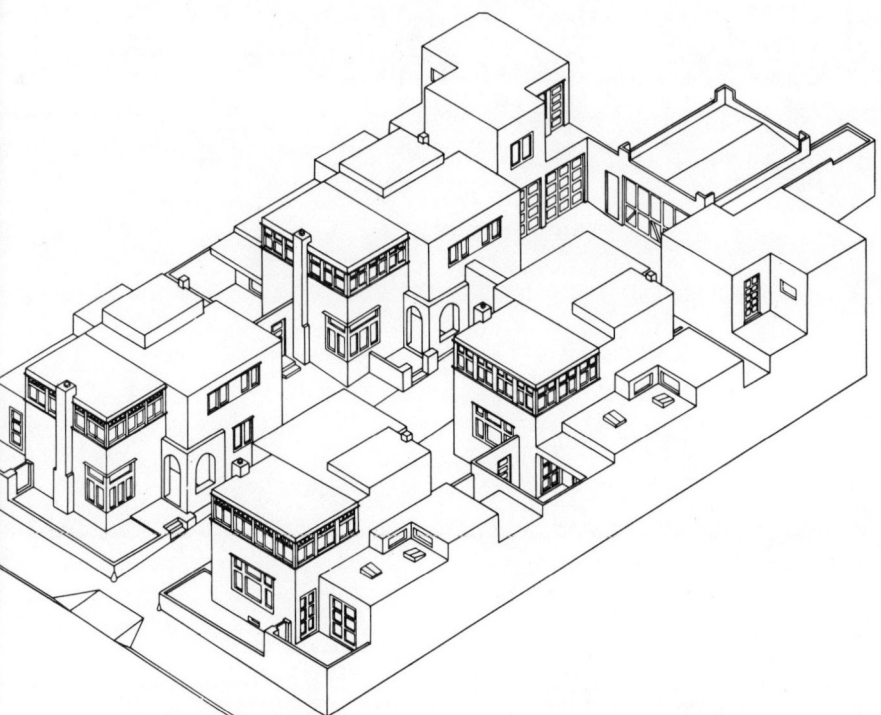

5.12 Irving Gill, Horatio West Courts, Santa Monica, 1919, axonometric drawing. (Courtesy of Margaret Bach)

drew from the bungalow courts and courtyard housing schemes of Los Angeles as the strongest local tradition for multi-family housing design. Projects such as Bowen Court in Pasadena in the Craftsman style by the Heinemann brothers, or the Andalusia in Hollywood, in the Mediterranean revival style by Arthur and Nina Zwebel, expressed many of the same commitments in program as Gill's work, but were a bit more flamboyant aesthetically.[60] In each case the use of lush landscaping and of local ceramic tiles heightened the sense of place. Today Los Angeles remains the American city with the most interesting multi-family housing stock on the courtyard model, and the best projects are still worth studying.

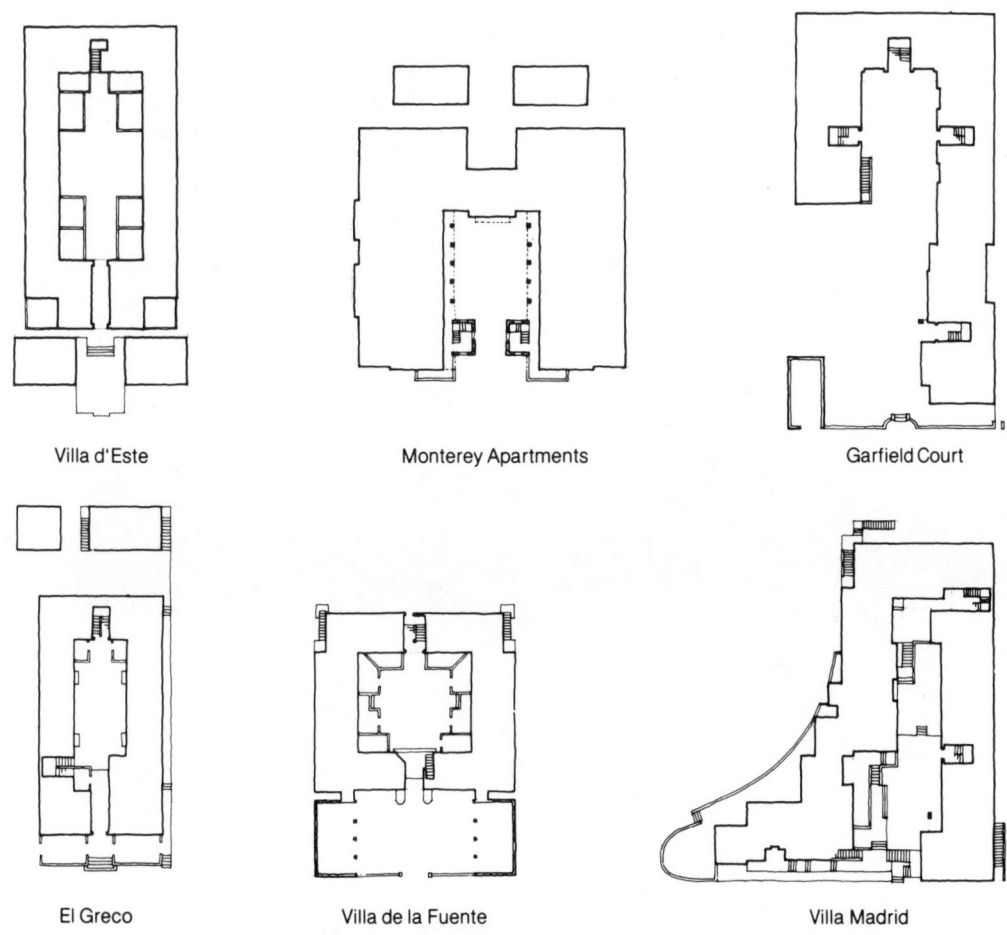

Villa d'Este   Monterey Apartments   Garfield Court

El Greco   Villa de la Fuente   Villa Madrid

5.13 Organizational diagrams of courtyard housing built in Southern California between 1920 and 1930. (After Polyzoides, Sherwood, and Tice, *Courtyard Housing in Los Angeles,* University of California Press, 1981)

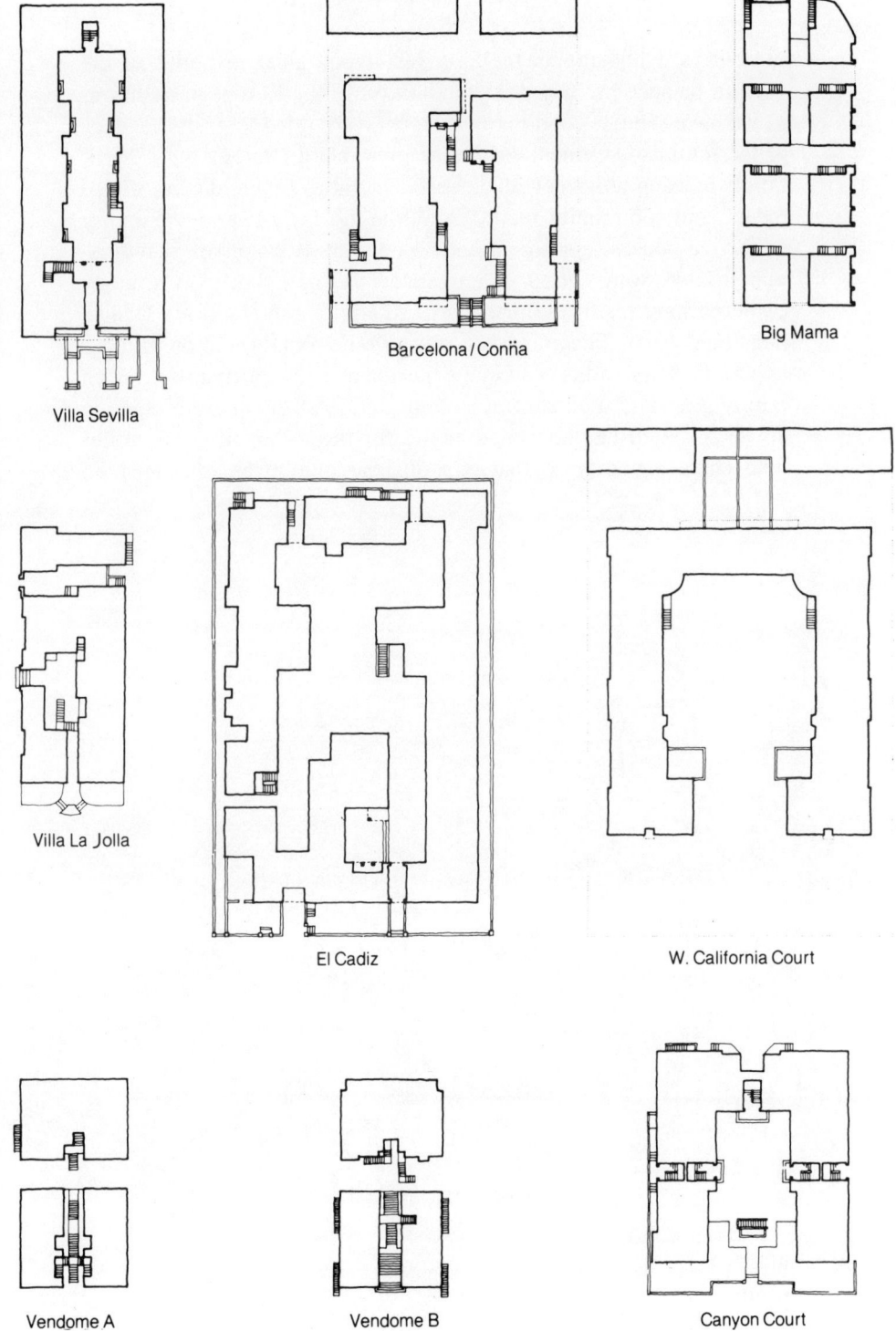

Villa Sevilla

Barcelona / Conña

Big Mama

Villa La Jolla

El Cadiz

W. California Court

Vendome A

Vendome B

Canyon Court

Courtyard housing is the strongest typological response to the need to balance privacy and community. In the European tradition, as we have seen, a good many designers struggled to graft the ideas of the feminist exponents of the neighborhood strategy onto multi-family housing projects with extensive facilities for child care, shared meals, and community facilities. While the early twentieth century collective houses, apartment hotels, and family hotels of Scandinavia provide some good examples of the neighborhood strategy explored in terms of the machine aesthetic, a contemporary Danish housing project, Tynggarden, carries on the social tradition of these experiments and adds aesthetic experiment with courtyards.[61] Each family gave up 10 percent of its allocated interior square footage to create a shared neighborhood center for the ten to fifteen families who share a courtyard that contains the mailboxes, the washing

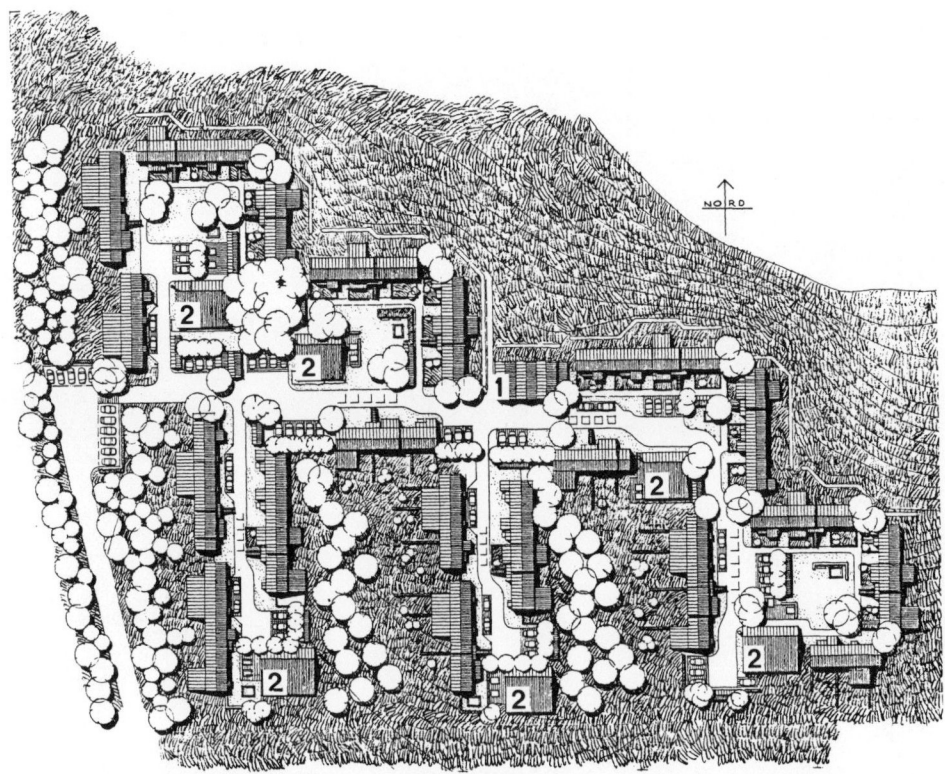

5.14 Tynggarden, outside of Copenhagen, Denmark. Site plan showing six courtyards housing about fifteen families each. (1) Central building with cafe and sports facilities; (2) multi-purpose community buildings.

5.15 Tynggarden. Views: *A*, community building, side view showing porch with mailboxes. Each family gave up 10 percent of their interior private space to help make this community building; *B*, courtyard with adventure playground; *C*, courtyard with grass; *D*, town house; *E*, parking.

machines and dryers, a community kitchen, and a large two-level space for activities planned by the residents, from child care to classes to political meetings. The designers also developed plans for the eventual expansion of the private units, to permit future flexibility for adding rental units or housing elderly dependents that the minimum square footages ruled out.

Their aesthetic favored massing, color, and wood siding similar to the large red and cream-colored Danish barns in the agricultural area surrounding the project. To these forms and colors they added a few metallic materials, so that the style of the Citroen "Deux Chevaux" car fits right in. At the same time, adventure playgrounds fill the active courtyards; grass, flowers, and vines are in the quiet courtyards. The entire project also has a community center with a cafe out front, in addition to the neighborhood centers.

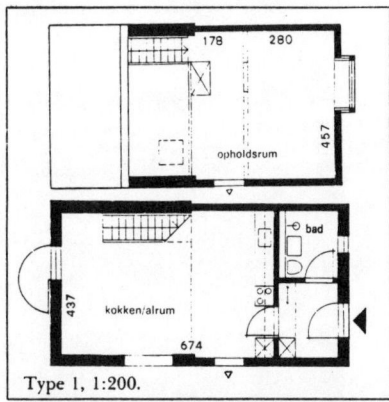

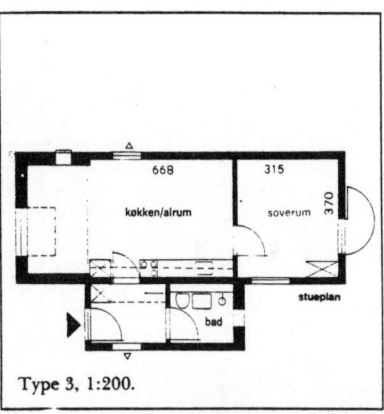

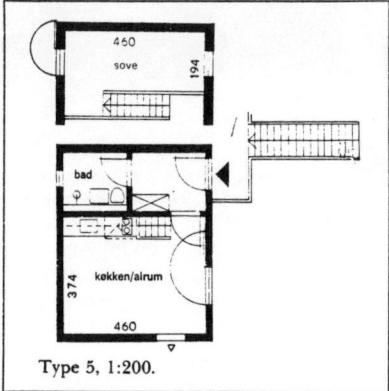

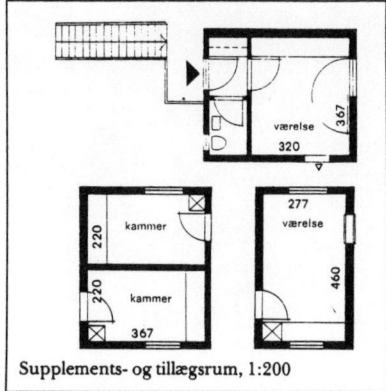

5.16 Tynggarden. Plans of typical town houses. The living spaces include kitchens. Types 1 and 5 have loft bedrooms. The "supplements" are rooms that can be added later.

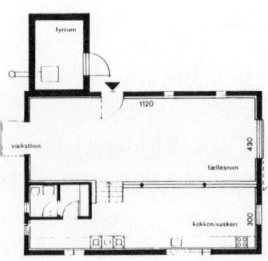

5.17 Tynggarden. Plan of community building located in each courtyard, a two-level space with kitchen, laundry, and bath on the lower level; open space for classes, meetings, day care, or work on the upper level. The porch area next to the entrance includes mailboxes.

Tynggarden is a successful project on many levels. It draws on the agricultural building types of the region, but goes beyond the recalling of stylistic details or the sacred-hut mentality to make a new community comfortable with a mixture of old and new spatial and technical forms: row houses and apartments, metal stairs, corrugated metal roofs, cars. The skyline of a village is simulated in the shed roofs of the community centers, with their place for solar panels, and their exaggeratedly tall chimneys, and what could be more sociable than a large front porch lined with mailboxes next to a bench? Unlike the cooperative quadrangles of the Garden Cities movement, which look a bit corny in their Tudor half-timbering, the courtyards of Tynggarden look backwards and forwards at the same time, carrying a complex social program and cultural agenda into fulfillment through a stylistic expression combining the old and the new.

Another European project of great interest is Aldo Van Eyck's courtyard housing complex for single-parent mothers in Amsterdam, Holland.[62] He has long been known as a talented designer giving care and attention to both social program and aesthetic realization. In this commission his client was an institution. He made

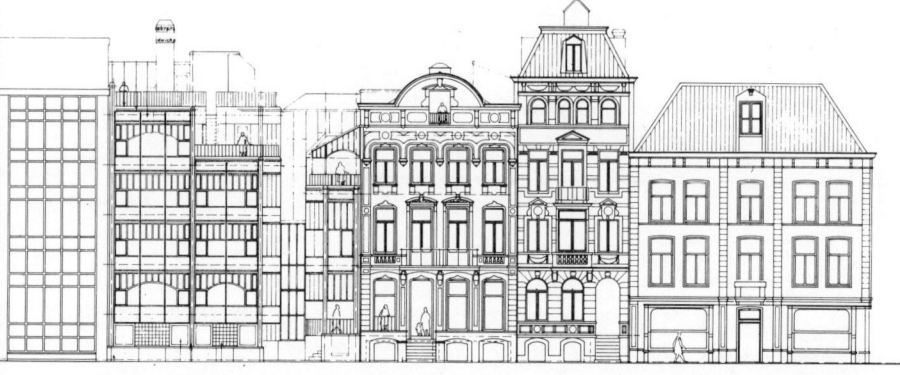

5.18 Aldo Van Eyck, The Mothers' House, Amsterdam, 1980, elevation of the street façade showing its integration with existing buildings.

housing for children, housing for parents, counseling spaces, and a common dining facility in addition to offices and outdoor space. "The Mothers' House" suggests what can be done to make institutional housing a truly supportive setting for the single-parent mother, in aesthetic as well as social terms. A rainbow of colors animates the building; the courtyard is beautiful and serene. The kibbutz-like nature of the child-rearing spaces may seem too communal for many households, but the project helps these single parents make a transition, rather than offering them a permanent residence. The Mothers' House is a project that helps sustain a new family form—the single-parent family—in urban society, rather than a model of a permanent collective settlement, such as the Israeli kibbutzim or American communes of the nineteenth and twentieth centuries, which go beyond a neighborhood strategy into a shared communal life.

5.19 The Mothers' House, plans. BASEMENT: (1) bicycles and prams; (2) laundry; (3) larder; (4) play areas in groups for children ages 1–6; (5) bedrooms for groups of children; (7) lobby; (8) store room; (9) outdoor play area with sculptured hill; (10) sand box; (11) office space. MEZZANINE: (1) entrance; (2) hall; (3) dining room; (4) kitchen; (5) guest room; (6) night assistant; (7) niches for playing; (9) meeting room; (8 and 10) administration. FIRST FLOOR: (1) hall; (2) work rooms; (3) doctor; (4) children 1–6; (5) loggia; (6) janitor's lodge. SECOND FLOOR: (1) hall; (2) work rooms; (3) babies' housing; (4) kitchen serving babies; (5) tableware; (6) parents' living rooms; (7) parents' bedrooms; (8) bathroom; (9) loggia; (10) terrace. THIRD FLOOR: (1) entrance; (2) meeting room; (3) babies; (4) sick bay; (5) parents' bedrooms; (6) bathroom; (7) loggia; (8) terrace. ATTIC: (1) heating system; (2) terrace; (3) bedrooms; (4) bathroom.

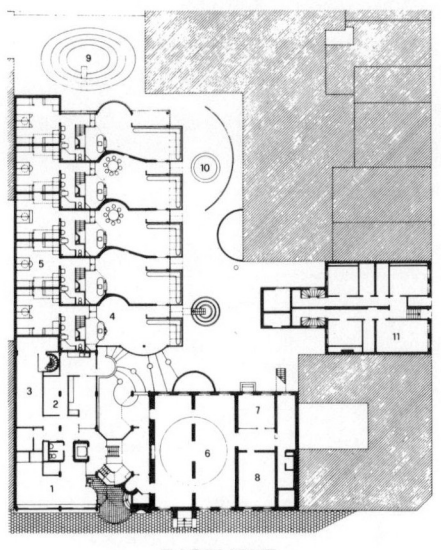

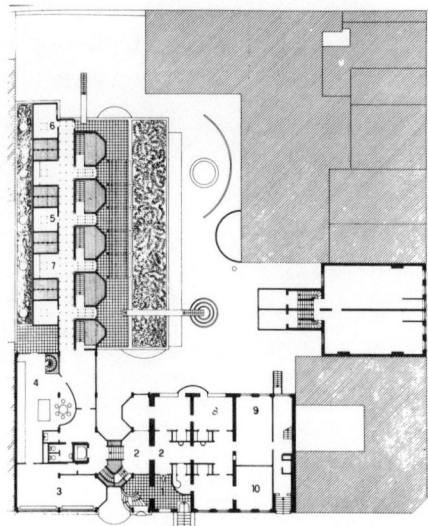

BASEMENT   MEZZANINE

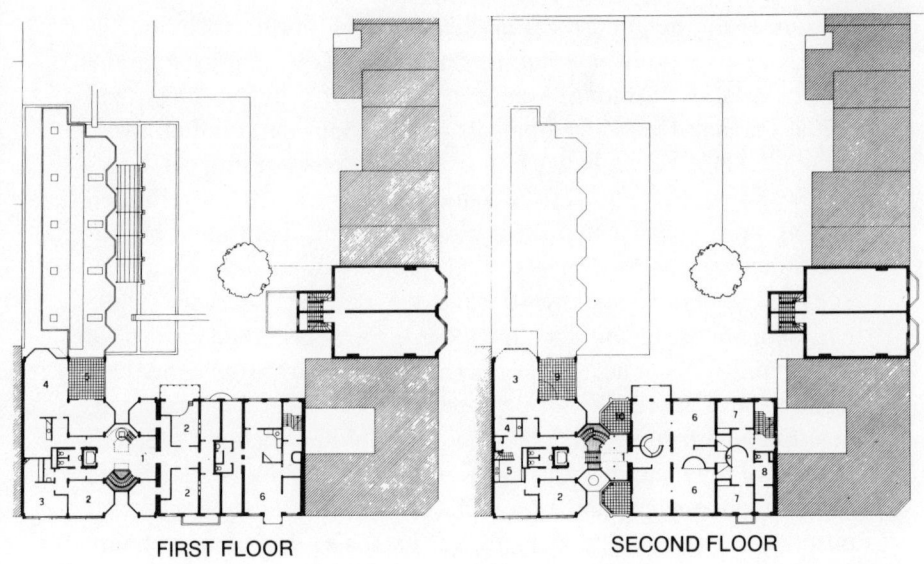

FIRST FLOOR

SECOND FLOOR

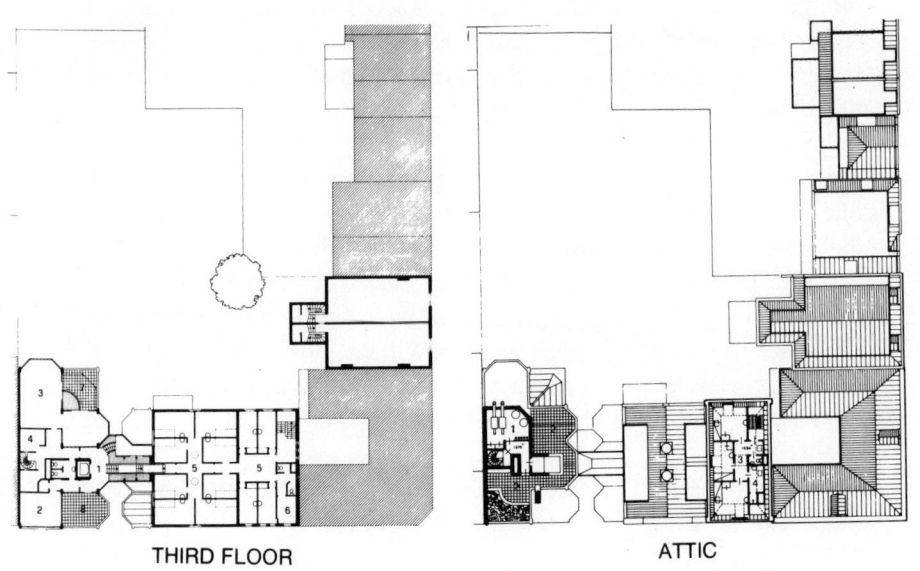

THIRD FLOOR

ATTIC

Condomania

Of course, the neighborhood aesthetic can be borrowed by developers who have profit in mind, as can any aesthetic approach or any vernacular style. Among American developers, in the 1960s and 1970s, Planned Unit Developments (PUDs) appeared to offer a way to imitate some of the better low-rise, high-density European housing developments, and, at the same time, a way to sell attached housing units cheaper than tract houses, or rent them more expensively than garden apartments. Such projects often were quite correctly presented as a way to save the natural landscape while regrouping housing units in a more convenient form than the typical single family residence (R-1) tract.[63] But the world of condoland began to look more like Disneyland than any local neighborhood. New England fishing village condos appeared in Phoenix; Mediterranean hill town condos arose in Kansas City. In almost every case the automobile wrecked the pre-industrial vernacular style (however unsuited to the site and climate) by its scale. Two cars per unit became standard parking requirements. So scraps of Old World building forms sat in between streets sized for the turning radii of new American Buicks and Fords.

Gone were the powerful arcades or pedestrian circulation systems crucial to this approach to programing and design. All the afterthoughts—carriage lamps, bollards, and artifical lakes—couldn't redeem the awkward juxtapositions of old and new. Prospective buyers were often encouraged to join the condominium "community" by purchasing a unit, but the community facilities tended to be a tennis court, a swimming pool, or a card room rather than child care or other services that connected to the basic needs of life. When one Los Angeles company (the Ring brothers) did experiment with day care in rental apartments, they quickly found it was far too complex to make profits, and switched back to mundane community card rooms in their next projects. Of course part of the charm of the monastic model or the pre-industrial village lies in the variety of economic activities that make such a complex self-sufficient. The condo development without small shops and small gardens has no chance of this aesthetic effect.

Recently the U.S. Department of Housing and Urban Development and the Urban Land Institute produced a report, *The Affordable Community: Growth, Change and Choice in the 80s,* that endorsed condominiums and the concept of "urban villages."[64] The examples of good practice shown in the booklet reverberate with the stylistic anxieties of condominimums trying to look like the old neighborhood; the Big Bad Wolf dressed as Grandma and waiting for Red Riding Hood comes to mind. This is a reworking of the neighborhood strategy agreed to by a committee composed of both developers and elected officials; it is not a call for better public housing design or better social service planning. The report defines "affordable housing" as multi-family condominiums, plus mobile homes (manufactured housing); houses without side yards (zero-lot-line housing); and four-family houses (four-unit cluster housing). Unfortunately the call for these choices is couched in terms of easing zoning and planning regulations to permit private developers to build cheaper space and sell it more profitably in the open market. With what planner Daniel Lauber has criticized as a "distinct developer bias," the authors of the report urge that the power of eminent domain be given to private or quasi-public organizations. They also propose that projects be allowed to proceed before all permits are awarded. And, on the topic of affordable rental housing, Lauber contends, "George Orwell would have been proud of the doublespeak."[65]

Yet as architect Roger Montgomery has pointed out, condominium developers provide the great bulk of commissions for American architects interested in more sophisticated housing design than the one-family tract houses of the 1950s.[66] As denser, more complicated projects than tract houses, they require skilled designers to handle the site planning and building design, and this represents a substantial opportunity for the design professions. Today, whenever housing starts are down, these same skilled practitioners are often underemployed or unemployed. As more building opportunities return, it will be especially important for designers to be very clear about priorities and models for future housing.

The neighborhood strategy depends on a social and economic program of mutual accountability to work, not merely swimming pools or peaked roof townhouses as symbols of organic community. It not only accommodates but really requires interdependencies of a more fundamental kind. The models of the cloister, the pre-industrial village, the village green, the college quadrangle hold their charm for all of us. But the economic and social pressures fragmenting these coherent spaces have been steady for the last century and a half, during the era of cheap energy, especially in the last eighty years of increasing automobile usage. Now standards are changing; if zero-lot-lines and manufactured boxes are possible, so are fewer cars, fewer garages, more day care, more public transit, more small scale economic activities, and stronger pedestrian spaces. The society that has more cars than children has a hard time shoe-horning itself into housing based on the pre-industrial village or the monk's cloister, unless some drastic new programing decisions are established for the sake of retaining human scale, social services, and economic activity in housing.

Three Architectural Strategies and the Future of Housing

Beecher, Bebel, and Peirce all stamped their conceptual models of home with the fears and desires of the mid-nineteenth century. The architectural programs derived from that time are all anachronistic: the hope of seclusion embodied in the hut; the fantasy of efficiency attached to the machine; the nostalgia for the intact community of village or cloister expressed in the neighborhood model. Yet each of these mid-nineteenth century architectural programs has per-sisted, with a strong aesthetic, and these programs may persist into the twenty-first century. Huts as manufactured boxes, computer controlled, are one frightening prospect; vast high-rises of 300-square-foot efficiencies are another; condoland disguised as Yankee villages yet a third.

The late twentieth century is not the best of times for new housing construction in the United States. In the years between 1963 and 1972 alone, the United States built 20 million new units—a mixture of hut, machine, and neighborhood models.[67] Now that household types are changing, the task is to look again at the products of that era and begin to see how to best use and adapt the 86 million units standing in the United States today. In 1977 Roger Montgomery argued that "The next decade will put enormous impetus behind conserving the standing stock of housing. . . . Conservation, recy-cling in currently fashionable jargon, perforce goes slowly, piece-meal, in very small scale units. To be in tune with the future, house architects and landscape architects will have to practice in equiva-lently small and piecemeal ways."[68] Yet if the scope of practice is to be small, the scope of the needs practice must meet is large, larger than ever when political and environmental questions are taken seriously. As the Soviets put it in 1926, "a new life demands new forms." Today Americans are often living the new life, with women employed, while not yet making the spatial changes that will provide new forms. One basic question recurs: how can Americans, having splurged on suburbia's detached houses, now afford any new forms? What are the three economic models of home life that correspond to the three social models of nurturing and the three architectural models of housing design?

6

GETTING AND SPENDING

The economic relationships between earning capability, housing design, and national economic development are still poorly formulated in advanced industrial societies, and this confusion works to the disadvantage of both women and men. Women suffer the double day, occupational segregation, and unequal pay; men suffer from too much pressure to be breadwinners and from too little family time. Getting and spending money takes up a major part of most adults' lives, yet it often seems an illogical process. Home life is the least understood part of economic activity, although Americans know housing is extremely expensive. To probe more deeply into the question of what the United States can or cannot afford in housing, it is crucial to establish some basic definitions of economic activity—what it is, what it is not, and how it relates to both housework and housing construction. Without such a framework of analysis, it is impossible to calculate the "costs" of any new housing arrangements to the society, to the household, to the individual, or to any group of workers.

Both neo-classical economists and Marxist economists have overemphasized wage work and rejected household work in their overall definitions of economic productivity, economic growth, and national product. These faulty definitions can be traced to the nineteenth-century doctrine of separate spheres for men and women. At the same time, neo-classical economists and state socialists have taken very different views of housing construction as an economic activity. In the United States, it is viewed as a key sector of production, crucial to stimulating the entire economy, sustaining banks and the real estate industry, creating jobs, and maximizing consumption of cars, appliances, and furnishings. In state socialist countries such as the USSR, China, and Cuba, an opposite view prevails. Housing construction is seen as resource consumption, and every effort is made to minimize the use of scarce resources by limiting space in housing units and limiting time and money spent on decorative effects and consumer goods. What both calculations of housing construction miss is the essential nature of home as a domestic workplace. Whether resource consumption is maximized or minimized, the single most important component of this spatial and economic equation concerning the reproduction of life is a parent's labor.

Housework, Earning Capability, and Economic Development

In 1979 the United Nations released a report that shattered economists' conventional views of labor and economic development: women, the report showed, perform two-thirds of the world's work hours, counting both paid and unpaid labor. They receive one-tenth of the world's wages. And they own one-one hundredth of the world's property.[1] Among American political leaders, one of the first to anticipate these numbers was Charles Percy, the Republican senator from Illinois. In 1977 he wrote the Percy amendment, which required American officials to complete a full economic impact statement of the effects of all new foreign aid programs on women's economic contributions and earnings.[2] While both Percy's amendment and the U.N. statistics have called attention to women's disadvantaged position in the world economy, and their meager economic recognition, the debates launched on these issues have not yet led to consistent national policies for the economic development of women in the United States. Jan Peterson, organizer of the National Congress of Neighborhood Women, an association of working-class women based in Brooklyn, New York, often asks: "Why don't we have a Percy Amendment for domestic spending, as well as for foreign aid?"[3]

We have seen that women in the United States work twenty-one more hours per week than men. What are they doing in economic terms? Economist Ann Markusen states: "Human energy is largely spent in one of two activities, the production of commodities for market exchange and the reproduction of labor power."[4] She explains that production of commodities takes place in "plants, shops, or offices, where employers hire workers." The reproduction of labor power takes place through government social services, such as schools and hospitals, and through the household. While cooks, nurses, and other public sector workers involved in the reproduction of labor power receive wages for their work, just as commodities production workers do, housewives and mothers do not. Instead, marriage, according to Markusen, "is an implicit rather than explicit contract for the exchange and organizational control of labor power in the household." Women work there, but no wages change hands.

Heidi Hartman, an economist with a special interest in domestic labor, argues that we should define the current U.S. economic situation as a capitalist mode of production harnessed to a pre-capitalist, patriarchal structuring of reproduction.[5] Crucial here are the "family" wage and the family home, both controlled by men. But a man must earn enough to acquire the physical plant, raw materials, and the labor power necessary for survival—that is, his home, his groceries and his wife's unpaid labor time. Most costly of these is the home, the "plant" where her unpaid labor is used. Because marriage (as a labor contract) represents a very large claim on her time and energy, when a woman also enters the wage labor market—to participate in production directly as well as indirectly—she is a disadvantaged worker. While all men, even childless, single men, now expect to receive "family" wages, nineteenth-century employers expected to pay all women, married or single, with or without children, even less than the cost of reproduction of their own labor power (can we call this "non-person" wages?), and most mid-twentieth-century wages for women barely meet subsistence needs.

Women's earnings have always reflected the ways the "labor of love" in the home turns into low-paying jobs outside the home. In 1980 American women earned less than three-fifths of men's earnings for full time, year round work. Both fathers and husbands of employed women should be dismayed to learn that not only has the earnings gap widened over the last 20 years; the gap also widens as women's educational qualifications increase. Female college graduates in full-time work average less than male high school dropouts.[6] In part this is because jobs requiring many of the traditional "womanly" skills of homemaking have been rated as unskilled work. As recently as 1975, a day-care worker was rated in the national *Dictionary of Occupational Titles* as less skilled than an attendant at a dog pound; a nursery school teacher as less skilled than an attendant at a parking lot.[7] These stereotypes about skill were reinforced by women's spatial disadvantages because of the location and design of their homes. Home was often the given, with paid work arranged around it; women put up with low-paying jobs to gain more flexible schedules or better commuting patterns in order to continue their unpaid labor of love.

Women's cheap, non-union, paid labor has been much sought after by employers in marginally profitable industries and in periods of boom, because employers do not have to commit themselves to a long-term relationship.[8] Industries can bring in women and use their labor to maximize the possibilities of expansion when the economy looks strong, and minimize the disruption of firing when the economy is weak. (Similar policies about women's paid employment have been developed by the state socialist economies of the USSR, China, Cuba, and Eastern Europe.) Ironically, when the use of female labor in this fashion still does not occur smoothly enough, women may be blamed for rising unemployment. Yet by drawing on women as a reserve army of labor, entrepreneurs have guided many major steps in the history of American economic development.

Young women staffed the cotton mills of Waltham and Lowell, which marked the birth of the American corporation in the early nineteenty century. As larger enterprises began to separate production from administration in the late nineteenth century, central city corporate headquarters developed where the new clerical staff was female. When service industries became important in the twentieth century, again the new workers were predominantly female. And as conglomerates and multi-national corporations attempt to move their capital from union to non-union areas in the late twentieth century, they prefer regions of the United States or developing countries where they can count on a non-union, female labor force. Robert Goodman, in *The Last Entrepreneurs,* has given numerous examples of local economic development planners who try to attract new industries to their areas by advertising that large numbers of dexterous but docile female workers are available to employers.[9]

National Economic Development

Men could not be persuaded to sacrifice their nights and days as tireless breadwinners, nor could women be manipulated in and out of the national labor market, unless woman's place was explicitly in the home. American policies on family wages for men, home-ownership for men, and wage labor as a measure of economic productivity were all developed within the crucial years following 1919 when, as we have seen, both production and reproduction were restructured around the concept of the single-family detached house. In 1920 the National Bureau of Economic Research was chartered in the United States, and its staff began to develop estimates of National Income and National Product. These economists decided to exclude all household work for which no wage was paid. During earlier debates on these issues, in the 1880s and 1890s, distinguished economists such as Richard T. Ely in the United States and Alfred Marshall in England had argued that household production was essential to all national economic calculations.[10] By the 1920s the NBER economists claimed that a mother's love had no price and should not be counted, a view later reiterated in Paul Samuelson's popular economics textbooks.[11]

As contemporary economist William Gauger contends, "Let's face it. If household work had traditionally been a man's job, it would always have been included in GNP."[12] Gauger points out that even the founders of the National Bureau of Economic Research conceded there might be two problems resulting from their 1920 decision. First, they noted, "comparisons are thrown askew between communities or classes that differ widely in the proportion of women who work at home and women who work for wages."[13] Second, and most important, they recognized that if more housewives did enter the paid labor force in succeeding decades, and if they produced fewer goods at home—home-grown vegetables, home-cooked foods, and homemade clothes—the amount of useful goods not paid for with money would shrink. Therefore, while national income would appear to grow, the official figures might actually hide a decline in quantity of goods and services produced. The figures might also hide a decline in quality, as homemade bread (not counted) was replaced with Wonderbread (fully counted).

The statistical evidence of steadily increasing female participation in the paid labor force from 1800 to 1920 was available to the men who made this decision. So was the knowledge that women had just achieved the right to vote and were demanding more power in public affairs and more access to jobs previously controlled by men. However, these economists were working at a time when lay-offs of women workers took place in the aftermath of World War I. These were the years when manufacturers were hoping to find that "Good homes make contented [male] workers," the years when Mr. Homeowner was supposed to get together with Mrs. Consumer. These economists put female labor-force data and female political participation aside, along with all their reservations about bad methodology, and banked on mother love as "priceless" and on "family" wages for men. They couldn't have made a more serious error.

Between 1920 and 1980, female participation in the paid labor force doubled. GNP became a systematic over-estimate of cumulative economic growth. Throughout the last half century the greatest visible economic gains have occurred in the expansion of consumer goods and services, exactly those which replace women's unpaid labor in the home and are the most impossible to calculate under the present system. Thus no one has known the real state of the American economy for decades. Economists' interventions to stimulate GNP growth or slow decline are clearly ineffectual. So, too, have been the struggles of many women, who find extreme difficulty in convincing members of their households that the nurturing they do is valuable within the conventional frameworks of market economics. And, at the same time, the struggles of some men to persuade their wives to enter the marketplace and obtain paid work are also ineffectual because of the mystique of "priceless" love and the reality of low wages for women.

The category of "housewife" as unpaid worker also leads to great confusion about national measurement of unemployment. If women are fired from paid work and discouraged about seeking new employment, they may be listed as housewives rather than as unemployed persons.[14] The phenomenon of the "displaced homemaker" has also shown that the housewife who is divorced or widowed may wind up desperate after a lifetime of unpaid labor. She needs an unemployment benefit but can't get it.[15] Similarly, all housewives

are ineligible for Social Security and for health and disability benefits given paid workers. In this respect, it may be noted that the
Social Security system, as originally established in the 1930s, was
not designed to suit either employed women or the two-earner family.[16] For decades it has provided different types of benefits to an
eligible woman as her husband's widow and as an earner in her own
right—and she has had to choose between these benefits, rather than
take both.[17] In addition, the housewife who gets divorced has no
vested rights to her husband's benefits. Only a single woman finds
her status the same as a single man. Currently the entire system is
in turmoil, but despite the panic, the imbalance between men's and
women's benefits is still thought too expensive to overhaul. Had
housewives been contributing to the system for the last five decades,
and been receiving more equitable benefits, both the system and the
female elderly would now be in better shape.

Underdevelopment of Women

Failure to analyze the national economic importance of the labor
of women has also led to disastrous, wasteful government spending
programs, as well as to inaccurate statistical measurements and
inability to predict economic growth or decline. Among the most
unwieldy policy areas are urban location theory, transportation
planning, social service economics, and housing economics. Each
one has been saddled with problems attributable to economists' and
planners' acceptance of Victorian definitions of male and female
activity patterns.

Transportation Planning

Ann Markusen notes that urban economists have usually studied the
male "head of household" to gain statistics about "journey to work"
or choices between "work" and "leisure."[18] Elaborate decisions
about the most efficient urban locations for public and private
investments (industrial location, social service location, and transport planning) made exclusively in terms of the male earner are
quite harmful to women and the efficient performance of their economic tasks. Economists' "journey to work" studies of this kind
overlook women twice. First, they ignore the unpaid work done in
and around the home and the transporation patterns necessary to its

accomplishment. Second, they overlook the fact that half of all married women are also in paid work and that they travel, not only to a paid job, but also to and from day-care facilities on the way to the paid job. Urban sociologist Gerda Wekerle notes that the authors of one of the few good studies on transportation, day care, and women workers, which was done in Paris, conclude that "women are subject to daily harassment in trying to coordinate work hours and commuting schedules with the hours of these facilities."[19] Or, as one American mother put it, "I was driving triangles all the time." If the simple male journey from home to job is the one planned for, and the complex female journey from home to day care to job is the one ignored, it is easy to see how women's time disappears when they attempt to overcome the separation of home and "work" that male economists and planners have created.

The field of time-space geography has introduced ways to represent women's and men's options graphically, showing the constraints upon mobility imposed by both time and distance in relation to daily tasks.[20] While time-space geography can illuminate the conflict within the two-earner family, this kind of analysis will lead to better regional studies as well. Markusen has observed that some patterns of urban and regional migration which have puzzled urban economists, such as the rehabilitation of older urban neighborhoods, the growth of small cities, and the decline of big cities, can also be predicted much more accurately by a two-earner location theory model. The growing areas may be physically or culturally less attractive, but women find they are better able to interweave housework, day care, and paid work because of manageable distances.[21]

Major decisions have also been made about public investments in transportation based on male patterns of movement. Such planning is wasteful in two ways. First, survey money is wasted in asking about men's "journey to work" and ignoring women's needs. Second, public transit money is wasted in planning routes to suit male needs, when actually many more female workers use public transit than male workers. The tendency of public transportation planners to disadvantage women workers is compounded by the fact that at the national level, American transportation planning has preferred to support the automobile industry through the construction of roads rather than to support public transit. The Federal Aid Highway Act of 1944 was a $1 billion public works project, and by 1980, one out of seven American workers earned a living building, selling, repairing, insuring, driving, or servicing vehicles or highways.[22] Almost all of these workers were male, so it can be argued that car culture in the United States represents economic development for male workers as well as convenience for male consumers. As transportation planner Martin Wachs has noted, "In some households the automobile is simply the man's domain. In many other households, a car is a shared resource, and quite simply it appears that male members of the household have systematically more control over the use of that resource."[23] In a suburban, one-car household, this situation contributes to women's powerlessness and isolation. Wachs finds that about three-quarters of the miles driven in the U.S.A. are driven by men, and while men make the majority of their auto trips as drivers, women make the majority as passengers. Wachs notes that when suburban women are drivers, they make over 11 percent of their trips solely to serve another passenger. That is, they are providing the transit service which the planners have chosen not to offer.

Still, many Americans have found car culture attractive, as planner Edith Perlman reminds us, "Once at the wheel, any boy could pretend he was a man. And any girl could pretend she was a boy." The automobile assisted women in their search for a spacious and private life in suburbia, although Perlman notes that it took women "a generation to discover that space meant loneliness, and privacy, privation." But meanwhile women were finding roles in the driver's seat. "There was superWife, on her way to execute half a dozen household errands. There was superMom, trundling the children to various enrichments. For the less domesticated, there were super-Bitch and superWhore, all played by Elizabeth Taylor with the top down. Most recently there has been superMs., racing toward a job whose salary maintains her smart little roadster." Still, Perlman maintains that women are losers: the automobile "requires and supports a detached life that isolates families from other families; the act of riding itself, with its grim, face-forward configuration, isolates members of the family even from each other."[24]

While transportation planners have often used women, explicitly or implicitly, to provide services for men and children, they have not used transport planning to provide services for women. Both sociologist Helena Lopata and Wachs emphasize the special problems car culture creates for the female elderly.[25] They are even less likely than younger women to have access to cars, and many endure extreme isolation. Wachs also cites a New York State study (excluding New York City) showing that four times as many women as men used transit for the journey to paid work. He also shows that in locations as diverse as Seattle, Washington, Davenport, Iowa, and Hicksville, New York, between two-thirds and four-fifths of all bus trips were made by women.[26] Having to rely on bad public transit limits women's job choices and hours. The even more ominous spatial consequence of female dependence on transit is underlined by Wachs: ". . . most assaults on women which are committed by persons who are not acquainted with the victim do occur in relatively deserted public places, when the victim is travelling or waiting to travel."[27] Two pioneering feminist groups in Madison and Milwaukee actually decided that creating a women's transit service was the most effective project their rape prevention group could undertake. Across the country, however, transportation policy works to the disadvantage of female workers and increases women's vulnerability to assault, largely because male work has been the heart of transport planning.

The difficulty of dislodging this policy is illustrated by the experience of Sandra Rosenbloom. Rosenbloom, Professor of Urban Planning at the University of Texas at Austin, is a nationally known expert in urban transportation planning. In 1977 she was asked by the Department of Transportation in Washington to organize a major conference on the effects of transportation policy on American women, to examine the ways in which women's needs were not being met by current programs. Since millions of dollars had already been spent for research on the "head of household's" choices that revolved around men's journeys, Rosenbloom had high hopes for the importance of the conference.

Then Senator William Proxmire, the Wisconsin Democrat, and his keen aides who ferret out our egregious examples of waste in federal government spending, decided that Professor Rosenbloom was an ideal candidate for his Golden Fleece award, given to those projects he considered to be fleecing the public treasury. Proxmire considered it extremely funny that anyone could possibly see differences between men and women in their relationship to buses, subways, and highways.[28] A senior HUD official, Donna Shalala, rushed to Proxmire's office to explain that women actually do use public transit two or three times more than men. The Golden Fleece was given to someone else. But the problem remains. Many public officials still believe in the ideal of a good city and a good society which has nothing to do with women's active involvement. If, implicitly, they believe that a woman's place is in the home, any urban research or urban program that involves women's labor or women's independent movement in the city seems peculiar.

Housing Construction and Economic Development

Suburban, single-family detached houses have provided economic benefits to financial institutions and to male construction workers and homeowners. Publically supported housing has had a similar role. In the 1940s American trade union leaders favored public housing as a source of jobs for their members, and thus saw housing projects as an economic development strategy for the workers in the construction trades. There was little concern for the prospective residents of the projects, who were often minority group members and women. These residents were excluded from most apprentice and training programs in the trades that benefited from constructing the housing.

Public housing programs have, in their design, also created great logistical and economic obstacles for mothers who wished to undertake any kind of paid work. Grim projects, planned without any local employment for women or day care services, have been filled with female heads of households. In the worst cases, these projects were also located away from urban centers, such as Boston's huge Columbia Point housing project, seven miles from downtown on the site of an old garbage dump. The residents of these projects were usually expected to subsist on such programs as Aid to Families with Dependent Children (AFDC) and Food Stamps, programs that simulated the traditional family with the welfare mother as homemaker cooking meals and minding children all day long, even though the male breadwinner was absent. Any forward-looking social service administrators who wished to find ways to locate jobs and day care in subsidized housing, and any progressive housing administrators who wished to integrate more services with dwellings, found obstacles to their collaboration in the myriad rules, regulations, and prohibitions set up by HUD and HHS that made the spatial connection of housing, jobs, and services a nightmare to administer.[29] Enterprising tenants, such as women who tried to make money serving dinners to their neighbors in the Williamsburg Houses in Brooklyn, were also frustrated by the charge that such "businesses" were illegal when run in housing space.

In the past few years neighborhood organizations and other groups involved with issues of housing, jobs, social services, and urban redevelopment have structured their programs with the goal of local economic development in mind. In contrast to those government programs that pushed the worlds of "home" and "work" farther apart, some new programs have attempted to see housing as a source of jobs and as a strategy for environmental conservation. Concepts of gender roles can keep such economic development efforts from achieving their fullest potential. This may be the case in both urban homesteading and solar rehabilitation efforts, if new efforts at housing construction are seen as a source of jobs primarily for men.

"There are three utilities in New York—Con Ed, Brooklyn Union Gas, and 519 East 11th Street," boasted one organizer at 519 East 11th Street.[30] At this building, also known as The Solar Tenement, the urban homesteading approach to the problems of inner city housing was developed in 1974 by Rabbit Nazario, Ruth Garcia, Travers Price, Michael Freedberg, and other architects and community organizers concerned with the abandonment of 30,000 units of deteriorated housing every year by landlords in New York City.[31] They determined to turn the situation around and create a model of cooperative home ownership by tenants whose labor on the rehabilitation of a tenement would be their only capital investment. The project involved training local male residents in construction skills, as well as experimenting with new technologies to create demonstrations of solar and wind energy. In the neighborhood, the residents of 519 also developed a community garden called El Sol Brillante on five vacant lots. When they lacked fertilizer, ingenuity in finding resources brought them to Ringling Brothers' circus, where they found free elephant manure. On the Lower East Side of New York, they raised a first crop of peanuts and sent some to the White House in the Carter administration as a public relations gesture.

While the phrases "urban homesteading" and "sweat equity" entered the vocabulary of many planners, and new projects were developed in Springfield, Massachusetts, Boston, Chicago, Hartford, Oakland, and Cleveland, the sweat equity approach is time-consuming. Freedberg notes that dealing with municipal bureaucracies in the cumbersome process of loan packaging and building rehabilitation "remains a deterrent to all but the most determined homesteaders."[32] And while the novelties of wind generation and

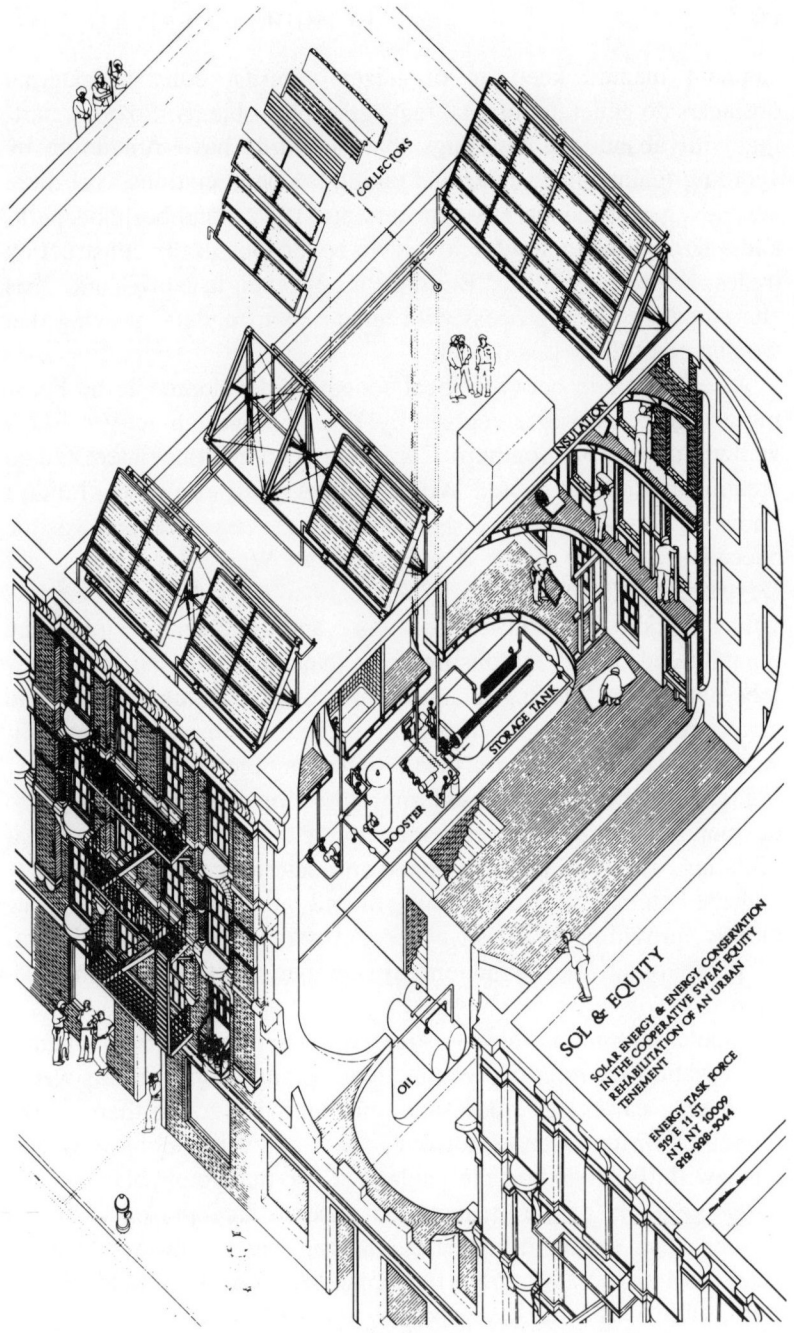

Labels within illustration: COLLECTORS, INSULATION, STORAGE TANK, BOOSTER, OIL

SOL & EQUITY

SOLAR ENERGY & ENERGY CONSERVATION
IN THE COOPERATIVE SWEAT EQUITY
REHABILITATION OF AN URBAN
TENEMENT

ENERGY TASK FORCE
519 E 11 ST
NY NY 10009
212-998-7044

6.1 The Solar Tenement, 519 East 11th Street, New York, New York.

elephant manure keep up organizers' spirits, constant external obstacles do generate internal management problems. So does starting with abandoned buildings that landlords have run down by avoiding maintenance costs and taking tax depreciations. Yet there are eleven new cooperative owners at 519, a neighborhood park, and a number of men who now have better jobs in the construction trades. A project called "Building for Women in New York" has attempted the same process with female ex-offenders, proving that women can follow this model.

A similar tie-in between local economic development and housing construction was developed by Valerie Pope, an activist Black welfare mother in Southern California who became interested in creating community jobs. "When I started in the early '70s, I didn't know solar from shinola," she commented.[33] By 1980 she was the executive director of the San Bernardino West Side Community Development Corporation, a group that had trained several hundred young workers for construction work and solar energy jobs, and rehabilitated over 400 housing units. Not only had she made new jobs and better housing available in a black community; she had also developed strategies to correct excessive domestic energy consumption. The CDC established a light manufacturing facility making solar panels to be used in retrofitting housing. They also developed an innovative program with the city for purchasing, rehabilitating, and reselling abandoned and deteriorated property. They launched an experiment in turning an old motel into housing for the elderly, providing solar hot water and space heating. Experiments in photovoltaic and wind energy are part of their current programs.[34]

Pope's program has always stressed job training in environmental conservation for minority youths: first, in summer programs weeding lawns, caring for sidewalks, and removing trash; then, in the rehabilitation of existing housing; next, and most ambitiously, in the new skills needed for the "solar age" so that young blacks could partake equally of the technical advances solar represents. Young women were absent from these job programs in substantial numbers, until a special program for female heads of households in San Bernardino was later developed by the local National Council of Negro Women. An anticrime drive made it clear that Pope wanted young men to stop vandalizing the built environment and start repairing it as a way to feel more positive about themselves and their community.

Urban homesteading and solar rehab provide some provocative examples of rethinking community approaches to housing as a source of jobs. The Solar Tenement project was a model for saving the inner-city's deteriorated housing stock and training residents in construction; Pope's program is a model of how to rehabilitate older suburbs and add new industrial uses. Both are models for motivating young men from minority groups. They provoke two questions: how can society rehabilitate existing housing to assist women gain more egalitarian family life, and how can society organize a building process to insure women's economic development as well as men's?

Women's Economic Security and Three Models of Home

Just as three models of home have been used to shape policy in industrial nations since the end of the nineteenth century, so three models have been used to define economic security for women. In the haven model, there have been campaigns for protection of women's right to be supported by their husbands and remain largely outside the paid labor force. This is expressed in rather pure form by far right ideologues such as Phyllis Schlafly, who campaigned against ERA while favoring Social Security reform to extend coverage to housewives. Some Moral Majority leaders also promote women's part-time earning from within the home, as a lesser evil than women's employment outside the home. At a Family Forum in Washington in August 1982, author Margie Johnson of Falls Church, Virginia, advised women to stay home: "If you work at home you only need to earn a third as much money." She suggested income tax preparation, sewing, and animal breeding as home occupations, as well as several services that could be undertaken around neighbors' homes, including shopping service, wallpapering, and housecleaning. She claimed there would be savings on childcare, lunches, and clothing for mothers choosing these occupations rather than regular paid employment.[35] At the same event, Nancy Motley of Rochester, New York, reported a spring cleaning club organized by her church: "We may take five or ten ladies and go into your home, wash the walls and windows and even your kid. Most of our ladies go away with $100." This resembles certain forms of housewives' cooperatives first started over a century ago, but the earnings are lower than nineteenth-century cooperators would have accepted.[36]

A rural approach to the haven model might also be expressed as a return to subsistence agriculture. A single person or a couple might simply try to drop out of the market economy as much as possible, and raise vegetables, run solar and wind devices for energy, and stay home. Yet in an urban society, paid work is essential for many, and the rural return to the nineteenth-century haven seems a personal solution rather than a social one.

The other two models of home give rise to more dynamic strategies for economic change. The economic equity approach develops Bebel's original industrial model of home by supporting women's activities as double workers. Successful examples of how to implement it come from various societies where female paid workers are in great demand. This strategy of economic equity involves making the public sphere, as it has been traditionally defined, more accessible to women. Thus it involves locating housing with reference to better jobs (with comparable and equal pay and adequate maternity leave), better public transportation, and better child care. The spatial reintegration model builds on Peirce's neighborhood strategy. This approach attempts to locate housing in order to reintegrate private and public economic activity and to maximize the choices and minimize the costs in both male and female workers' lives. "Home" and "work" are no longer two disparate worlds, as they are for the male worker, or two different workplaces, as they are for the female worker. Successful projects of this kind are often those created for poor single parents, women with the least to lose and the most to gain from risking dramatic strategies for economic change. Examples of these show how grass-roots community groups, employers, and government can act to deal with both economic and spatial issues through more sensitive approaches. They show how serious, sustained consideration of the problems women have faced as double workers can, with the help of architectural and economic innovation, strengthen both industrial production and residential neighborhoods.

Economic Equity for Women and Men

When employers provide services to women, there are usually bonanza profits to be made; when the state intervenes to provide services for employed women, there are usually national labor shortages. These crisis times reveal just how much effort is necessary to avoid penalizing women for being both parents and paid workers, and to support women's economic activities fully. The American example of housing and collective services developed for female workers and their families, justified as a wartime emergency project, at Kaiser Shipyards in Vanport City, Oregon, was an impressive demonstration of how employer supports for women can make a difference. In less than one year, as we have seen, Kaiser management created a dazzling array of inducements for mothers with children to take on jobs as welders, riveters, and heavy construction workers. The speed with which private industry tackled women's needs and met them should encourage reformers to have confidence in the possibilities of rapid implementation of economic equity under sustained economic pressure.

Nine thousand of the Vanport City residents were children. For them Kaiser built six nursery schools, several kindergartens, five grade schools, and seventeen supervised playgrounds. The director of the child care project, James L. Hymes, noted that "In the past, good nursery schools have been a luxury for the wealthy. The Kaiser Child Service Centers are among the first places where working people, people of average means, have been able to afford good nursery education for their children."[37] For eight-hour child-care service, parents paid only $.75 per day for the first child, and $.50 per day for each additional one. The range of services offered to mothers by an American employer was unprecedented; but the wartime profits were also.

Edgar J. Kaiser and his management team linked their economic success in production to their concern for women's labor power: "The way people live and the way their families are cared for is bound to be reflected in production,"[38] said one Kaiser official. But these supportive conditions for women workers did not outlast the war and the wartime profits of defense industries. In 1945 women workers throughout the United States were laid off and their jobs given to returning veterans. The skilled female riveters and welders interviewed by oral historians in the remarkable film *Rosie the Riveter* became cafeteria workers, dishwashers, maids, and supermarket clerks. Most wartime employers and most states discontinued their day-care programs immediately. Supports for American women workers still have not become a right of citizenship, despite steadily increasing paid labor-force participation by women in the last four decades.

Swedish policies guarantee women and men workers more rights to economic supports for parenting, but this has an interesting political history. Politicians agreed that more Swedish women in the paid labor force were preferable to large numbers of guest workers (migrant laborers), for political reasons. So, during the 1960s and 1970s, elaborate maternity insurance, child-care provisions, and incentives to employers evolved in order to avoid bringing guest workers from Southern Europe into the country in large numbers. Eventually, by 1980, 69 percent of Swedish women had joined the paid labor force; Swedish Parent Insurance was a monument to their economic importance to the nation, and to their role as mothers.

Swedish Parent Insurance, established in 1974, provides for economic benefits and leaves from paid work for either new mothers or new fathers. As Sheila Kamerman, a specialist in the comparative analysis of social welfare programs, has described it, "this is a universal, fully paid, wage-related, taxable cash benefit covering the eight months after childbirth."[39] Either parent can remain home to care for the infant, and the cash benefit can be split any way the couple chooses. Kamerman explains how it might work: "a woman might use the benefit to cover four months of full time leave and stay home. Then each might, in turn, work two months at half time, followed by two months at three-quarter time (a six-hour day). Employers are required to accept part-time employment as part of this benefit, for childcare purposes." Only 10 percent of the eligible men used this benefit in 1976, so not all men felt they could and should take advantage of it. However, Kamerman reports that men do use an additional benefit which provides between twelve and eighteen days of paid leave per child for either parent to care for sick children at home.

In some parts of Sweden, Kamerman notes that workers will also come to the house to care for a sick child so that both parents may go to work, and another Swedish program offers state subsidies for employers who hire women in fields dominated by men, or hire men in fields dominated by women. This program recognizes that there may be economic disruption caused by giving equal work to women and men, where jobs previously were segregated, and it makes it possible for employers to recoup some of the time this social change may take from production. Here we have several models of strong attempts to provide economic benefits for ending gender discrimination. This is the kind of economic equity that can improve the lives of both women and men.

Spatial Reintegration

To recognize the desire of women and men to be both paid workers and parents is to search for a way to overcome the physical separation of paid jobs and parenting inherent in many urban settings. One of the first and most successful architectural designs aimed at reintegrating these activities was developed in Sweden in the 1930s. Of all the collective houses, service houses, family hotels, and apartment hotels that were part of the neighborhood strategy of housing, this project was the most successful in adding work space to new housing forms. In 1935 the feminist Alva Myrdal (recently awarded the Nobel Prize for her work on world peace) collaborated with architect Sven Markelius to create housing with office space, food service, and child care available. Their project in the center of Stockholm included fifty-seven small apartments of very elegant design. Some of them could also be used as offices or studios. Not only did Markelius design these, he moved into the building himself and served as an unofficial handyman for thirty years in order to make sure the nuts and bolts of this scheme worked.[40]

After ten years of operation, *Life* magazine praised this project as a model for post–World War II reorganization of American housing: the reporter suggested that Americans should copy its services for women in the wartime labor force who wished to continue their careers.[41] The only disadvantage which eventually appeared was that most residents did not wish to leave after their children were grown, and new parents could not find space in the building. The day-care center ultimately had to take in neighborhood children as well as residents' children to stay in business; the restaurant food was good but it became less economically competitive when cheap eating places appeared in large numbers in the city.

Another European project of the 1960s also brought homes and jobs together for single parents. Nina West, a housewife and mother in London, England, was divorced in the early 1960s. She didn't know how she could possibly support her young children and take care of them at the same time. She had no alimony or child support, and didn't want welfare. She didn't know how to find day care, housing, and a job, let alone find all three together. She was a typical single parent, a decade and a half before single parents constituted a substantial proportion of American households.

Nina West recognized the economic and social dimensions of her

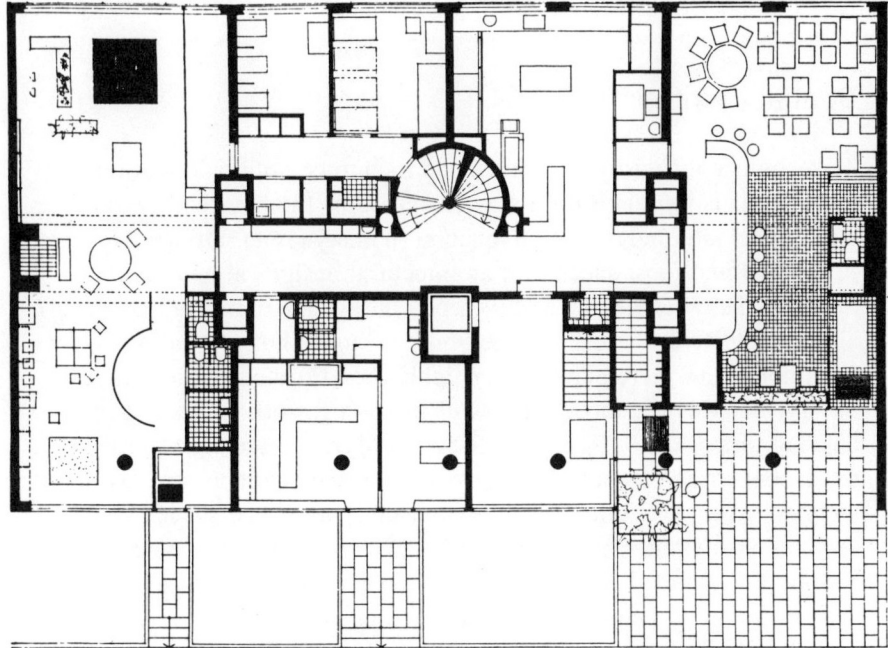

FIRST FLOOR

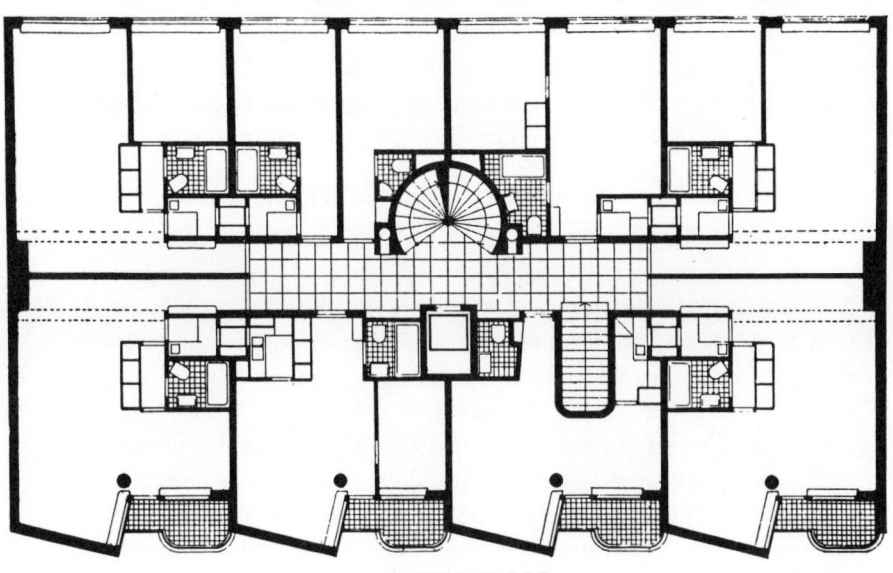

SECOND FLOOR

6.2 *Life* recommended Sven Markelius's and Alva Myrdal's Collective House, built in Stockholm in 1935, as a model for housing American mothers who wished to keep their jobs after World War II. The first floor plan includes a restaurant and child-care center. Food could be sent up to private apartments in "food lifts." The second-floor plan shows elegantly designed private apartments that could also be used as studios or offices.

predicament, as well as the personal ones. She tackled the problem of bridging private life and paid employment in her creation of a pioneering housing project. She began with a small building including several apartments and a day-care center serving the entire neighborhood. Single parents (male or female) could occupy the housing, use the day care to free themselves for paid employment, and in some cases, even find suitable employment in the day-care center itself. She had socialized one aspect of reproduction—child care—found a way to make it generate income, and connected this to affordable housing. She had built a bridge between private and public life.

As her first project provided a successful base for single parents, Nina West began to expand her operations. She bought more small buildings in different locations around London and organized them in the same way. She received state support and charitable contributions. And ultimately she was able to hire an architect, Sylvester Bone, and build a new building. Fiona House, opened in 1972, offered many design features to help single parents.[42] The interior corridors doubled as playrooms, with carpeted floors and windows

6.3 Nina West Homes, London, England, view, 1972. This project was designed by Sylvester Bone for single parents and their children.

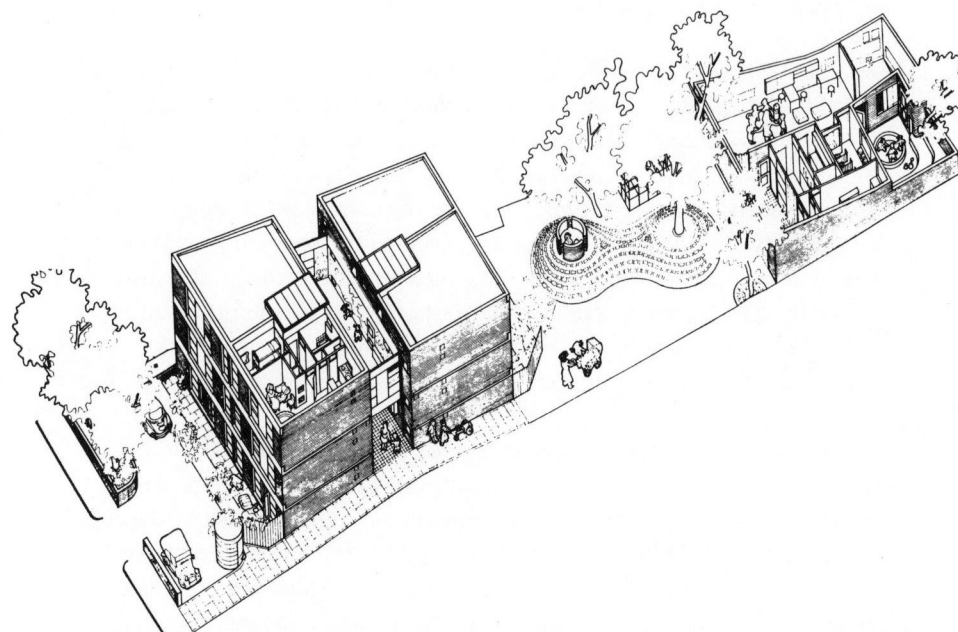

6.4 Nina West Homes, axonometric drawing. The child-care center is at the back of the site on the ground level; the corridor between apartments also serves as a children's play area. Kitchen windows offer easy observation of the corridor, and intercoms link units for easier baby-sitting.

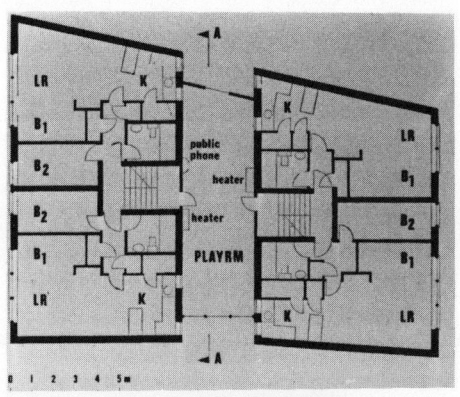

6.5 Nina West Homes, plan of housing units and corridor used as playroom.

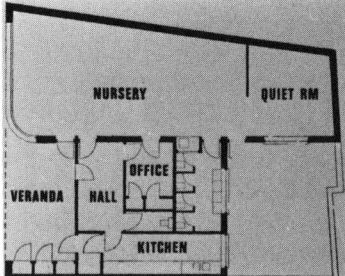

6.6 Nina West Homes, plan of child-care center.

from each apartment looking in, so that a parent cooking could watch a child at play. Intercoms linked apartments, enabling parents to baby-sit for each other by turning on the intercom and listening for children crying. By 1980 Nina West had several other projects under construction, and visitors from many parts of the world were studying her operations.

West's success represented several significant advances over earlier projects. First, she recognized that single parents are usually very poor. All of her housing units are tiny by American standards—efficiencies or one bedroom apartments. But they were a realistic response to the economic situation of single parents. And she avoided the conflict between affluent women and service workers, which some of the earliest Scandinavian service house builders such as Fick and Myrdal had encountered. Second, West argued that the residents would have to find a market for their services in the neighborhood if they intended to establish new jobs on their housing site. This attempt to generate both jobs and housing controlled by women gave West an economic base most housing providers lacked. Myrdal and Markelius' project had the day care, but they never thought of asking residents to work there. West did begin to get extensive state support for her housing services in the 1970s, so one cannot describe her activities as self-sustaining. In addition, although she was able to replicate her original project, it has not offered a permanent community to its residents. It helps them to make an economic transition over one or two years' time, but after that, residents are expected to seek jobs on their own and other housing of a traditional kind.

A recent American experiment takes these approaches one step further. Joan Forrester Sprague, Katrin Adam, and Susan Aitcheson are architects who taught at a successful summer school for women students in architecture and urban planning from all over the United States in the 1970s. All three felt the need to go further, to work closely with low income urban women, many of them single parents, in order to develop an economic and spatial program that would meet women's needs. They called their project Housing with Economic Development, and their organization, the Women's Development Corporation. For six years they prepared the project while working at other jobs.

They started operations in 1978 in the inner-city area of Elmwood in Providence, Rhode Island.[43] Here they made connections with numerous church and community organizations, as well as with city, state, and national agencies. They surveyed run-down housing and located ten residential buildings suitable for rehabilitation. They examined commercial spaces and discussed the problems of sustaining local small businesses with economic development experts. They established an informal day-care network so that women could come to meetings, and began training women in self-help concepts.

In a community with 10 percent Hispanic, 25 percent white, 40 percent Black, and 25 percent Laotian households, they found that over half the households were headed by single, widowed, or divorced women. Most of these were below poverty level. Yet, as Sprague has noted, the women had distinctive skills—the Hmong women from Laos could create magnificent handicrafts but had few markets for them; another local woman ran tours by bus from Providence to New York but didn't see herself as a potential travel agent until the organizers suggested this; others wanted to be trained as building maintenance workers and construction workers.

Slowly the Women's Development Corporation found a constituency in Providence, and by 1980 225 women were registered as participants in the program, many of them single parents in their twenties, with from one to eight children. Twelve women became active in the housing program, intending to rehabilitate buildings and make them small limited-equity housing cooperatives owned by residents. The residents would be able to pay the monthly charges because they had established new jobs and new small businesses (through a Small Business Administration training program) to revitalize a nearby commercial street. In fact, by 1983 the project was focused on rental housing with a mix of new construction and rehabilitation, drawing on federal support and local corporate co-sponsorship. Practical success along these lines has meant postponing their earlier, more ambitious scheme of economic development, such as a mix of traditional and nontraditional jobs, from beauty culture and needlework to construction work. However, they have still built on a broader base of economic activities than has Nina West's child-care center and are actively combatting the gender segregation of the well-paid construction trades by establishing jobs for women as builders and developers. They are also extending their economic activities into the community, contributing to a larger urban revitalization project by giving attention to a declining commercial street.

The Women's Development Corporation has struggled against women's problems in obtaining housing and jobs simultaneously

and emphasized economic self-sufficiency and long-term physical
rehabilitation of the neighborhood. They have moved from identi-
fying single parents' need for safe and affordable housing to creating a program for social reconstruction as a result of their substantial
experience both in community organizing and in building. They want
to develop a project which can be replicated in rural areas as well
as urban areas, and they are well on their way to inspiring imitation.
As they said in their prospectus, "Many women need reinforcement, support, and a chance to plan positively for their own and
their children's futures."[44]

These few examples of struggles for economic equity and spatial
reintegration suggest the ways Americans might begin to reevaluate
planning and housing budgets. A standard for evaluation must be,
does a particular economic arrangement reward all the men and
women who participate in it? Does it reward some women and men
at the expense of other women? Or does it simply encourage women
to go on nurturing men and children? One can also ask, does a
housing program recognize a community's energy resources and job
training needs? Does a housing or job program support full economic recognition for traditional homemaking skills, and does it
develop new skills and capabilities the society will reward? Most of
all, one must ask if a housing or job program diminishes the double
day, or if, in its basic definitions of separate spheres of "home"
and "work," it denies that many paid workers are parents, and that
most parents are paid workers.

Only when economic equity and spatial reintegration have been
accepted as logical, cost-effective approaches to economic planning
for women and men, will any society be able to develop the program necessary to move beyond the conventions of gender imbed-
ded in traditional housing design as well as in concepts of consuming.
Given our existing American housing and settlement patterns, to
realize such an economic program is a major challenge. However,
female workers and their families constitute a majority of American
citizens. This is a large group of people who will find it to their
advantage to reformulate getting and spending by finding new
approaches to housework and housing construction. The neighborhood strategy first articulated by housewives and employed women
in the nineteenth century contains the most appropriate theoretical
statement of an egalitarian approach. The architectural form most
congenial to that strategy is the courtyard or neighborhood of residential space complete with open spaces and shared economic activi-

ties. The answers to the social question of how to balance ''home'' and ''work'' and to the aesthetic question of how to animate housing converge in the economic strategy of spatial reintegration.

A new neighborhood strategy connecting nurturing and paid work in one space, connecting private housing units to collective services, and promoting economic development for all citizens (not just those traditionally involved in making cars or houses, or in making banking or real estate deals about cars or houses) has a strong political attraction based on the goal of redistributing resources. A new neighborhood strategy would not require huge government expenditures (which should please fiscal conservatives) but it would promise to have direct effect on the poorest citizens (which should please liberals, feminists, and civil rights advocates). But what does a new neighborhood strategy involving increased residential densities mean to the United States, as a country covered with low-density small private houses? Perhaps some urban problems that have long seemed insoluble—shortages of social services and shortages of affordable housing—may have complementary solutions.

I see this day the People beginning their landmarks, (all others give way;) Never were such sharp questions ask'd as this day.

Walt Whitman

Where will our children live?

California builders

part III

Rethinking Public Life

> There's theoretical love; and then there's applied love.
> *Bill McLarney*

> The cost of a thing is the amount of what I call life which is required to be exchanged for it, immediately or in the long run.
> *Henry David Thoreau*

7

RECONSTRUCTING DOMESTIC SPACE

Dody Green has been attending every recent zoning meeting in Springdale, Connecticut, where she and her husband have lived for eighteen years. "There have been a lot of changes in the suburbs, most of them for the worse," she says. "But now they are trying to carve up the American Dream itself—the family home—and I'm going to fight it."[1]

The mayor of Springdale wants to legalize small accessory apartments created within the three- and four-bedroom houses of her neighborhood. Mrs. Green told William Geist of the *New York Times* that she doesn't like it: "They are doing this in the name of the elderly, and for the struggling young couple. But I don't see this. I see greedy neighbors who are trying to make a few dollars off of a housing shortage and I see officials looking the other way. We have to fight it. They bring in experts to tell us how wonderful this is for everyone. Well, I have had experience in this, and it isn't as nice as they say. Apartments are a sign of deterioration. It takes the sparkle out of the American Dream just knowing there are apartments on the block."

On either side of Mr. and Mrs. Green's house, neighbors have built rental units in their houses. Across the United States, the carving up of suburbia is proceeding apace: as you read, hundreds of do-it-yourself builders are remodeling their attics, basements, or garages to make illegal apartments, altering the character of their property and their neighborhoods. In many ways the new apartments make sense. Never before has the single-family house been so expensive. Never before has owning a house been so precarious, because of high prices, high interest rates, and taxes. Never before has ownership been so inflexible; rarely has it been so difficult to sell a single-family house in order to accommodate a life change: to divorce, relocate, retire, or realize one's equity to meet other expenses. While there is more housing space per capita in this country than anywhere else in the world—more rooms per person, more rooms per household, and more land per household—the built environment now represents the wrong physical configuration for the society. Inflexible house designs and rigid zoning in R-1 neighborhoods were made more acceptable between the 1940s and 1960s by low interest rates and a fluid housing market enabling households to move over the life cycle. Now Americans need more adaptable and sophisticated spatial designs, with fewer inducements to achieve greater residential satisfaction by moving.

House sizes have been increasing for thirty years, from 800 square feet and one and a half baths, to 1600 square feet and two and a half baths.[2] Meanwhile average household sizes have been decreasing, from 3.37 persons in 1950 to 2.75 persons in 1980.[3] The misfit between buildings and families represents both problems and opportunities.[4] One elderly woman interviewed by planner Patrick Hare complained, "I don't want to spend my golden years cleaning three bathrooms."[5] At the same time that the elderly are seeking smaller units, the demand for smaller homes is also increasing among the young. Division of the existing housing stock seems desirable, yet the ideal of the intact one-family home dies hard. As Dody Green protested at her zoning meeting: "This was my dream, a house on a quiet street in the suburbs. There have been enough changes . . . now they want to undermine the foundation of the dream itself, the house, by subdividing it. We will fight them to the finish."

Mrs. Green's phrases, "take the sparkle out of the American Dream," "carve up the American Dream," reflect her fearful assessment of the situation. One could observe, more optimistically, that costs of new housing create commitment to staying in one's house and neighborhood, staying with the American dream and updating it. Commitment means looking again at the usefulness of houses, as opposed to their theoretical market prices; it involves reexamining the basic needs of households, as opposed to the rising costs of foodstuffs, household commodities and energy; it involves reappraising the mutual assistance families give (or don't give) to their neighbors, as opposed to the costs of new commercial services or of new government services. A leading ecologist has noted, "There is theoretical love and then there's applied love."[6] There is the theoretical American dream of the one-family house, wearing a bit thin, and the applied one, that depends on continued ingenuity, resourcefulness, and neighborliness. American citizens and designers need a way to balance the new needs of American households with the high standards of those homeowners who want few changes.

Here is a test of our national character: to devise a process of improving and perfecting American housing that can satisfy many different constituencies, a process that can give the phrase "American dream" new meaning. It would involve replanning single-family neighborhoods where there is pressure for accessory apartments. At the same time, it would require improvements in the programing of new housing for new household types as well as rehabilitation of the existing public housing stock. For all this to happen, a coalition of planners, designers, citizens, and political leaders must emerge to direct and regulate the efforts of the building industry.

The Builders' Approach

During the Reagan administration, various housing task forces and policy advisers have taken the position that the building industry can provide the solution to American social and economic needs. The building industry proposes to add 30 million new units for smaller households to the more than 54 million units the industry has constructed between 1950 and 1980. While there might be good reason to build on the model of such innovative designs as Myrdal and Markelius' Stockholm project, the Nina West Homes, or the Danish experiment at Tynggarden, this is not what most American builders have in mind. Developers, banks, realtors, and government officials have proposed much less subtle solutions that include tiny condos, mobile homes, and government bail outs for developers. The 1982 *Report of the President's Commission on Housing* boils down to a single conclusion: that builders should be free to create tracts of smaller units, including mobile homes, placed closer together, on any land they like, and to transfer many infrastructure costs to local governments.[7] The Urban Land Institute's study, *The Affordable Community,* co-sponsored by HUD, makes the same plea for relaxation of existing controls to favor new construction and new purchases of homes. Yet the grass roots response is overwhelmingly in favor of conservation and adaptive *re-use* of existing housing. The homeowners of America want to keep their towns the way they are, or increase densities and change the configuration of housing on their own terms. They do not want to see their towns ringed with new construction on the developers' terms.

By the year 2000, the United States will need perhaps 20 million more units to accommodate new households—but 70 percent to 80 percent of these new households are estimated to be single-parent or one-person households.[8] We will also need as many as 10 to 13 million units to make up for deteriorated housing stock if current levels of abandonment (600,000–800,000 units per year) are unchecked.[9] What does this need for new units mean in terms of economic development? Well, if the construction industry were to build some 30 million new units, and ask the towns and cities of America to pay for the infrastructure to support them, most towns and cities would be wary of such blanket requests. Officials in Madison, Wisconsin, calculate the city's cost of sanitary sewers, storm drainage, water mains, and local streets at $16,500 per acre of new development, excluding schools, fire stations, and arterial streets.[10] San Diego, under Republican Mayor Pete Wilson, estimated overall costs to the city of one new detached suburban house at $13,500 and began billing this infrastructure charge to startled developers.[11] Fairfield, California, estimated that total tax revenues from new housing development would cover half the cost of police services and nothing more.[12]

Most of the towns and cities of the United States simply cannot afford this kind of new development: not the infrastructure cost, or the service cost, or the energy cost. The development of new detached housing units also assumes that all householders want to live alone. But do those 17 million new single-parent and single-adult households—split between the elderly and the young—really want the same degree of privacy as larger families? These groups will not thrive in new developments of mobile homes (manufactured housing) or cheap, tiny, condominiums. New approaches to their housing should be coordinated with jobs, services, transportation, and landscaping. For this coordination to be effective, new accounting processes are necessary to assess the real costs and benefits of choices about nurturing, earning, and the built environment. What may be of greatest advantage to a neighborhood, town, or region will not be the same package favored by land developers.[13] As economist David Morris has observed, many cities now deal with the problem of unequal resource flows in and out of a specific area by developing a "domestic" policy and a "foreign policy" much as if these were "balance-of-payments" questions.[14] Local economic planning at the level of the city and the neighborhood is important now; in ten or twenty years time, local economic planning may be operating at the level of the apartment house or the block as well.

The Alternative Approach: Tougher Economic Planning and More Sensitive Social Planning

Projections of household forms and sizes in 1990, 2000, or 2010 concur about the predominance of single people and the elderly, employed women and single-parent families. Projections of energy costs suggest that gas to run an automobile will cost an exorbitant amount.[15] How can planning boards respond with something other than miniaturized condo efficiency units and miniaturized cars? The need to reunite social planning, economic development, and physical planning is clear: no one sector of change can be resolved without considering all the private-public relationships.

Planners can structure changes so that economic development for the entire neighborhood counts more than speculation. After all, marketing experts understand the increasing importance of groups once considered to be marginal (women, the elderly, and the young). The chief securities analyst at Merrill, Lynch, Pierce, Fenner and Smith described himself as "bullish" on those businesses which sell services to working mothers in the 1980s. And a successful realtor, who built the United States' largest chain of franchise real estate offices, Century 21, now plans to develop 10,000 "Mr. Build" franchises for building contractors interested in home remodeling, to handle the projected demand for accessory apartments.[16] But new realms of economic activity do not have to become profit-making possibilities for big corporations, national franchises, and their stockholders. There is also the potential for citizens to end the owner-speculation on one-family houses, halt the flood of new commercial products and services that do little to help our current crisis about the nature of housing and family life, and create local economic development instead.

What are the economic precedents for neighbors to organize and make new agreements about how to re-use the residential landscape? No one wants to be tied into the lockstep of a completely planned social and economic regimen. But when resources are finite, new economic incentives emerge. Existing mutual aid groups are already present in most suburban and urban neighborhoods, as well as small-scale economic activities of the kind that enhance neighborhood options. There are neighbors involved with making vacant lots into parks and playgrounds. There are baby-sitting co-ops and car pools that represent agreements for shared labor, usually by parents of children of the same age. There are some centers where newspapers, tin cans, glass bottles, and used appliances are recycled. Garage sales are also recycling efforts. In addition, there are small licensed day-care providers, and homemakers who run catering, cosmetics, or Tupperware businesses. There are professionals who work at home, typists, editors, free-lance writers, graphic designers, doctors, architects, and lawyers. Always, there are teenagers who want to earn money after school or on vacations. And sometimes scout troops or local grade schools are interested in raising money and in environmental education. All of these bits and pieces of economic activity can be developed into more coherent patterns. These patterns can then be related to existing social service programs.

What would be the scope of a practical program for change? A program broad enough to transform housework, housing design, and the economics of residential neighborhoods must, first, support women's and men's participation in the unpaid labor associated with housekeeping and child care on an equal basis; second, support women's and men's participation in the paid-labor force on an equal basis; third, reduce residential segregation by income, race, and age; fourth, minimize wasteful energy consumption; fifth, maximize real choices about recreation and sociability; and sixth, retain privacy in housing while adding new dwellings and new service options. While there are many partial reforms which can support these goals, a piecemeal strategy alone cannot achieve them because of the split between private and public life which is at the heart of the problem. The reorganization of the built environment involves both the economic restructuring of a local community development program and the architectural restructuring of neighborhood space.

Examples of community development projects from our own culture and from other countries can provide essential models, and can offer essential experience about what may work, and what may not. While it is important to draw on the examples of successful projects of all kinds, it is important to remember that most employed adults in the United States are not interested in moving toward communal groups, nor are they interested in having new bureaucracies run family life. They desire community services to support the private household, rather than an end to private life altogether. They also desire solutions which reinforce their economic independence and enhance personal choices about child rearing and sociability. And they want home ownership, as an American tradition, albeit one that can be improved.

Each of the alternatives to new speculative housing involves a different set of planning issues and a slightly different constituency. Three areas need examination: first, existing single-family neighborhoods and the potential of rehabilitation with more units achieved by accessory apartments; second, existing public housing and the potential of rehabilitation with fewer units but more space for jobs and services; and third, new construction of multi-family housing to meet the special needs of special groups.

Accessory Apartments: The Zoning Crisis in Single-Family Neighborhoods

Assuming that most towns and cities reject expensive new housing development as too costly, citizens and planners have three choices about how to proceed with the existing single-family housing stock of 53.9 million units. It can be remodeled illegally, on a piecemeal basis; it can be remodeled legally, on a piecemeal basis; or it can be remodeled legally within the context of replanned blocks. In towns choosing the third option it is possible to encourage incremental changes with accessory apartments, while planning for the whole to become more than the sum of the parts. Instead of updating our single-family houses as primitive sacred huts, Americans can coax, push, and nudge whole blocks of hut owners toward the model of the neighborhood, where accountability is a stronger value than privacy. This could be done by refusing zoning variances and building permits to owners who wish to build accessory apartments unless they comply with an agreed-upon neighborhood improvement plan. For instance, they could pay for additional amenities such as street trees, underground wiring, off-street parking, and community green space whenever they add a rental unit to their property.

At the moment, unfortunately, many planners have decided that the best way to deal with illegal housing conversions is to wink and look the other way.[17] Planners may argue that changing the traditional R-1 zoning is too difficult politically. They may feel that calling attention to the problem will decrease the supply of affordable housing and even cause hardship to families where the second unit is intended for an elderly parent (who would otherwise be in a nursing home), or a young daughter or son (whose alternative is a cheap rental unit where grandparents can't babysit for them). Some planners estimate that there are already up to two and a half million illegal conversions, however, and at this scale, piecemeal remodeling in suburbia causes planning problems: loss of acoustical privacy, strain on existing utilities, fire hazards, and lack of street parking, to name a few.

Certain planners have attempted to attack the issues by introducing legislation favoring the new units. According to Patrick Hare's report *Accessory Apartments: Using Surplus Space in Single-Family Houses,* areas actively promoting the legal conversion of excess

7.1 A typical tract of single-family houses without any common space, 1970s. Imagine every house becoming a duplex or a triplex in the next twenty years as accessory apartments are added, legally or illegally.

space in one-family houses into rental units include Portland, Oregon; New Castle, Babylon, and Lydenhurst, New York; Weston, Connecticut; Montclair and Princeton, New Jersey; Fairfax, Virginia; Concord and Lincoln, Massachusetts; Belvedere and San Anselmo, California. In these towns, in neighborhoods ranging from working class to upper class, with housing stock ranging from Victorian mansions to post–World War II split levels, conversions are legal, under certain circumstances.

These conversions may be restricted to houses of a certain size (Portland) or to lots of a certain size (Princeton) or to houses of a certain age (Montclair). This last provision discourages new houses in one-family districts designed for instant conversion to two-family houses. Accessory apartments may also be restricted to owner-occupied houses (Portland and New Castle) or even restricted to relatives of the homeowners (Fairfax and Montclair). They may be subject to intensive review processes—by neighbors, zoning boards, or special accessory apartment boards—with particular concerns for off-street parking (Lincoln); adequate sewage facilities; and indicators of one-family neighborhood character, such as only one front entrance visible from the front yard (Babylon); or "no external evidence of occupancy by more than one family" (Brookline, Massachusetts).[18] To many citizens and planners these legal restrictions and review processes guarantee a smooth transition between the current state of R-1 neighborhoods and the better use of housing resources in the future. Some towns even require yearly code of occupancy reviews; the most sensitive planners have offered a little extra flexibility in physical design requirements to encourage barrier-free conversions for the handicapped.[19]

Even so, the legally restricted remodeling of single-family houses is not an answer to the full range of planning, design, and landscaping needs embodied in the current housing crisis; nor is it a full exercise of the opportunities available in suburban R-1 districts. The relaxed zoning laws suggest how short-term private investments of time and money can be used to support homeowners' longer term investments, and they provide safeguards for neighbors who do not want the quality of their neighborhoods to deteriorate. Yet, implicitly, the house-by-house approach denies that over two or three decades most of the single family housing stock and most of the R-1 neighborhoods will change to reflect the basic demographic shifts the United States faces.

Legalizing house-by-house conversions not only denies the scale of demographic change; it denies the economics. While some of the ordinances prohibit absentee owners from gaining the appreciation in property values a rental unit provides, none deal with the economic question of the owner-speculator who sees the rental unit as a way to increase the value of his or her own property at the expense of neighbors' property values, which may be sustained by low densities and quiet, traffic-free streets. Some cities, such as Davis, California, and Washington, D.C., have begun to restrict the owner speculator. In Davis no one can buy a single-family home unless he or she is willing to live in it as a principal place of residence for one year; in Washington, D.C., a graduated capital gains tax penalizes those who buy and sell property quickly.[20] Santa Cruz, California, does acknowledge the plight of the renter by requiring that accessory apartments be rented only to low and moderate income tenants. When Dody Green complained about "greedy neighbors who are trying to make a few dollars off of a housing shortage," she had this problem of the owner-speculators in Springdale, Connecticut, clearly on target.

To develop a broader perspective citizens, planners, and designers must cast an interested eye on the whole suburban and urban landscape, and begin to think at the scale of the block, the neighborhood, and the city or town. The time horizon for this broader analysis must extend two or three decades, not two or three years. The questions are more obvious then. Just as some cities now bill infrastructure charges or demand other amenities built by large-scale commercial developers operating within their bounds, so some neighborhoods will scrutinize the public costs and private benefits of what homeowners want to do, and bill them accordingly.

Building a Constituency for Replanning Neighborhoods with Accessory Apartments

What actual and potential groups might be interested in becoming part of an effort to transform R-1 neighborhoods? Such groups would need to lobby for more comprehensive planning efforts, including changes in zoning, incentives to local economic development, and reorganization of local social services. As a consultant to the American Association of Retired Persons, Patrick Hare believes that one constituency is older homeowners: "They are politically unassailable and would be acting out of legitimate self-interest. A related group would be the sons and daughters of older homeowners who cannot take their parents into their own homes, but do not want to see them forced into nursing homes or other institutions.''[21] (He concedes that there are problems with the grown children as lobbyists because they may not live in the same towns as their parents; this, he believes, will lead to lobbying at the county, state, and national level for zoning changes.) Ultimately, Hare argues, elderly homeowners may acquire new bargaining power in American society through their creative concern for the unused space in their homes. They control "the nation's largest untapped housing resource,''[22] which Hare estimates as 14 percent of the owner-occupied housing stock.

Many sociologists have observed that the elderly do not choose to move from their homes, even when their health or financial situation becomes precarious: many elderly cannot bear the psychological losses associated with losing ties to their dwellings and communities.[23] So for elderly homeowners to insist on changes in the ways the existing housing stock is used is appropriate. In addition, the elderly in good health may want accessory apartments either for income or for tenants who will help with maintenance. Their children often want zoning permission for apartments or "elder cottages" for the frail elderly.

A second constituency for change consists of young people who are now tenants of apartments and their middle-aged parents who are owners. Many young single people and young childless couples simply cannot afford to buy houses in the towns where they grew up. Their parents are empty-nesters who would like to see more of their children and help their children economically. In the past, the parents might have provided their children with the down payment on a small house near their own; now, all they can provide is one or more accessory apartments in their own home. By accommodating more young single people and more young couples, as well as the single elderly, the old R-1 neighborhoods can house diverse age groups and diverse household types that can bring more varied family ties and friendships into the lives of suburban residents.[24] New kinds of financial arrangments and architectural arrangements might make it more attractive for younger people to live in or near their parents' homes, while preserving privacy and autonomy as young adults. If they could, for instance, become co-owners of private spaces within their parents' houses rather than heirs, it might add to the attraction of living in a separate apartment in the same dwelling.

A third potential constituency consists of single parents, male and female, and their children. The national association Parents Without Partners seeks housing options for its members, and in his book *Going It Alone,* sociologist Robert Weiss noted that housing has always been a major problem for this group.[25] Some single parents have tried shared housing—two parents inhabiting a single-family house—but this has met with mixed success. The existing housing stock in suburbia needs to be modified architecturally to meet single parents' needs for privacy as well as support. Shared housing programs do not acknowledge that the significant spatial conventions most of us carry with us are not so much a function of square footages as they are of a series of gradual spatial transitions from community to privacy. A house designed for one family cannot accommodate two unless these physical transitions are redesigned.

Women are a fourth constituency.[26] Women care about the survival of neighborhood kinship networks across generations. They also have a special interest in developing day care as a community service, and in creating local jobs to ease commuting for employed mothers.

A fifth constituency consists of environmental activists. In such an effort, conservation minded citizens, makers of solar equipment, and small designers, carpenters, and builders might find common interests.[27]

A sixth constituency is minority Americans, both owners and renters, who have experienced difficulties in finding, renting, buying, and reselling suburban dwellings. The research of Robert Lake and Thomas Clark shows that racial discrimination has limited minority participation in the capital accumulation that many white homeowners have achieved, although the number of blacks in suburbia has increased in the 1970s.[28] Minority suburban homeowners and renters are (however involuntarily) less mobile, more committed to certain neighborhoods. They are a potential constituency for projects that play down the role of the owner speculator in favor of greater neighborhood improvements available to the community.

A seventh potential constituency consists of the Dody Greens of America who can't stand noise, too many cars, or greedy neighbors. At the moment Mr. and Mrs. Green are living in a rapidly changing neighborhood, fighting a rear guard action. The alternative for them, and for other homeowners concerned about the amenities of their R-1 neighborhoods, is to insist that changes be made to the highest .

standards of quality in planning and design. The benefits to the Greens of joining forces to replan and redesign their neighborhood, rather than simply fighting those who want it to be rezoned, are substantial. The planners and designers who care about quality need the Greens on their team to speak up in favor of quiet, trees, and public transportation, and to fulminate against owner-speculators. This last constituency of house-proud owners is the key to the homelike world if their high standards can be orchestrated as zeal for quality rather than as resistance to change.

Reorganizing the Dream Houses

The architectural and landscaping possibilities presented by accessory apartments are complex and exciting ones. Consider a stereotypical tract of the 1950s and 1960s. A typical suburban block will have been divided into plots of a quarter to half an acre each. If there are, say, thirteen houses, then thirteen driveways might be used by twenty-six cars; ten garden sheds, ten swings, thirteen lawn mowers, thirteen outdoor dining tables being to suggest the duplication of existing amenities. Yet in the R-1 design there are few transitions between the public streets and the private homes, no community park, no space to socialize with neighbors because all space is either strictly private or strictly public. The typical one-family houses—ranch, split level, or colonial—will probably include three bedrooms and den, two and a half baths, laundry rooms, porches, and two-car garages, if they were constructed in the 1950s or 1960s.

It is easy to see how such suburban single-family houses could be remodeled to become duplexes and triplexes. (Architecture student Hattie Hartman has developed a handbook to show the many variations).[29] A 1400-square-foot house can become a triplex, with a two-bedroom unit; a one-bedroom unit; and an efficiency unit (for a single person or elderly person). The three units can share a porch and entry hall. While the remodeled apartments are small (400–600 sq. ft.) they are not as tiny as some that developers have proposed or even executed as new construction.[30] Many experiments can take place with regard to the sizes and shapes of new apartments. They can be in the garage, extending into the backyard, under the roof, or at the bottom levels of a split level design. A good architect can make many of these plans work; designing for acoustical privacy is especially important.

Relandscaping the Dream Neighborhoods: Room for New Village Greens

Unless the entire block is relandscaped to create more common green space, the conversion of one house to two or three apartments won't be especially pleasant in its connection of indoor and outdoor spaces. A minimum recommendation would be to provide private outdoor space for each unit. Perferably this would be a small garden, but possibly porches and decks for first and second floor apartments. Ae˟thetically the neighborhood as a whole would be improved if empty front lawns were replaced with diverse, small, private gardens, and new porches. But an even greater aesthetic impact can be achieved if residents start to create new common land by joining parts of their yards. Most American suburban tracts are large enough to accommodate private gardens and new common land as well. Pedestrian paths and sidewalks can be created to link housing with such central spaces. Private porches, garages, and tool sheds could also be more intensely utilized as semi-public or public spaces. Precedents for this approach were proposed in the post-World War II era, as well as in more recent years.

In redefining the American suburban block spatially, there are two alternatives: a zone of greater activity at the street or at the

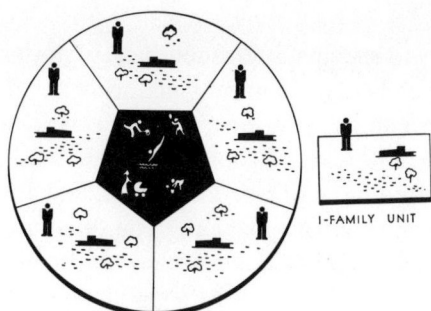

7.2 Architect's diagram from the 1940s proposing suburban community with shared child care and recreation space. The roles were traditional but not the land use.

center of the block. Urban neighborhoods may wish to emphasize the public aspects of street life; Raquel Ramati's book *How to Save Your Own Street*[31] suggests this in her Manhattan urban design approach. But in suburbia, there are great advantages to turning the block inside out for community use away from the auto. Clarence Stein clearly delineated this second approach as correct land use in "the motor age," with cars segregated from residents' green spaces and spaces for children. At Radburn, New Jersey, and in the Baldwin Hills Village in Los Angeles, as we have seen, Stein achieved remarkably luxurious results (at a density of about seven units to the acre) by this method, since multiple-unit housing always bordered a lush parkland without automobile traffic. Stein's projects demonstrated this success most dramatically, but a revitalized suburban block with lots as small as a quarter of an acre can be reorganized to yield a similar effect. Shared green space of this kind is also the tradition in some of the most expensive and exclusive row house blocks in New York, and, interesting enough, in the seven villages the Amana community built in Iowa in the nineteenth century.[32]

At the same time, some new built space for the entire neighborhood might be appropriate. The Certosa di Pavia offers the memorable image of single units joined by an arcade framing the collective open space. Irving Gill's Lewis Courts suggest the possibility of trellises and arched gateways connecting units to enclose a common space. Other ways to connect and frame green space will suggest themselves as architects and landscape architects ponder the best uses for each site, along with the desires of residents, based on age, income, and ethnicity. Some neighborhoods will find the model of the traditional village greens of New England a powerful inspiration, and many Americans could have town greens again, by literally carving out the heart of every converted suburban block for shared open space where new neighborhood activities could be accommodated. The experience of one European city and two American cities can demonstrate the various ways in which backyard rehabilitations have been accomplished.

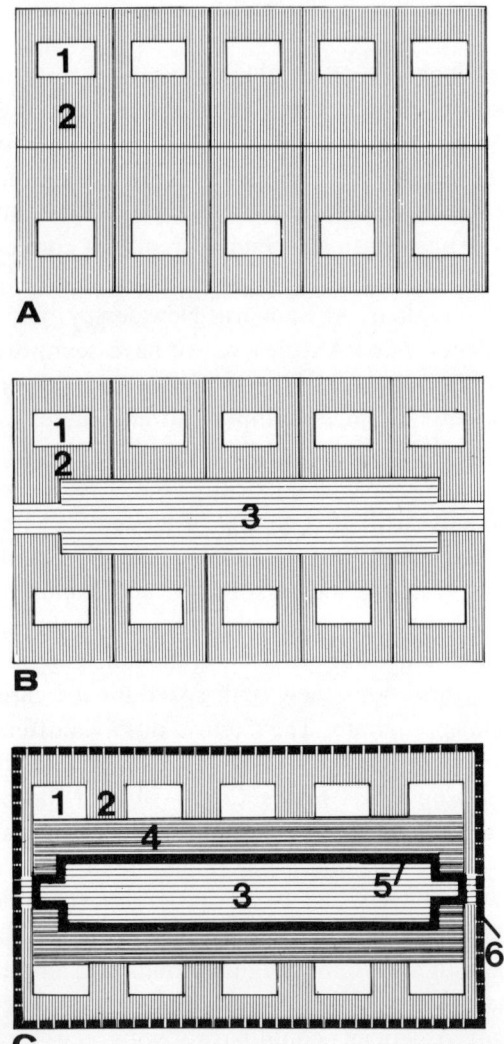

7.3 Diagram showing some of the possibilities of reorganizing a typical suburban block through rezoning, rebuilding, and relandscaping. *A,* ten single-family houses (1) on ten private lots (2); *B,* the same houses (1) with smaller private lots (2) after a backyard rehabilitation program has created a new village green (3) at the heart of the block; *C,* the same houses (1) and many small private gardens (2) with a new village green (3) surrounded by a zone for new services and accessory apartments (4) connected by a new sidewalk or arcade (5) and surrounded by a new border of street trees (6). In Figure *C,* (4) can include space for such activities as day care, elderly care, laundry, and food service as well as housing, while (3) can accommodate a children's play area, vegetable or flower gardens, and outdoor seating. (5) may be a sidewalk, a vine-covered trellis, or a formal arcade. The narrow ends of the block can be emphasized as collective entrances with gates (to which residents have keys), leading to new accessory apartments entered from the arcade or sidewalk. In the densest possible situations, (3) may be alley and parking lot, if existing street parking and public transit are not adequate.

Experiences in Relandscaping

The work of architect Hans Wirz of Zurich, Switzerland, who has exploited the potential of his city's back yards, alleys, and service entrances, provides an extensive, urban case study of how to relandscape residential blocks. Wirz succeeded in getting his city to vote $300,000 in funds to sponsor such projects, as well as to establish a city agency to "encourage, motivate, and coordinate involved property owners," conduct the often lengthy negotiations, and participate in the design process and actual construction. By 1979 his efforts resulted in twenty completed block rehabilitations of backyard spaces in Zurich.

With the city agency providing technical, legal, and financial assistance to groups of homeowners, tenant organizations, and housing cooperatives, the projects proceeded with voluntary participation and private initiative. Four basic categories developed. (1) In projects emphasizing private and semi-public space, private yards were reduced in depth to half their size, and the remaining land was developed as a cooperatively owned central open space accessible to each private yard. (2) The common open space approach is similar, but the whole back yard area was turned into common space accessible to all. (3) The complementary facilities approach involved making community services, such as day-care centers, in the new common spaces. (4) The intensive, low-rise projects—for the most urbanized areas with a mixture of shops and housing—involved creating expensive, underground parking in the rear yards and building an accessible roof deck over the parking as common open space, because commercial uses could help finance this.

Wirz has noted that his main obstacle was "the skepticism of home owners that an agreement can be reached among the neighbors regarding the legal, financial, and other design considerations involved." He believes that "it is essential that a third party—such as Zurich's special agency for rear yard rehabilitation—be available to channel and coordinate individual interests and initiatives.[33] And Wirz notes that the United States looks like a place with great potential for this kind of activity. There are similar problems, but even greater opportunities with more generous lot sizes than the Swiss often started with. Either a town's planning and zoning agency or a neighborhood association could undertake such activities.

American ingenuity provides another model of how some groups might build upon Wirz's work. A solar greenhouse run by a community development corporation in Cheyenne, Wyoming, generates income from a commercial nursery, food from a community garden, and environmental education for all. The project underlines the importance of building and gardening activities to developing a sense of citizen accountability, since the Cheyenne solar greenhouse involves the young, the middle aged, and the old. It is the kind of project that could be undertaken by a group that had already made a backyard common open space.

The Cheyenne project began in 1976 as a program employing fifteen low-income community youths to build three small 16'-by-20' solar greenhouses on vacant lots. The youths worked on these as an alternative to going to jail; the greenhouses provided food for a group home of thirty-five handicapped people. The success of the small greenhouses led to a larger community undertaking in 1977 involving the design and construction of a three-stage, three-growing-climate, 500-square-foot greenhouse. In spite of heavy snow and long winters, the greenhouse produced its first harvest in May of 1978. Designer Gary Garber reports that the project attracted about eighty gardeners ranging in age from ten to ninety-two, including retirees and the handicapped.

What seems most distinctive about the Cheyenne system, as compared with the outdoor community gardens found in Santa Monica, California, or many other towns where city residents cultivate private plots and socialize across the plot lines, is that the cultivation proceeds collectively. The greenhouse's paid staff select plantings, make up work schedules, and assign participants to jobs. Harvesting is more remarkable: ". . . individuals simply take what they need. In some cases, people who may work at the greenhouse three or four days a week for several hours a day may choose to take little or nothing, while an individual with less time to spend but more need might take whatever is ready to pick." According to designer Gary Garber, "so far, after two complete winter and summer seasons, there have been no problems with this system of distribution. It seems that people get to know each other through working side-by-side in the structure and develop strong bonds of mutual understanding and respect. This has been one of the least anticipated and most heartening aspects of the project."[34]

Yields are constantly increasing; two sections of the greenhouse produce foods such as tomatoes, onions, spinach, and herbs in two growing seasons, while the third section of the greenhouse is used for commercial production of plants to generate income. Environmental education is also essential to the experience: ''A visitor at the greenhouse may be greeted by a retired school teacher, a little girl, or a weather-beaten old cowboy. Any of them will gladly conduct a tour and explain how everything works. A visitor will see a cross-section of the community—young and old, rich and poor—working side-by-side. Some are there to socialize, some to learn, while others need the food.'' One can conclude, with Garber, that this project ''is an alternative energy park where people can learn not only how to save energy, but how to create it.''[35]

Richard Britz, landscape architect and author of *The Edible City,* and several other advocates of urban agriculture whose work appears in *Resettling America,* believe that all Americans will need to become self-sufficient in food production in the next few decades.[36] Not every neighborhood will be so ambitious that they will want a solar greenhouse, as well as a new village green. But demographics suggest that one facility sure to be in demand is community day care, along with home maintenance help for the elderly. The outdoor play space for children that a day care facility requires is especially well-suited to a new green heart for every block. On Derby Street, in Berkeley, California, in the 1970s, residents pooled land at the heart of the block and created a parents' cooperative day-care center in just this configuration. One absentee landlord refused to join, but the common green simply flowed around his fenced yard.

Like this man who refused to have anything to do with the Derby Street block remodeling, there are many Americans who want to keep their land all their own. However attractive the options of shared open space, community gardens, and day care, many Americans will choose the private walled garden, and such choices should be protected in every neighborhood plan. As entire blocks of detached houses are converted to a more complex mix of duplexes, triplexes, and community service uses, the new densities will demand as much skill in protecting privacy as enhancing community. Whether or not residents favor community uses of land, if extensive residential conversions are underway, a sophisticated landscape plan for the whole block is still necessary.

Homeownership in a Period of Change

At the same time, additional issues of ownership and proprietorship
need to be faced. Homeownership has long been associated with the
"each farmer on his own farm" sort of territoriality, which can turn
into fences and guard dogs in some suburban areas. New neighborhood densities are certain to cause friction. While financial need
will be pressing some owners to accept new densities, the American
non-verbal conventions and "hidden dimensions" of personal space
attached to suburban homeownership will be violated.[37] The only
answer to this issue is to take a closer look at homeownership in
comparison to other forms of domestic proprietorship, to see if it,
too, can be renegotiated over several decades as part of reorganizing
the American dream house and dream neighborhood.

Suppose every neighborhood trying to deal with accessory apartments on a long-term basis organized itself to ease the transition,
economically, socially, and physically, to a situation where there
would be homeownership without speculation. This would mean
attempting to form a limited-equity cooperative of owners, which
over time, would assure that the housing—whether old units or new
ones—would remain affordable. It would imply devising a strategy
to remove units from the housing market, which would not be ineq-
uitable to present owners, but would discourage absentee landlords
and speculators.

Homeownership is still our most powerful national inducement
for any policy change, whether it is wielded in favor of those who
want to retain it or those who want to achieve it. There is nothing
wrong with the American tradition of homeownership, if it is available to all without regard to gender or race; if owners do not receive
tax benefits unavailable to renters; and if owners do not speculate
on their homes and deprive the next generation of the chance for
ownership. As an alternative to current forms of homeownership,
Americans can explore the limited-equity cooperative. Such an
organization holds a blanket mortgage on many housing units,
maintains them all and the common land. Owners receive all personal income tax deductions that single mortgage holders do, but
they sell their shares back to the coop when they leave, rather than
selling a unit on the open housing market. The rate of appreciation
is determined in their membership agreement. In many neighborhoods, a limited equity cooperative association concerned with tak-

ing care of buildings and common land could be a way to nurture commitment to a specific place; to encourage accountability to a group; to educate the young about the necessary work of society; and to carry out the responsibilities every generation has to those older and younger.

Here is how such an arrangement might develop in a neighborhood with a long-term landscape plan and a policy of strict enforcement of zoning and building codes. Let's say that owner A wants a permit to convert excess space in a $70,000 house into an extra apartment. Suppose the tough local planning board offers owner A two choices. First: Owner A can subdivide the house into a legal duplex, and sell the second unit for the market price, $35,000, provided that both Owner A and the new duplex owner then enter into a limited equity cooperative association, which fixes the future appreciation of each unit and handles neighborhood improvements. Second: Owner A can subdivide the house by making one legal accessory apartment for rental income subject to a special assessment for neighborhood improvements by the neighbors' association. If Owner A wants cash, he or she will subdivide and sell. If Owner A wants income, he or she will subdivide, pay the neighborhood assessment, and collect rent. The second approach can lead to the first after some years. Either way, a local planning authority or a neighborhood association can begin to gain the power to plan more changes over time as owners feel the pressure to make legal conversions to realize part of their equity, or to increase their income. Some owners who would probably like to sell part but not all of their property would be those who feel the pressure of foreclosure, those who are elderly, and those who are getting divorced or separated. Other owners who would like to rent would be households with extra space but no money problems (who could afford the neighborhood assessment), or households needing help with maintenance, baby-sitting, or elderly care.

The Route Two Cooperative in Los Angeles provides a model for the shared ownership of existing houses by new types of households; although it is *not* a model of how to start such a process, because it all began with a proposal for a freeway. In the pressure to expand the Los Angeles freeway system of the 1960s, Caltrans, the California transportation agency, condemned 124 small single-family houses and 90 apartment buildings containing 350 units for a 2.4 mile extension of Route 2—the Glendale Freeway. For fourteen years the low and moderate income housing units sat, deteriorating, in the projected path of the freeway and, when the freeway extension was held up by protest groups, Caltrans rented them on a temporary basis. Finally the freeway plan was abandoned and the state proposed to resell the housing units at market prices. The former owners protested that years had gone by and they could not afford to repurchase their own houses; the tenants joined them in protests.[38]

After an heroic organizing drive over several years, aided by the Los Angeles Community Design Center, the Route Two Tenants Association won support for a different proposal. Caltrans agreed to rehabilitate these properties and to offer all the tenants (and former owners) the first chance to purchase them. But because a public agency was involved, everyone agreed that they had to produce affordable units and prohibit speculation in order to keep them affordable. House prices range from $25,000 to $60,000; apartments in a limited-equity cooperative on scattered sites cost about $20,000.[39] The FHA is insuring mortgages arranged by a consortium of local lenders. After years of being threatened by eviction, the dream of homeownership is coming true—but without the possibility of speculative profit. The resale of any unit will be handled by the cooperative residents' association and restricted to other low and moderate income families.

A limited equity cooperative structure has several other advantages besides easing the psychological and economic transition from lower to higher densities. It also solves maintenance problems of common land and it can introduce new economic activities to combine jobs and services with housing. Any new suburban parks, courtyards, arcades, or greens imply shared maintenance, or proprietorship, as Ronald Fleming and Lauri Halderman point out in *On Common Ground*.[40] Their concept of proprietorship is derived from New England Puritan covenant communities. In each town, the greens were established as common lands by the original settlers, called the Proprietors, in their covenant. Proprietorship can of course mean many different forms of ownership, management, and concern, but any shared space needs care by its owners or users. If the shared space includes shared economic and social activities, even more organization is required. How much are neighbors capable of doing together? Legal redefinitions of privacy and community of the kind a housing coop provides are crucial to the answer. Gradual involvement in projects that provide real gains to an entire neighborhood can reassure neighbors that the struggle to organize and work collectively actually produces results that are worth the long meetings, economic risks, and social challenges.

Public Housing: Breaking the Stereotypes

Public housing represents a relatively small part of the American housing stock, even a very small part of the multi-family housing stock, but it is a crucial area for improvement in the combination of housing, jobs, and services for residents. The majority of public housing tenants are female-headed families and the female elderly. Both kinds of households suffer from all of the restrictions on women's earning capability and independent movement in the city that have already been explored. One group already making changes on this front is the National Congress of Neighborhood Women in Brooklyn, New York, a multi-ethnic, multi-racial coalition of working-class and poor women aimed at finding new approaches. Jan Peterson, one of their leaders, has developed a program in three public housing projects to help residents get job training and job placement, along with better day-care services. Bertha Gilkey of

7.4 Public housing, Columbia Point, Dorchester, Massachusetts. Many aging housing projects are in need of job development programs for women residents and services such as child care.

Saint Louis, organizer of the tenants group in public housing there, is another leader in this field, who has introduced many new jobs, services, and activities, in a tenant management setting. In each case organizers may actually choose to eliminate a small number of residential units in order to attract new services and jobs.

In older cities, there is the increasing problem of abandoned housing that has become city property. When landlords have drained a building's assets, taken their depreciation, and then stopped paying property taxes, the city becomes the owner by default. This abandoned stock not only needs a similar infusion of jobs and day-care services; it also often requires extensive repair work. Some cities have managed to make such buildings acceptable and even turn them into limited equity coops, but until the landlord's tax structure is changed, this will always be an uphill battle.

A third category of publically supported housing which should probably be considered are all rent-subsidy arrangements. Private developers may build housing at market rates and then receive subsidies for taking low income tenants. If the developer is a non-profit group such as a church or a labor union this arrangement may be satisfactory, but for profit-making developers, the use of public funds can lead to abuses. Another form of public support is to give housing assistance directly to the poor as some form of "voucher" to be passed on to private developers. This only exacerbates the possibilities for developer exploitation, yet too much federal and local intervention makes for a bureaucratic tangle and uninteresting buildings.

An alternative to some of these federal, state and local rent subsidies for multi-family housing would be greater concern for the special needs of specific groups who currently inhabit most subsidized housing, and a focusing of funds on services directed at rehabilitating and enriching these environments. This could be justified if the conversion of existing R-1 housing stock to duplexes and triplexes proceeds fast enough to increase the supply of affordable housing, and is also monitored by planners to assure integration of minorities, the elderly, and single parents, who now constitute the bulk of tenants in subsidized projects. At a national level, sympathetic members of Congress would need to tie strict fair housing provisions to any new aid for conversion programs to make this work.

Housing, Special Needs, and
the Ideal of Normal Family Life

The one type of new housing construction that the United States can probably justify in the next few decades is housing programed and designed to meet the special needs of the elderly, single parents, battered wives, and, possibly, single people. All of these groups have received scant attention from planners and designers in the last forty years, since the ideal of normal family life tended to shape the units professionals designed for them, even if the gender and age stereotypes didn't fit. This "normal" unit prevailed even though each one of these groups was sometimes ghettoized—in elderly housing or retirement homes, in public housing, and in swinging singles complexes. (A few congregate housing projects for the elderly were an exception.) For each of these groups, the route to more autonomy and independent living will require rethinking the standard apartment. This means integrating it with support services, such as meals on wheels, part-time employment, day care, or counseling, all spatially integrated into the building or neighborhood setting, but not produced in such a way as to make residents feel that they are unusual or abnormal for needing them.

The handicapped form a special needs group that *has* succeeded in lobbying effectively for environmental changes in the last decade. Led by Vietnam veterans and other activists, handicapped citizens have insisted that much of the urban built environment in the United States be modified to become barrier-free. The financial cost of this was high. Women, children, and the elderly represent a much more substantial majority of American citizens who also need spatial assistance to lead fuller lives, and surely when their needs are articulated, the economic resources to meet them should be forth coming. These groups need to make it clear that they have outgrown the model of traditional family life embodied in a suburban, prescriptive architecture of gender. Reprograming housing to suit their specific needs is a complex task, whether it leads to new construction or renovation. Yet a few examples of successful reprograming suggest how important new shared facilities can be. While these examples may come from affluent or highly politicized groups, the needs they meet are more generally felt.

An Inn for the Elderly in New England

New Canaan, Connecticut, is one town where residents struggled to meet the housing needs of the elderly who could no longer afford to live alone in their houses, or who could not manage the driving or physical maintenance that suburban houses required. As the towns-people assessed the situation, they saw that there were few moderately priced rentals, and only one small inn in town taking a few elderly guests. As one man summed up the situation: "Many of our older citizens, who had contributed so much to the town, had had to move elsewhere in their later years. Or they had continued to live alone in their own homes, coping as best they could with problems of safety, loneliness, isolated locations, maintenance of their properties, and meal preparation. Our desire was to provide a conveniently located residence for seniors where they could live comfortably under one roof, but with dignity, privacy, and independence." So residents decided to establish The New Canaan Inn, open to town residents over sixty-two and to elderly relatives of town residents. It is a non-profit corporation without any government funding.

The residence was designed as an inn rather than as a home for the elderly, in order to convey the sense of public life and personal independence available to guests in the dining room, library, living room, and recreation areas. Residents enjoy three meals a day and invite guests for meals when they like; it is a short walk to shops and the post office. The former librarian likes it because she still feels in the center of things happening in town; other residents write for the local paper or take part in various activities. An innkeeper who lives on the premises supervises a twenty-four hour staff. The project provides an excellent way to reuse a large old house or even a small inn. It suggests a use compatible with existing residential neighborhoods.[41]

Rehabilitation for Singles or the Elderly

The remodeling of larger one-family houses can also take place under the control of a sensitive preservationist, developer, or architect with a special interest in new kinds of households and their needs. Of course, there is the disadvantage of segregating singles, be they young or old, from families with children or other household types, but some argue that the new facilities provided outweigh the disadvantages. A community of people of a common age or situation in life can be more congenial to some than having grandmothers next to young singles.

Existing tax incentives for historic preservation have encouraged entrepreneurs to create more shared space within housing. Catherine Davis of Los Angeles, California, is a preservationist taking advantage of the Economic Recovery Tax Act of 1981, by acquiring historic houses, restoring them, and renting them. She began by helping a friend create a shelter for battered wives and their children. Then she explored how to find new kinds of tenants for large old houses— young single professionals or two or more families. She argues that traditionalists like to live in fine old houses—the sense of history pleases them—and states that renting in this way to a group of single adults generates more income than a one-family rental. In addition, transitional neighborhoods are strengthened for further preservation efforts, by permitting slow appreciation rather than quick resale. Davis's projects include this one: "A Craftsman house in Pasadena, designed by Greene and Greene. It's home to a group of art students. They use the airy living room as a gallery, the inglenook as a drafting room, the sleeping porches as a sculpture studio and an upstairs bathtub for soaking their watercolor paper."[42] She has also rehabilitated a Mediterranean villa of the 1920s in the Hollywood Hills, where young professionals share the large living and dining rooms and terraces for entertaining; and she turned a Colonial Revival mansion in Dallas into a duplex. Davis gives new life to physical settings designed for large affluent households by redesigning for moderate-income single adults. She offers homes that go beyond the options usually available to singles: efficiencies, shared apartments or the swinging single complex. She is also creating a social context with both privacy and community for adults who might not have the capital, the skills, or the time to commit to such preservation projects themselves.

Gwen Rønø, a developer and architect in Cambridge, Massachusetts, has undertaken the restoration and expansion of a nineteenth century parsonage on Harvard Street. Eight households with members over sixty-one years of age can own small, private condominiums and share a common living, dining, and kitchen area, and gardens. There is also one guest room that all residents can use for visitors. Rønø designed this project not only with the needs of older people in mind but for those who would like to be close to lectures, concerts, bookstores, and the range of activities in a university town. She also asked Jean Mason, an experienced social worker and group therapist, to help the six tenants work out their approach to group living and management of the condominium. Mason's services were included in the purchase price, as part of an experiment to see if congregate spaces would attract residents to the project. Mason worked out a "Common Area and Shared Living Arrangement," which all of the purchasers signed as part of their commitment to the project.[43]

The efforts of Catherine Davis and Gwen Rønø suggest how much can be done to transform older housing and extend new possibilities, when special needs are well understood. They have served relatively affluent residents, but a similar project in Massachusetts operates with a state subsidy. At Captain Clarence Eldridge House in Hyannis, a New England sea captain's house was rehabilitated and extended to become congregate housing for the elderly. Architect Barry Korobkin, sociologist John Zeisel, and associated architects Donham and Sweeney developed the design for the state's

7.5 An old parsonage converted to condominiums for the elderly with a common living and dining area by Gwen Rønø, Cambridge, Massachusetts, 1982.

Office of Communities and Development, the sponsor of over a dozen similar projects. As their carefully annotated plans show, patterns of social activity were researched before any decisions were made about private spaces and shared facilities.

7.6 Captain Clarence Eldridge House, Hyannis, Massachusetts, by Barry Korobkin, 1981, views and plans. Residents share the front porch, laundry, tv room, living, and dining areas, but individual kitchenettes, bed-sitting rooms, and toilets maximize privacy. (*Progressive Architecture,* August 1981, photos courtesy Reinhold Publications)

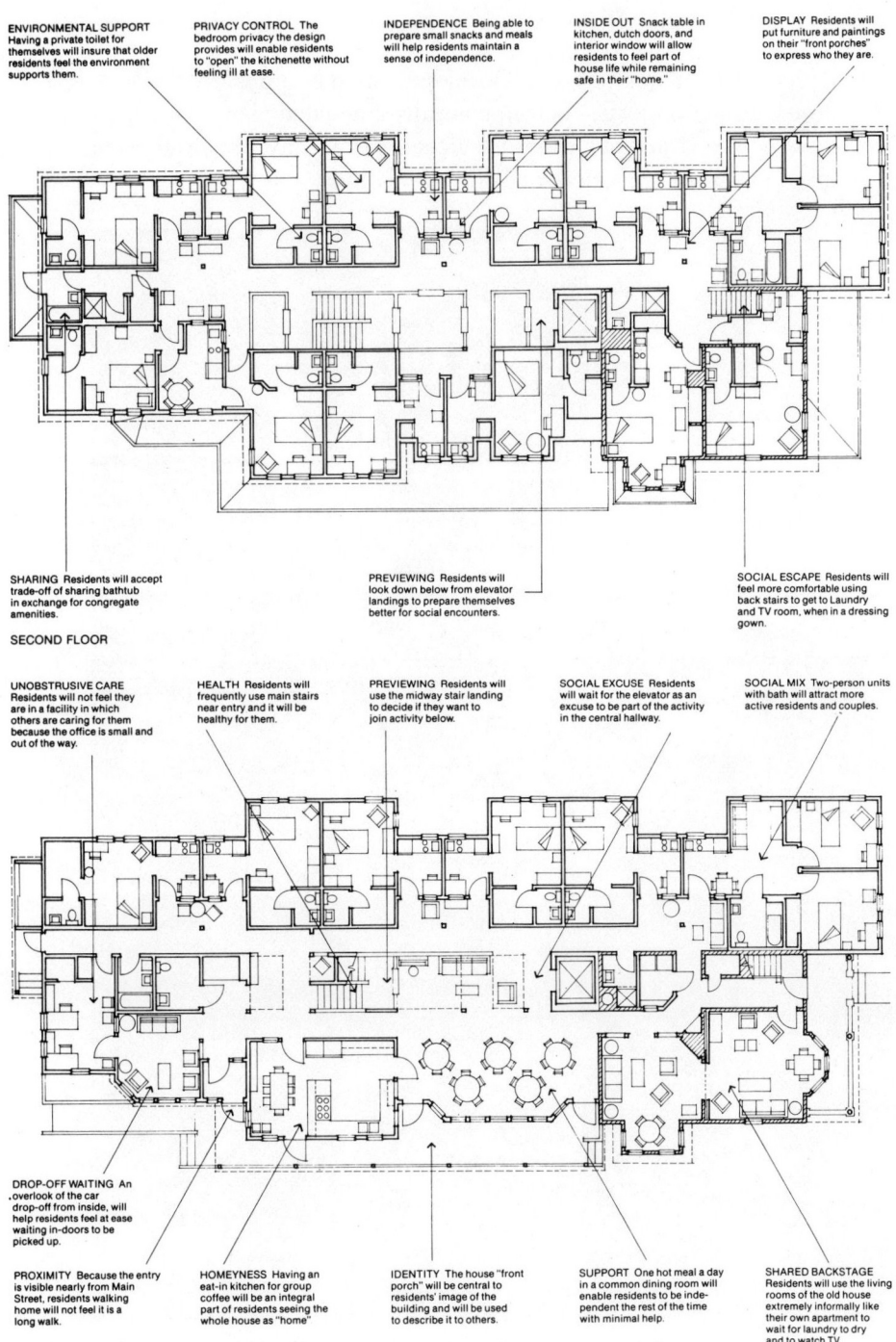

ENVIRONMENTAL SUPPORT
Having a private toilet for themselves will insure that older residents feel the environment supports them.

PRIVACY CONTROL The bedroom privacy the design provides will enable residents to "open" the kitchenette without feeling ill at ease.

INDEPENDENCE Being able to prepare small snacks and meals will help residents maintain a sense of independence.

INSIDE OUT Snack table in kitchen, dutch doors, and interior window will allow residents to feel part of house life while remaining safe in their "home."

DISPLAY Residents will put furniture and paintings on their "front porches" to express who they are.

SHARING Residents will accept trade-off of sharing bathtub in exchange for congregate amenities.

PREVIEWING Residents will look down below from elevator landings to decide if themselves better for social encounters.

SOCIAL ESCAPE Residents will feel more comfortable using back stairs to get to Laundry and TV room, when in a dressing gown.

SECOND FLOOR

UNOBSTRUSIVE CARE Residents will not feel they are in a facility in which others are caring for them because the office is small and out of the way.

HEALTH Residents will frequently use main stairs near main entry and it will be healthy for them.

PREVIEWING Residents will use the midway stair landing to decide if they want to join activity below.

SOCIAL EXCUSE Residents will wait for the elevator as an excuse to be part of the activity in the central hallway.

SOCIAL MIX Two-person units with bath will attract more active residents and couples.

DROP-OFF WAITING An overlook of the car drop-off from inside, will help residents feel at ease waiting in-doors to be picked up.

PROXIMITY Because the entry is visible nearly from Main Street, residents walking home will not feel it is a long walk.

HOMEYNESS Having an eat-in kitchen for group coffee will be an integral part of residents seeing the whole house as "home"

IDENTITY The house "front porch" will be central to residents' image of the building and will be used to describe it to others.

SUPPORT One hot meal a day in a common dining room will enable residents to be independent the rest of the time with minimal help.

SHARED BACKSTAGE Residents will use the living rooms of the old house extremely informally like their own apartment to wait for laundry to dry and to watch TV.

FIRST FLOOR   N↑   ⊢———⊢—⌐—⊢——⌐——⊣ 20'/6m

7.6 (Continued) Annotated plans of Captain Clarence Eldridge House.

Congregate Housing Designed
for Privacy and Community

The entrance to the Captain Clarence Eldridge House is placed for
easy visibility from Main Street in Hyannis, so residents "will not
feel it is a long walk" home. A waiting room with windows over-
looking the entry allows for comfortable, indoor seating next to the
automobile drop-off. Nearby is the main office, unobtrusively sited.
All entrances and the dining room open out into a broad front porch
that wraps the extended sea captain's dwelling in a familiar architectural symbol of home, amenity, and comfort.

Inside, on the ground floor, two main rooms of the original house
(at the lower left in the plans), serve as informal living rooms for
the new residents. The designers call this a "backstage" where they
can watch TV, chat, or wait for their laundry to be done in a nearby
room with washer and dryer. The social spaces next to this living
area include a formal dining room where residents eat one meal per
day together. A large kitchen includes a table and chairs in an alcove for "homeyness," or sitting around chatting and drinking coffee, as well as space for the efficient preparation of the meals to be
served next door.

Circulation within the building is designed to balance sociability
and privacy, exercise and ease. The front stair is formal. The back
stair connects apartments to the "backstage" and allows residents
to watch TV in dressing gowns and slippers. An elevator is stationed
in the most sociable space next to the dining room. Seating nearby
is overlooked by both a mid-stair landing and an elevator landing so
residents can "preview" the social scene and "decide if they want
to join activity below."

The eighteen private apartments are small but designed to maximize both sociability and privacy. Two-person units include a dining area, small kitchenette, dining table, full bath, and two bedrooms. One-person units provide a bedsitting room, half bath,
kitchenette, and dining area. Independence is stressed by making it
possible for residents to eat alone, yet the private dining tables are
placed next to interior windows opening into the corridor. This corridor area widens where it includes kitchen windows and doors for
two units and the designers call this a shared, interior "front porch."
It is large enough for the display of some personal furnishings or
paintings.

Whether or not a space like the interior "front porch" works for all residents, all of the time, it is an example of the kind of architectural experimentation that can lead to new patterns of community and amenity. The delicate balancing of private space, space shared by residents, and space shared by residents with outsiders must go on all the time in housing design. New designs that make unexpected trade-offs—say a shared bathtub room in return for private kitchenettes—expand the sense of what is possible, socially and architecturally. Ultimately the goal is never to enforce communal living against the residents' wishes. Rather it is to reinforce autonomy and privacy by providing designed support in the form of social services. The designers of this project express the idea perfectly in their 1985 manual of architectural advice on congregate housing entitled *Independence through Interdependence*. Independence is strengthened through skillful deployment of shared resources. Their concept is applicable to housing for young families with children needing child care or to single young people, as well as to the frail elderly. As the end of the twentieth century approaches, more and more Americans are going to be looking for ways to live happily after sixty-five.

7.7   Common space at the center of an old California bungalow court converted to housing for battered wives. Each of the ten bungalows is shared by two women and their children.

A Court for Battered Wives

In Pasadena, California, Haven House offers yet another model of a special needs conversion. Here the residents are battered wives and their children who share the old bungalows of a Classical Revival bungalow court. A child-care space has been created and the housing design keeps the feeling of a homey place with privacy for residents, despite the fact that the program only offers housing on a temporary basis. Here the sense of place generated by the original design adds to the feeling that all participate in a shared home, since the court was originally built on the model of the neighborhood strategy.

Implementing Change: Idealism, Cynicism, and the Long View

Architecture can't bring about revolution; spatial change by itself can't effect social change. American housing reform movements over the last two centuries have often been blessed with a multitude of good ideas and cursed with a lack of economic power. Until land and residential buildings are no longer treated as commodities in this society, until government policies such as depreciation allowances and other tax breaks favoring real estate developers are ended, this society will always have housing problems. Yet, it seems crucial to reiterate the underlying potential in a difficult situation. This moment of concern about affordable housing is a time when a coalition of concerned citizens, local officials, planners, and designers can provide leadership for a transformation in the way we live. What is important is for ordinary citizens to gain a clearer sense of their spatial needs.

The story of "Lonelyville" should underscore just how important this moment is in historical terms. In the years just after the Civil War, affluent young New Yorkers confronted a housing crisis, a dilemma that was somewhat similar to our own suburban crisis. At that time the preeminent model of an urban dwelling for a middle-class family and their servants in New York City was a brick row house, with a basement, two or three additional habitable floors, and an attic. In many ways this house form promoted good urban design because row houses joined with others to form graceful urban streets and, in the best situations, row houses formed handsome squares or crescents. In other ways, this house form was overgenerous, because it was based on a zoning law of 1811 that decreed a grid of 25'-by-100' lots covering the best part of Manhattan Island "to facilitate the buying and selling of land." Large back yards complemented the row houses' unified street fronts, and the unified fronts also provided the face-to-face contact between households that was important for social continuity. The manners cherished by Henry James and Edith Wharton were rooted here. But the system was too expensive to sustain in the face of post–Civil War industrial and commercial development.

Young couples in Manhattan found that they could not afford to buy lots of this size and build three-story houses on them as their parents and grandparents had. And while they might have liked the same amount of space, they confronted a shortage of servants to maintain the space. They also had smaller families, and more modern ideas about how to entertain. One obvious physical solution was to divide row houses horizontally, but the young couples considered this socially unacceptable. The middle-class social strictures against having anyone live above or below oneself—sharing a horizontal surface such as a floor or ceiling—seem quaint now, but they caused panic then. Families simply couldn't believe that they could continue to exist without the row houses they knew and loved, but they wouldn't subdivide them.

Another spatial option was sharing land costs with other families to build multi-family buildings with common services, but this was even less agreeable. It suggested working-class poverty, or the unrespectable, bohemian life of flats or hotels, or European-style apartment houses. Another, temporary alternative for a young couple was boarding somewhere until they could afford to buy a row house or build one, but this simply postponed the problem. The last resort was to move to "Lonelyville," as one young wife called it, the remote suburbs reached by railroad (or perhaps streetcar) where land was cheaper. As described in *Good Housekeeping:* "The busy men leave on early trains and are at once plunged into the rush of their accustomed life among their usual associates, while the suburban woman remains at home, standing behind the struggling young vines of her brand new Piazza."[44]

Despite women's reservations, affluent Lonelyvilles proliferated in response to the row house crisis. Yet other changes evolved over time. After several decades new housing types such as apartments became somewhat acceptable for Manhattan's middle-class families and, at the same time, some families began to subdivide the large old row houses into small apartments, or into apartments, office, and shops. Some became slums, and were only rediscovered recently. But eventually the row houses began to be recycled for smaller families and new uses. They form some districts of New York that include some of the most sought after housing today. However small the row house apartments are, when these neighborhoods are well cared for, they are still the most desirable of all urban and suburban areas anywhere.

The context of this story cannot be overemphasized: the years of that housing crisis for the upper classes and upper middle classes of Manhattan were also the years of the greatest slum problems, when immigrants huddled six to a room in tenement districts, and densities in New York's slums were among the highest in the world, close to today's densities in places like Calcutta. The middle class fears of social ostracism based on shared spaces not only seem silly to us now; those fears also seemed silly to the poor of the 1870s.

Today's housing crisis has a similar social and economic context. The middle-class ideal of the detached, single-family suburban house is becoming less and less affordable, while inner-city slums are plagued by abandonment and vandalism. The solutions for suburbanites—moving to remote exurban locations (new Lonelyvilles), or sharing houses with other families—seem equally undesirable to many young couples; postponing the purchase in the hope interest rates will drop does little to solve the problem. Most of all, like the Manhattan affluent in the 1870s, today's suburbanites often lack a sense of the world context of their housing problems. Our two-car garages are often larger than basic shelter for a family in a developing country.

The question of how to sustain (or divide) our seven-room houses is not the economic problem itself, but a symptom of a larger, underlying economic problem. The affluent Manhattan residents rationalized that in time the tenement dwellers of their era could perhaps move to better accommodations, and in fact, they got away with this response, but this was a temporary respite. The other side of the Manhattan solution still remains valid. The adaptation of suburban house forms to new uses is as inevitable as was the adaptation of brick row houses and brownstones and the introduction of mixed uses, higher densities, and new building types that accompanied it. This adaptation can be carried out brilliantly or half-heartedly.

Housing stock can deteriorate and become slummy or it can be correctly preserved; neighborhoods can create fear and unease or generate a better social context for new smaller units. These are the choices in terms of housing, and they reverberate with implications for the larger public domain. If reconstructing domestic space will make life easier for American families, domesticating public space is also essential to new forms of private and public life.

> Make the whole world homelike.
>
> *Frances Willard*

> This new adventure demands psychological maturity, as the boyish heroism of the old adventures did not.
>
> *Lewis Mumford*

8

DOMESTICATING URBAN SPACE

The phrase "A woman's place is in the home" has defined much housing policy and urban design in American society. The query "What's a nice girl like you doing in a place like this?" has reflected the prevailing attitude toward women in public, urban space. Both phrases have their roots in a Victorian model of private and public life. The first involves the patriarchal home as haven; the second defines the Victorian male double standard of sexual morality. Both are implicit rather than explicit principles of urban planning; neither will be found stated in large type in textbooks on land use. Both attitudes are linked to a set of nineteenth-century beliefs about female passivity and propriety in the domestic setting ("woman's sphere") versus male combativeness and aggression in the public setting ("man's world").

When nineteenth-century men (and women) argued that the good woman was at home in the kitchen with her husband, they implied that no decent woman was out in city streets, going places where men went. Thus, it was "unladylike" for a woman to earn her own

8.1 A temperance banner of the 1850s attacks the male sexual double standard: corseted wife in white offers water; the 'fallen' women in black with loose robes and flowing hair flaunts wine, dice, and cards. While the temperance reformers meant this as a lesson, the male really didn't have to choose. (Library of Congress.)

living. Because the working woman was no *one* urban man's property (her father or her husband had failed to keep her at home), she was *every* urban man's property. She was the potential victim of harassment in the factory, in the office, on the street, in restaurants, and in places of amusement such as theaters or parks. While the numbers of employed women and women in active public life have increased, many of these spatial stereotypes and patterns of behavior remain. Just as the haven houses hobble employed women, so the double standard harasses them when they are alone or with their children.[1] Men do not escape the problem. As husbands and fathers they share the stresses of the isolated houses and the violent streets they and their wives and children must negotiate. But rarely do men attribute the problems of housing and the city to the Victorian patriarchal views that reserved urban, public life for men only.[2]

The Freedom of the City

At a theoretical level, women have never explicitly demanded or enjoyed the *droit de la ville*, the medieval right to the freedom of the city that distinguished urban citizens from feudal serfs.[3] The existing literature on urban history and theory conveys this in dozens of titles like *City of Man* or *The Fall of Public Man*. The experiences of women in urban space are absent from the content of many academic studies as well as from the titles.[4] The implicit assumption has been that either respectable women (and children) had the same urban experiences as men when they were with men, or else that women (and children) had no urban experiences, since their place was in the home or other segregated spaces. The closest that American women of all classes and races have come to challenging this view was in the Progressive Era, when Frances Willard attacked the double standard as expressed in saloons and the ward-boss political culture of the late nineteenth century and attempted to domesticate the American city.

8.2 Public space on the male double standard is shown in J. N. Hyde's "Running the Gauntlet," New York City, 1874. A respectable woman walks down the street with ten men ogling as if she were a prostitute. Her body is tense and corseted, her eyes averted; the men lounge and stare boldly, providing a graphic example of what Nancy Henley calls "body politics," the dominance of one race, class, or gender over another shown through positioning of bodies in space.

Some historians and critics have suggested that women failed to establish lasting power in the public sphere in the Progressive Era because they failed to develop an urban political theory suited to their needs.[5] Critics who complain of women's lack of "ideology" might first examine definitions of the nature of political theory and political activity. As long as the domestic world remains a romantic haven "outside" of public life and the political economy, politically active women can always be sent back to it, and men can justify the exclusion of women and children from their public debates and analyses. Yet the reverse is also true. If women can overcome what Lyn Lofland has called the "thereness" of women,[6] if they can transcend what Jessie Bernard has defined as "the female world" of a segregated place,[7] new kinds of homes and neighborhoods might become the most powerful base in America for progressive political coalitions on urban issues.

A political program to overcome the "thereness" of women and win all female and male citizens, and their children, access to safe, public urban space requires that the presence of women (and their children) in public space be established as a political right; and that gender stereotypes be eliminated from architecture, urban design, and graphic design in public space. Such a political program would share many common features with Olmsted's attempt to create public space accessible to all in his parks; it would share many goals of the campaign Frances Willard launched in the 1890s for a "home-like world" in America's cities; it would require many new institutions like Jane Addams' Hull-House, a public center for community organizing on the model of a collective home open to all; it would link the campaigns of the Anti-flirt club of the 1920s to the "Take Back the Night" marches of the 1970s.

Many professionals in the design fields are ready to support the political struggles necessary to bring domestic standards of amenity and safety into public space. In the recent past, disdainful speculators and politicians have claimed that the men engaged in these causes were not "real men," and the women were "little old ladies in tennis shoes," but on this subject, Lewis Mumford can be very reassuring. Calling for a serious study of resources and settlement design in 1956, Mumford challenged Americans to go beyond the old machismo of previous urban development patterns. "This new adventure," he said, "demands psychological maturity as the boyish heroism of the old adventures did not; for it is an exploration in depth, to fathom all the potential resources of a region . . . and to assess its possibilities for continued enjoyment. . . ."[8] The ultimate proof of maturity is the ability to nurture and protect human life, to develop public safety, public mobility, public amenities. Small, commonsense improvements in urban design can be linked to larger ideas about nurturing to help end the split between private life and public life.

8.3 Inhospitable environments. Older women wait for a bus while the car culture passes them by; a young woman waits for a bus while "Kim" advertises the double standard.

8.4 Charter members of the Anti-flirt Club, formed by female office workers to combat street harassment of women, Washington, D.C., 1920s. The problem of comfort in public space continues as women enter paid employment in larger numbers, but are hassled on the streets. (Library of Congress)

Recapturing Public Space for the
Needs of Parents

Anyone who has ever cared for babies or small children, even for a
few hours away from a domestic environment, knows how little
thought has been spent on making public space accessible to parents. When they begin a family, parents find that having a baby puts
great spatial limits on their public, urban life. Although a first priority is to have adequate infant care and day care in residential neighborhoods for parents, it is also necessary to make it easier for adults
to move in public space with their children. Other countries do this.
In Denmark banks provide children's play areas with small furniture
and toys while parents do their banking; in New Zealand, department stores offer day care to customers.[9]

To develop public facilities with the expectation that parents and
grandparents with babies and young children will be using them is
not a technically difficult task: it requires a commitment to better
programing and a little imagination. Baby-changing spaces as a
standard feature of both men's rooms and women's rooms would
help; well-located seating and small children's furniture in banks,
stores, and restaurants suggest that children are expected and wel-
comed with their fathers or mothers; windows at children's eye
levels, as well as adults', are attractive in spaces where children
represent a substantial number of users. Such changes in scale to
accommodate children add liveliness and diversity to the urban scene.
Concern for building materials and interior finishes neither too fragile nor too rough also helps define places that children can use. Play
spaces can add a sense of joy for people of all ages, especially when
they are organized to incorporate trees and flowers, public art or
local landmarks such as ruins of old buildings, traces of past settlement patterns, or artifacts conveying economic history. Public space
for children is, at its best, not only warm and educational but also
fun: Linda Hollis' exhibit, "Childspace," alerts parents and designers to the potential of both planned and spontaneous possibilities, as
Colin Ward, Robin Moore, and Clare Cooper have done in more
scholarly ways.[10]

Greenlights and Safehouses

Many adult Americans are afraid of public urban space. In 1967 the U.S. President's Commission on Law Enforcement and the Administration of Justice concluded that "One-third of a representative sample of all Americans say it is unsafe to walk alone at night in their neighborhoods."[11] Another study by a Congressional Committee in 1978 reported that fully one-half of all Americans were afraid to go out at night.[12] Yet another study by sociologists in Chicago stated that one-half of all women and 20 percent of all men were afraid to walk alone in their neighborhoods at night.[13]

Two programs designed to bring a greater sense of security into the lives of citizens are the Greenlight Program developed by the Women's Safety Committee of a group called City Lights in Jamaica Plain, Massachusetts, and the Safehouse program created by Tenderloin Tenants for Safer Streets in San Francisco. As one reporter put it, "Safehouses, the traditional refuges of intelligence agents, fugitive radicals—and more recently havens for battered wives—now are being established for senior citizens. . . ."[14]

Both programs attempt to extend a sense of domestic security into the public realm. Greenlight aims to make women feel more secure from mugging and rape. Any house in the neighborhood showing a green light in the window is a place where a frightened woman can find shelter, a telephone, and emergency counseling. The Safehouse program, identified by signs showing a peaked roof and a dove, operates in stores, bars, and hotels in a very rough district of San Francisco. All people in distress are welcome to enter and ask for safety, help in getting to the hospital, or assistance from the police. The group distributes maps of the area to show the locations of the refuges, and encourages residents to patronize them.

Obviously neither green lights nor safehouse signs can prevent crime. However these two efforts do show how citizens and planners can begin to give public space a more homelike quality.

Reclaiming Access to Public Space: Better Public Transportation

When most Americans think of public transportation, the New York subways come to mind, covered inside and outside with the spray-paint graffiti of young men and women who found the subway yards a place to paint and who enjoy "Watching My Name Go By" in letters eight feet high. Often the only pristine surfaces are the advertisements. Cars without air-conditioning, frequent breakdowns, and violent muggings add to the grim picture, but one can contrast New York with the new Washington, D.C., Metro system, with its magnificent arch-spanned stations, dramatic coffered ceilings, and silent, sleek trains. Most of the United States' expenditures on transportation in the last thirty years have supported freeway construction and car culture rather than projects like the Metro. The United States urgently needs better public transit systems. In the meantime, the services of existing public transit—subways, commuter railroads, and buses—must be improved by better social programing and by recognition that minorities, the young, the elderly, and women are most often the citizens without private cars.

Access to the public domain is especially difficult for older women. After age sixty-five, many women reap the results of a lifetime of low earnings, limited mobility, and self-sacrifice. In a study of 82,000 widows in Chicago, Helena Lopata found that over half of them did not go to public places, and over a fifth did not even go visiting. While 82 percent were not in a position to offer transportation to others, 45 percent had no one, of any age, to rely on for transportation.[15] There are many ways that bus schedules and fares can be tailored for older people. Security issues can be worked on for both female passengers and the elderly, who are apprehensive about long waiting periods, especially at night, in deserted bus stops, train stations, and subway stations. Child-oriented and elderly oriented schedules offer a further bonus: they relieve adults, usually women, from the responsibility of driving the elderly and the young, and at the same time encourage independence and self-reliance.

Good transportation is also a key factor in rape prevention. Recent estimates suggest that one woman in three in the United States will experience an attempted or completed rape in her lifetime.[16] Of course, if most citizens, including politicians and police officers, believe that a woman's place is in the home to begin with, they will not necessarily be concerned about unsafe streets. Instead, they may blame the rape victim for being in urban public space. Several innovative transportation projects, documented by Rebecca Dreis and Gerda Wekerle, meet the demand for greater safety on the streets by adding needed, flexible transportation.[17] In 1973 the Madison, Wisconsin, Women's Transit Authority began a service operating two cars seven nights a week, serving 1,000 women per month, on a fixed route shuttle service plus a flexible service within a four mile radius of the University of Wisconsin campus. Volunteers drive; the university, city and county pay the costs of the vehicles. In White-horse, Alaska, the Yukon Women's Minibus Society reached an even broader constituency. Women concerned about access to pub-lic space and about security created a system of four minibuses with sixteen seats each that now serve 700 passengers per day. The wom-en's project provided the first bus system for the whole commu-nity.[18]

Public transportation not only provides safe access to public space, it can also educate riders about their city and about political strug-gles to make public space hospitable for everyone. This can range from adult education classes on commuter trains, such as those ini-tiated by Michael Young in England, to exhibits in key places—bus shelters and subway stations, and on buses and subways—that can provide essential information about cities, infrastructure, and public safety. Riders are thus united as a constituency for better services.

Advertisements, Pornography, and Public Space

Americans need to look more consciously at the ways in which the public domain is misused for spatial displays of gender stereotypes. These appear in outdoor advertising, and to a lesser extent in com-mercial displays, architectural decoration, and public sculpture. While the commercial tone and violence of the American city is often criticized, there is little analysis of the routine way that crude stereotypes appear in public, urban spaces as the staple themes of commercial art. Most Americans are accustomed to seeing giant females in various states of undress smiling and caressing products such as whiskey, food, and records. Male models also sell goods, but they are usually active and clothed—recent ad campaigns aimed at gay men seem to be the first major exception. Several geogra-phers have established that men are most often shown doing active things, posed in the great outdoors; women are shown in reflective postures responding to male demands in interior spaces. As the nineteenth-century sexual double standard is preserved by the urban advertising, many twentieth-century urban men behave as if good women are at home while bad ones adorn the billboards and travel on their own in urban space; at the same time, many urban women are encouraged to think of emotionlessness, war-mongering, and sexual inexhaustibility as natural to the Marlboro cowboy, war heroes' statues, and every other male adult.

8.5 The male double standard today: pedestrian passing a billboard for *The Bitch,* a movie starring Joan Collins, Los Angeles, 1981. Vulgar graffiti has been inflicted on "the bitch," but this kind of advertising makes urban space danger-ous for all women.

This double standard is the result of advertising practices, graphic design, and urban design. Sanctioned by the zoning laws, billboards are approved by the same urban planning boards who will not permit child care centers or mother-in-law apartments in many residential districts. But the problem with billboards is not only aesthetic degradation. By presenting gender stereotypes in the form of nonverbal body language, fifty feet long and thirty feet high, billboards turn the public space of the city into a stage set for a drama starring enticing women and stern men.

Let us observe outdoor advertising and other urban design phenomena with similar effects, as they are experienced by two women on an urban commuting trip along the Sunset Strip in Los Angeles in June 1981. Standing on a street corner, the two women are waiting for a bus to go to work. The bus arrives, bearing a placard on the side advertising a local night club. It shows strippers doing their act, their headless bodies naked from neck to crotch except for a few blue sequins. The two women get on the bus and find seats for the ride along Sunset Boulevard. They look out the windows. As the bus pulls away, their heads appear incongruously above the voluptuous cardboard female bodies displayed on the side. They ride through a district of record company headquarters and film offices, one of the most prosperous in L.A.

Their first views reveal rows of billboards. Silent Marlboro man rides the range; husky, khaki-clad Camel man stares at green hills; gigantic, uniformed professional athletes catch passes and hit home runs on behalf of booze. These are the male images. Then, on a billboard for whiskey, a horizontal blonde in a backless black velvet dress, slit to the thigh, invites men to "Try on a little Black Velvet." Next, a billboard shows a well-known actress, reclining with legs spread, who notes that avocadoes are only sixteen calories a slice. "Would this body lie to you?" she asks coyly, emphasizing that the body language which communicates blatant sexual availability is only meant to bring attention to her thin figure. Bo Derek offers a pastoral contrast garbed in nothing but a few bits of fur and leather, as she swings on a vine of green leaves, promoting *Tarzan, the Ape Man*.

Next the bus riders pass a club called the Body Shop that advertises "live, nude girls." Two reclining, realistic nudes, one in blue tones in front of a moonlight cityscape, one in orange sunshine tones, stretch their thirty-foot bodies along the sidewalk. This is the same neighborhood where a billboard advertising a Rolling Stones' record album called "Black and Blue" made news ten years ago. A man-acled, spread-legged woman with torn clothes proclaimed "I'm Black and Blue from the Rolling Stones—and I love it!" Members of a group called Women Against Violence Against Women (WAVAW) arrived with cans of spray paint and climbed the scaffolding to make small, uneven letters of protest: "This is a crime against women." Demonstrations and boycotts eventually succeeded in achieving the removal of that image, but not in eliminating the graphic design problem. "Black and Blue" has been replaced by James Bond in a tuxedo, pistol in hand, viewed through the spread legs and buttocks of a giant woman in a bathing suit and improbably high heels, captioned "For Your Eyes Only."

When the two women get off the bus in Hollywood, they experience more gender stereotypes as pedestrians. First, they walk past a department store. In the windows mannequins suggest the prevailing ideals of sartorial elegance. The male torsos lean forward, as if they are about to clinch a deal. The female torsos, pin-headed, tip backward and sideways, at odd angles, as if they are about to be pushed over onto a bed. The themes of gender advertisements are trumpeted here in the mannequins' body language as well as on billboards. Next, the women pass an apartment building. Two neo-classical caryatids support the entablature over the front door. Their breasts are bared, their heads carry the load. They recall the architecture of the Erechtheum on the Acropolis in Athens, dating from the 5th century B.C., where the sculptured stone forms of female slaves were used as support for a porch in place of traditional columns and capitals. This is an ancient image of servitude.

After the neo-classical apartment house, the commuters approach a construction site. Here they are subject to an activity traditionally called "running the gauntlet," but referred to as "girl watching" by urban sociologist William H. Whyte. Twelve workers stop whatever they are doing, whistle, and yell: "Hey, baby!" The women put their heads down, and walk faster, tense with anger. The construction workers take delight in causing exactly this response: "You're cute when you're mad!" Whyte regards this type of behavior as charming, pedestrian fun in "Street Life," where he even takes pleasure in tracing its historic antecedents, but he has never been whistled at, hooted at, and had the dimensions of his body parts analyzed out loud on a public street.[19]

Finally, these women get to the office building where they work. It has two statues out front of women. Their bronze breasts culminate in erect nipples. After they pass this last erotic public display of women's flesh, sanctioned as fine art, they walk in the door to begin the day's work. Their journey has taken them through an urban landscape filled with images of men as sexual aggressors and women as submissive sexual objects.

The transient quality of male and female interaction in public streets makes the behavior provoked by billboards and their public design images particularly difficult to attack. Psychologist Erving Goffman has analyzed both print ads and billboards as *Gender Advertisements* because art directors use exaggerated body language to suggest that consumers buy not products but images of masculinity or feminity.[20] If passers-by are driving at fifty miles per hour, these gender cues cannot be subtle. In *Ways of Seeing*, art historian John Berger describes the cumulative problem that gender stereotypes in advertising create for woman as "split consciousness."[21] While many women guard themselves, some men assume that ogling is part of normal public life. Women are always wary, watching men watch them, and wondering if and when something is going to happen to them.

Urban residents also encounter even more explicit sexual images in urban space. Tawdry strip clubs, X-rated films, "adult" bookstores and sex shops are not uncommon sights. Pornographic video arcades are the next wave to come. Pornography is a bigger, more profitable industry in the United States than all legitimate film and record business combined.[22] It spills over into soft-porn, quasi-porn, and tasteless public imagery everywhere. In the midst of this sexploitation, if one sees a real prostitute, there is mild surprise. Yet soliciting is still a crime. Of course, the male customer of an adult prostitute is almost never arrested, but the graphic designer, the urban designer, and the urban planner never come under suspicion for their contributions to a commercial public landscape that preserves the sexual double standard in a brutal and vulgar way.

Feminist Laura Shapiro calls our society a "rape culture."[23] Adrienne Rich has written of "a world masculinity made unfit for women or men."[24] But surely most Americans do not consciously, deliberately accept public space given over to commercial exploitation, violence and harassment of women. Indeed, the success of the "Moral Majority" displays how a few activists were able to tap public concern effectively about commercialized sexuality, albeit in a narrow, anti-humanist way. In contrast, the example of the Women's Christian Temperance Union under Frances Willard's leader-

8.6   The same problem abroad: *Beau Père,* movie ad Paris, 1981.

ship, and the parks movement under Olmsted's, show religious idealism, love of nature, and concern for female safety can be activated into dynamic urban reform movements that enlarge domestic values into urban values, instead of diminishing them into domestic pieties.

Creating Innovative Institutions to Link Private Life and Public Space

In the process of domesticating public space, cultural institutions that exist somewhere between the private domain and the public domain play a key role in initiating ideas, organizing financial support, and supplying the designers or administrators to make the whole more than the sum of the parts. One such institution is the Los Angeles Woman's Building, a public center for women's culture that carries on many projects in the tradition of Willard and Olmsted. To get there you have to get off the freeway and wind around empty streets lined with old warehouses, cross the railroad tracks, and keep going past sidings filled with boxcars marked Southern Cross and Southern Pacific. The Los Angeles Woman's Building is housed on three floors of an old factory, and serves as a gathering place for painters, graphic designers, video artists, performance artists, novelists, and playwrights. It includes gallery space, artists' studio space, performance space, and offices.[25]

The Woman's Building was designed to create a political and cultural bridge between public and private life. The group encourages members to make public art about their lives. Sheila de Bretteville, one of the founders of the Building and a graphic designer, initiated a project called "Private Conversations and Public Places." She described her aims: "We will be creating graphic works for and about public places with personal meaning in Los Angeles." She aimed to pose questions about "our voice and images in public places." Her group designed posters about sites ranging from beauty parlors to the county jail, posted them in these public places, and arranged events to highlight taking their art into the public sphere. Maria Karras, a photographer and graphic designer at the Building, did another project on work. She interviewed employed women from six or eight different ethnic groups in the city, asking them about both their paid jobs and their work in their households. Handsome bus cards with photographs and texts in two languages were placed on public buses to be seen and read by men and women traveling to work. A performance artist, Suzanne Lacy, created "Three Weeks in May" in 1977. Lacy wished to increase public awareness of the numbers of rapes that occurred in the neighborhoods of Los Angeles. She gathered police reports and stamped RAPE in three-inch-high red letters on a large map of the city whenever an attempted or completed rape occurred. She also arranged for extensive television coverage of the map-stamping rituals. By the end of one week, millions of men and women had seen Lacy's work on television or in the newspapers. Public indignation about the prevalance of rape has increased dramatically, as well as knowledge of prevention techniques.

All these projects address various issues of concern to urban citizens—fear of the city, skills of balancing home and career, difficulties of avoiding rape. The Woman's Building has also had real success in bringing together women of diverse ethnic backgrounds. Chicanas, Blacks, Chinese-Americans, Japanese-Americans, and white women of Greek, Jewish, and Irish-American ancestry all work together. By emphasizing graphics and performances, they have solved the problems of making public art with little money. Their efforts indicate many directions for similar urban cultural ventures, intentionally located midway between the home and the street; placing the products of their love, care, and creativity in public space evokes positive responses so important to the "homelike world." While these activists expand the feminist aspects of Frances

Willard's "municipal housekeeping" approach, other groups such as Partners for Livable Places, in Washington, D.C., and The Townscape Institute, in Cambridge, Massachusetts, have a similar goal of strengthening ties between private and public life.

The First Steps

These small, common-sense approaches are indications of ways in which citizens, politicians, and designers might approach urban design in the future. Although they do not directly attack the immiseration of ghetto populations that causes crime, they do suggest how to focus on gender, and how to spend energy and money to help poor women, some of the most disadvantaged citizens. And they do attempt to rebuild spatial connections between old and young, black and white, male and female. If they are non-reformist reforms, it is because the process of winning and implementing them would enable many more female citizens to have the confidence and security to fight harder on additional urban economic issues. These are not only American issues—worldwide, street harassment is a reminder of how many cultures have denied women the freedom of the city— although on topics such as supports for children and the elderly, many urban societies do better than the United States.

In 1961 Lewis Mumford wrote: ". . . the prime need of the city today is for an intensification of collective self-knowledge, a deeper insight into the processes of history, as a first step toward discipline and control: such a knowledge as is achieved by a neurotic patient in facing a long buried infantile trauma that has stood in the way of his normal growth and integration."[26] He was referring to a male infatuation with automobile technology and metropolitan expansion, but his metaphor of urban citizens as neurotic patients is a powerful one with wider applicability to the example of the Victorian double standard of male and female behavior. Until girls and boys, men and women achieve equal citizenship in the city which is created and sustained by the labors of both sexes, Mumford's metaphor of a long-standing urban neurosis blocking growth and integration will remain valid. When women, men, and children of all classes and races can identify the public domain as the place where they feel most comfortable as citizens, Americans will finally have domesticated urban space.

> I remembered the end of my first semester at Penn when, after months of talk in our housing course, learning unfamiliar acronyms and digesting strange statistics, I finally realized that all the talk and all the figures suggested no remedy, but masked the scandal that Americans with houses don't care about those who don't have them. "But what are you going to *do?*" "I don't know," said Wheaton, doyen of housers, walker of Washington corridors, drafter of legislation: "What are *you* going to do?"
>
> *Denise Scott Brown*

> "My God, Ned, I'm going to have to win this one on its merits."
>
> *lawyer for tract developer Ned Eichler*

9

BEYOND THE ARCHITECTURE OF GENDER

One or two decades ago, the cities of the United States appeared to be wealthy enough to sustain their unique spatial structure. In addition to having the highest rate of homeownership, the U.S. had the very tallest skyscrapers in the world. Spatial patterns—skyscrapers downtown and detached single-family houses in suburbia—were imitated from Paris to Nairobi. Yet both the skyscrapers and the suburban houses reflected patterns of speculation designed to benefit landlords, real estate developers, and home owners rather than the entire citizenry.

Now, in the last decade, the United States has experienced an urban fiscal crisis as well as a housing crisis.[1] The old urban infrastructure—roads, bridges, railroads, public transit systems, water and sewer systems—is weak from age and lack of maintenance. At the same time, much new infrastructure, such as nuclear power, looks problematic.[2] Old industrial plants are closing, taking jobs away from already poor areas where unemployment is high. Old housing is abandoned by landlords, while newer housing looks like a hasty investment. For those who attempt to improve the urban situation, there will be intense competition for resources. In such an era, the spatial needs of non-traditional households have significant implications for the redistribution of resources and for the success of any new housing or urban design strategies. Design solutions for the 1980s and 1990s will not work unless they repudiate the Victorian gender stereotypes glorified in the post–World War II patterns of development.

Two Basic Ideas Behind Change

Before planners, designers, citizens' groups and local officials can form an effective constituency for affordable housing, two ideas must be held in common. First, housing issues must include "work" as well as "home." Better spatial planning and design requires concern for employment patterns and household work as the basic eco-

9.1 "The Dream House." (Brad Holland, © 1977 by the New York Times Company)

nomic issues connected to residential neighborhoods. Private life and public life, private space and public space are bound together, despite all the cultural pressures to separate them. Privacy is indeed a crucial element in our personal lives. At the same time, a much richer and more complex set of transitional spaces and activities is required to connect private life and public life effectively. Then home is no longer seen as "a women's place" and women in public places are not asked, "What's a nice girl like you doing in a place like this?"

Second, suburban neighborhoods are part of urban problems. As workers in the Civil Rights movement used to put it, "If you are not part of the solution, you are part of the problem." The American spatial patterns of deteriorated ghettos, skyscraper congestion, and low density dreamhouses are inextricably related to land speculation and depreciation. To deal with these problems, Americans need sophisticated legal and economic sanctions as well as better skills in spatial planning and design.

Major changes in the national political economy are necessary to deal with these issues. To correct the artificial split between "home" and "work" would require a new definition of the GNP and all national accounting methods. To correct patterns of land speculation and building depreciation, it would be necessary to change the taxation policies that are at the core of banking and real estate development activity.

These are the fundamental issues that should frame all discussion and action about housing on the national level. They are very difficult ones to resolve. However, citizen activity on the local level can help to move concerned Americans toward the necessary larger national solutions. In working incrementally, we can distinguish simplistic partial solutions from significant ones. One can ask, of any new proposal: does it support the two largest ideas about change, or does it support the status quo in economic analysis and real estate development?

Avoiding Simplistic Solutions

Simplistic corporate solutions to our housing crisis are framed in the rhetoric of developers promoting new projects and marketing directors selling new products. They include: introducing tiny houses, condominiums, and apartments; advocating mobile homes as cheap housing; promoting home computers and robots to make cramped condos and mobile homes seem modern and technologically sophisticated; and selling new commercial services to make housewives feel they are dealing efficiently with their double workload. Examples of such commercial services include fast food, profit-making nursing homes, and franchise day care systems.

Simplistic political solutions, however well intentioned, are also too close to the old economic models and real estate models. The proposals of labor, environmental groups, civil rights, and women's groups are often too narrow. It is not helpful to argue for new construction to make more jobs available to building trades workers without considering the design of that construction and without making efforts to bring women and minorities into these unions. It is shortsighted to promote solar design without considering larger patterns of energy consumption. It is too simple to advocate role reversals for women and men without looking at gender roles in terms of time and space. It is not enough to advocate racial integration of white, male homeowner culture without examining the quality of that culture.

Neither the simple corporate responses nor the simple political responses will work. All real estate development proposals and corporate marketing proposals need to be evaluated for their social costs. Developers should have to win every single case on its merits, or not at all. All single-issue political proposals need to be studied for their fullest implications for class, race, and gender. Activists must weave all these issues together rather than pit one group's partial solution against another group's partial solution.

Making Economic, Social, and Physical Changes Work Together

Housing involves a complex, interlocked set of economic, social, and physical design components. We have looked at the experiences of many innovative groups that have tried to build creatively, such as the Solar Tenement group, the Women's Development Corporation, the Tynggarden residents group, the Cheyenne greenhouse, and the Zurich backyard rehabilitation agency. Each group managed to create an ingenious package that was more than the sum of its parts. Taken together, these experiences suggest the rewards for national, state, and local governments that support small, self-sustaining projects. The results are infinitely preferable to million dollar tax write-offs for slumlords.

In the area of social planning, we have also seen ingenious attempts to renegotiate the boundary between private life and public life. The Women's Transportation Service, the Greenlight Program, and Nina West homes are only a few examples. While a national daycare policy—one that also covers after-school hours—is desperately needed, a social service approach alone is not enough. Many women spend their lives trying to reconnect the divided city; more original approaches should reach out to jobs, housing, transportation, child care, and care of the elderly as parts of a better solution.

What are the design components of better proposals? In the area of architecture and planning, no great changes can occur until the economic and social policies already discussed have been agreed upon. Then planners can begin to implement significant zoning reforms. Architects and planners must recognize that different residential neighborhoods will require different design solutions. In aging tracts of single family houses and deteriorated public housing projects, intensive reprograming and redesign efforts are needed. In one-family residential neighborhoods (R-1), the acceptance of higher densities through accessory apartments should involve an exchange of benefits. For instance, the owner who increases the number of units on a given site should also be required to contribute amenities to the neighborhood.

New housing construction also requires careful economic and social programing so that housing is integrated with transportation, jobs, and social services for specific constituencies. If this is done, the mistakes of earlier suburban developments and earlier public housing projects will not be repeated. Private space needs attention as well. It is necessary to preserve acoustical and visual privacy, but when sizes of dwelling units are reduced, new kinds of semi-private and semi-public spaces such as courtyards, stairs, and services can assure security at the same time that variety and pedestrian scale are introduced.

In commercial areas, zoning changes should be aimed at regulating the excesses of outdoor advertising. Public safety for children, the elderly, and men must also be priorities as well as ending the street harassment and rape of women. One can only defeat women's isolation in the home, and the sexual double standard outside the home, by simultaneous action.

Developing Leadership and Tactics

Between any urban context and any new design product there lies a long negotiating process. Many local city councils and planning boards consist of responsible, progressive people who care about their towns and know the day-to-day needs of their citizens. Yet those officials are often pressured by real estate interests who want to promote unchecked development. Some elected officials resist well-funded developers' lobbying groups, while others serve these interests all too well. With focussed citizen support, both planners and politicians can handle these pressures and deal with housing issues more effectively. Denise Scott Brown has suggested that the United States is a country where people "with houses don't care about those who don't have them."[3] But this situation is changing: both people with houses (who want to expand them) and those without houses are importuning planners and politicians. National political groups of environmentalists, women, minorities, single parents, and retired persons are taking up housing issues as well. Here officials and politicians can find support to challenge the real estate lobby, the largest private interest group in the country.

In such a volatile, politicized time, it is important for as many Americans as possible to agree about the large changes that are necessary. "Starting from zero," the cry of housing architects after World War I and after the October Revolution, is not possible. Nor is the post-World War II devastation of Europe our call to action, wryly described by Martin Pawley in the phrase, "Bombers are a plan's best friend."[4] We cannot even take advantage of the large-scale rubble of 1950s urban renewal, or the swath-like decay of 1960s "planning blight" caused by such long-term decisions as highway locations. Instead, in the 1980s, we have to begin to solve our housing problems room by room and block by block, starting with our existing dwellings. But we cannot just modify each lot by adding such inventions as an organic garden, an acquaculture pond, a movable granny-house on wheels, or a single accessory apartment in the attic. Neighborhood renovation by groups of citizens, guided by planners, landscape architects, and architects, with the support of politicians and government officials, is crucial. Such concerted action will depend, above all, on the initiative of women.

Housing and urban design ultimately represent labor issues—not lifestyle issues—for women. Strikes are labor's traditional source

of political clout. From the wildcat strikes of small groups of workers spontaneously agreeing to lay down their tools, to the general
strikes that are often a prelude to revolution, the paid workers of the
world have used this technique. Terms like "rent strike" show how
tenants have borrowed this concept to explain the witholding of rent
in equally forceful terms. Lately two new forms of the strike have
appeared that are particularly promising for social movements dealing with housework, housing, and urban design.

A wildcat strike of fifteen housewives took place in Smithfield,
Rhode Island, just before Christmas 1982. These women were
inspired by a Des Moines housewife who struck alone for six days
in the summer of 1982, sitting in front of her house with a sign.
Some of the Smithfield women had economic equity issues to air,
others wanted husband participation in household work. A coffee
klatsch led to their strike. Placards were posted on front lawns, and
these housewives appeared on national tv to publicize their
demands.[5] While this event suggests the power that organized women
can have on a local basis, the experience of the first group to mount
a general strike of women is equally suggestive.

In 1975 the women of Iceland organized a general strike—
housewifes, nurses, secretaries, architects, cabinet ministers. Family life stopped, offices stopped, factories stopped. 25,000 women,
old and young, flooded into the main square of the capital city,
Rekjavik, to demonstrate for equal rights. It was the first nationally
organized general strike of women citizens anywhere in the world.
It lasted but one day. Yet the image of that day remains. The traditional medieval "droit de la ville," the right to the city that characterized the urban citizen, is a right that Iceland's women took and
held for twenty-four hours that day. The news photographs of that
day are astonishing documents.

For the last two centuries, the quintessential American intellectual, political, and architectural dilemma has been: dream house or
ideal city? We have seen how Americans have wavered over these
alternatives, and how costly this hesitation has been for an urban
society. Yet within our own culture Americans can find the roots of
housing solutions as well as the roots of the housing problem. The
common sense of Emerson and Thoreau; the urban visions of Whitman and Olmsted; the feminist campaigns of the municipal housekeeping advocates, the settlement workers, and the material feminists
offer a wealth of social concern. Other societies such as Denmark,

Sweden, England, Cuba, and Holland also offer examples of more service-oriented approaches to nurturing and earning. But no country has yet created an urban fabric and an urban culture to support men and women on equal terms as citizens and workers.

The world awaits the non-sexist city. The poems of Whitman and Adrienne Rich offer glimpses of its streets and rooms. The architecture of Markelius and the graphics of the Woman's Building suggest its culture of professional craft and political activism. The programs of Neighbors in Community Helping Environments and of the National Congress of Neighborhood Women prefigure its personal approach to nurturing work and social services. Yet Americans still have to come to terms with their current needs and their own best traditions, to go beyond the architecture of gender and build the "city of the faithfulest friends."

NOTES

Chapter 1. Housing and American Life

1. "Designed for 24 Hour Child Care," *Architectural Record* (March 1944) 86.
2. "Nation's Biggest Housebuilder," *Life* (May 22, 1950) 75–76; "Up From the Potato Fields," *Time* (July 3, 1950) 68.
3. Levitt in an interview with the *Saturday Evening Post* (Aug. 7, 1954) 72. For a full study of this company and its policies, see Herbert Gans, *The Levittowners: Ways of Life and Politics in a New Suburban Community* (1967; New York: Columbia University Press, 1982).
4. Gwendolyn Wright, *Building the Dream: A Social History of Housing in America* (New York: Pantheon, 1981) 247–48; Esther McCoy, "Gregory Ain's Social Housing," *Arts and Architecture* 1 (Winter 1981), 66–70.
5. "Vanport City," *Architectural Forum* (Aug. 1943) 53.
6. Eric Larrabee, "The Six Thousand Houses That Levitt Built," *Harpers* (Sept. 1948) 84.
7. "Houses Off the Line: Burns and Kaiser Throw the Switch," *Architectural Forum* (Oct. 1946) 10.
8. Clarence Stein, *Toward New Towns for America* (1957; Cambridge, Mass.: MIT Press, 1971) 188–216, 218.
9. Personal interview with a former administrator for the schools in that area, 1982.
10. Leverett Richards, "And So a City Died," *Oregonian* (Dec. 3, 1975); Kate Huang, "Women, War, and Work," unpublished paper, 1982; the Northwest Women's History Project in Portland, Oregon, has done some oral history and a slide show on shipyard workers; Sherna Gluck of California State University, Long Beach, has also researched an extensive oral history, "Rosie the Riveter Revisited."

11. U.S. Department of Commerce, Bureau of the Census, *1980 Census of Population and Housing: Provisional Estimates* (Washington, D.C.: U.S.G.P.O., 1982) 3, 80; George Sternlieb, James W. Hughes, et al., *America's Housing: Prospects and Problems* (New Brunswick, New Jersey: Rutgers University Press, 1980) 26.

12. Allan Heskin, *Tenants and the American Dream* (New York: Praeger, 1983).

13. *Los Angeles Times* (Nov. 21, 1982) VII, 24.

14. Martin Wachs, *Transportation for the Elderly: Changing Lifestyles, Changing Needs* (Berkeley and Los Angeles: University of California Press, 1979).

15. Carol Brown, "Spatial Inequalities and Divorced Mothers," paper delivered at the American Sociological Association Annual Meeting, San Francisco, Sept. 6, 1978; Jacqueline Leavitt, "Aunt Mary and the Shelter-Service Crisis for Single Parents," paper delivered at the Association of Collegiate Schools of Planning Annual Meeting, Chicago, Oct. 21–24, 1982.

16. "Burning the House to Roast the Pig: Unrelated Individuals and Single Family Zoning's Blood Relation Criterion," *Cornell Law Review* 58 (1972) 138–65.

17. Rita A. Calvan, "Children and Families—the Latest Victims of Exclusionary Land Use Practices," in *Management and Control of Growth: Updating the Law,* ed. Frank Schnidman and Jane Silverman, vol. 3 (Washington, D.C.: Urban Land Institute, 1980).

18. Patrick Hare, "Rethinking Single Family Zoning: Growing Old in American Neighborhoods," *New England Journal of Human Services,* (Summer 1981) 32–35; Wendy Schuman, "The Return of Togetherness," *New York Times,* Mar. 20, 1977, 1. Also see Martin Gellen, "Underutilization in American Housing," and "A Home in Every Garage: The Economics of Secondary Units," Working Papers, U.C. Berkeley College of Environmental Design, 1982.

19. John Betz Willmann, "Mortgage Delinquency Dangerous," *Los Angeles Times,* VII, Jan. 17, 1982, 8; Doris A. Byron, "Mortgage Delinquencies at Highest Level in 17 Years," *Los Angeles Times* III, Mar. 6, 1982, 14.

20. Kathryn P. Nelson, "Recent Suburbanization of Blacks: How Much, Who, and Where," *American Planning Association Journal,* 46 (1980) 287–300.

21. Iver Peterson, "Congress Is Urged to Help Homeless," *New York Times,* Dec. 16, 1982, 9; "Millions Hit Bottom in the Streets," *Los Angeles Times,* Dec. 26, 1982, 1.

Chapter 2. From Ideal City to Dream House

1. "Home Shopper Survey," *Housing* (Nov., 1979), gives a builder's view of "amenities" of this kind and how to market them. On interior design, see Joseph Giovannini, "Sex Stereotyping in Design," *New York Times,* Dec. 16, 1982, C1.

2. Wright, *Building the Dream,* surveys housing in these communities and subsequent forms.

3. Ronald Lee Fleming and Lauri Halderman, *On Common Ground* (Harvard, Mass.: Harvard Common Press, 1982), appendix, lists all locations.

4. Dolores Hayden, *Seven American Utopias: The Architecture of Communitar-*

ian Socialism, 1790–1975 (Cambridge, Mass.: MIT Press, 1976), surveys these town building experiments.

5. Catharine E. Beecher and Harriet Beecher Stowe, *The American Woman's Home,* (New York: J.B. Ford, 1869); Catharine E. Beecher, "How to Redeem Woman's Profession from Dishonor," *Harper's* 31 (Nov. 1865), 712; also see Dolores Hayden, "Catharine Beecher and the Politics of Housework," in S. Torre, ed., *Women in American Architecture: An Historic and Contemporary Perspective,* (New York: Whitney Library of Design, 1977), 40–49.

6. Walt Whitman, "Song of the Broad-Axe," in *Complete Poetry and Selected Prose,* ed. James E. Miller, Jr., (Boston: Houghton Mifflin, 1959), 136, 141.

7. *Ibid.,* 138, 141, 142.

8. Walt Whitman, "Poem of Remembrance for a Girl or Boy of These States," in *Complete Poetry,* 393.

9. Walt Whitman, "In the New Garden, in All Its Parts," in *Complete Poetry,* 399.

10. Walt Whitman, "I Dream'd in a Dream," in *Complete Poetry,* 96.

11. Walt Whitman, *Democratic Vistas,* in *Complete Poetry,* 462.

12. Frederick Law Olmsted, *Public Parks and the Englargement of Towns* (Cambridge, Mass.: American Social Science Association, 1870).

13. *Ibid.,* 7–9. See, for background, Laura Roper, *FLO: A Biography of Frederick Law Olmsted* (Baltimore: Johns Hopkins University Press, 1973; Francesco Dal Co, "From Parks to the Region," in G. Ciucci, M. Tafuri, F. Dal Co, *The American City* (Cambridge, Mass.: MIT Press, 1977); Albert Fein, *Frederick Law Olmsted and the American Environmental Tradition* (New York: Braziller, 1972).

14. For a broad review of these ideas, see Dolores Hayden, *The Grand Domestic Revolution: A History of Feminist Designs for American Homes, Neighborhoods, and Cities* (Cambridge, Mass.: MIT Press, 1981); also on Peirce, see her "Cooperative Housekeeping II," *Atlantic Monthly* 22, (Dec. 1868), 684; Zona Gale, "Shall the Kitchen in Our Home Go?" *Ladies' Home Journal* 36 (Mar. 1919), 35.

15. Ruth Bordin, *Women and Temperance: The Quest for Power and Liberty, 1873–1900* (Philadelphia: Temple University Press, 1972), 33.

16. *Ibid.,* 29–30.

17. *Id.*

18. *Id.*

19. Frances Willard, quoted in Sheila Rothman, *Woman's Proper Place: A History of Changing Ideals and Practices, 1870 to the Present* (New York: Basic Books, 1978) 67.

20. *Id.;* Marlene S. Wortman, "Domesticating the American City," *Prospects* (Philadelphia: American Studies Association, 1979).

21. Florence Kelley, ed., *Hull-House Maps and Papers* (1895; New York: Arno, 1975).

22. Sam Bass Warner, Jr., *The Urban Wilderness* (New York: Harper and Row, 1972); David Gordon, "Capitalist Development and the History of American Cities," in W. Tabb and L. Sawyers, eds., *Marxism and the Metropolis* (New York: Oxford University Press, 1978), 25–63; Richard Walker, "The Suburban Solution," Ph.D. dissertation, Department of Geography, Johns Hopkins University, 1977.

23. For a good account of the Red Scare in this period, see J. Stanley Lemons, *The Woman Citizen: Social Feminism in the 1920s* (Urbana, Illinois: University of Illinois Press, 1973), 209–27.

24. Barbara Ehrenreich and Deidre English, *For Her Own Good: 150 Years of the Experts' Advice to Women* (Garden City, N.Y.: Anchor/Doubleday, 1978), 134. (They quote an unidentified corporate official interviewed by Charles Whitaker about 1920.); Industrial Housing Associates, *Good Homes Make Contented Workers*, (Philadelphia: Industrial Housing Associates, 1919); the last of these quotes is printed on an old textile used in a quilt. A review essay covering many approaches to home ownership is Carol Duncan, "Home Ownership and Social Theory," in *Housing and Identity*, ed. James Duncan (London: Croom Helm, 1981).

25. Daniel Luria, "Suburbanization, Ethnicity, and Party Base: Spatial Aspects of the Decline of American Socialism," *Antipode* 11 (Fall 1979), 76–79.

26. Stuart Ewen, *Captains of Consciousness: Advertising and the Social Roots of the Consumer Culture* (New York: McGraw Hill, 1976).

27. Christine Frederick, *Selling Mrs. Consumer* (New York: Business Bourse, 1929), 244–45, 388–94.

28. Reports from *The President's Conference on Home Building and Home Ownership*, (Washington: U.S. Government Printing Office, 1932).

29. R. Slitor, "The Federal Income Tax in Relation to Housing Research," Report No. 5, National Commission on Urban Problems (Washington, D.C.: U.S.G.P.O., 1968). On public housing initiatives in this era, see Catherine Bauer, *Modern Housing* (Boston: Houghton Mifflin, 1934); Eugenie Birch, "Woman-Made America: The Case of Early Public Housing Policy," *Journal of the American Institute of Planners* 44 (Apr. 1978); and Timothy A. McDonnell, *The Wagner Housing Act* (Loyola University Press, 1975).

30. Luria, "Suburbanization . . ." 79.

31. *Survey of AFL-CIO Members' Housing, 1975* (Washington, D.C.: AFL-CIO, 1976), 16.

32. U.S. Bureau of the Census, *Historical Statistics of the United States, Colonial Times to 1970* (Washington, D.C., U.S.G.P.O., 1975), Part I, 8; *1980 Census of Population and Housing: Provisional Estimates* (Washington, D.C., U.S.G.P.O., 1982), 3, 70.

33. *Historical Statistics*, 8; *1980 Census*, 80.

34. *1980 Census*, 80.

35. Sternlieb and Hughes, eds., *America's Housing: Prospects and Problems*, 80–81; 26.

36. Fred J. Napolitano, "Housing—A Priority to Preserve the American Dream," *Newsweek* (Sept. 13, 1982) 20.

Chapter 3. Awakening from the Dream

1. Susanne Greaves, "Levittown Revisited," New York *Herald Tribune* magazine, (Aug. 16, 1964), 9–12.

2. "Same Rooms, Varied Decor," *Life* (Jan. 14, 1952).

3. Wright, *Building the Dream*, 251.

4. Barbara Miller Lane, *Architecture and Politics in Germany, 1918–1945*,

(Cambridge, Mass.: Harvard University Press, 1968).

5. Hayden, *Grand Domestic Revolution*, 228–65.

6. *Progressive Architecture* 63 (Jan. 1982), 112–35, exemplifies current taste.

7. For a sampling of the vast literature on suburbia, see: Philip C. Dolce, ed., *Suburbia: The American Dream and Dilemma* (Garden City, N.Y.: Doubleday Anchor, 1976); Robert Goldstone, *Suburbia: Civic Denial* (New York: Macmillan, 1970): Charles Haar, *The End of Innocence: A Suburban Reader* (Glenview, Illinois: Scott, Foresman, 1972); Bennett M. Berger, *Working Class Suburb: A Study of Auto Workers in Suburbia* (Berkeley, Calif.: University of California Press, 1971); William Michelson, *Environmental Choice, Human Behavior, and Residential Satisfaction* (New York: Oxford University Press, 1977); Donald N. Rothblatt, Daniel J. Garr, and Jo Sprague, *The Suburban Environment and Women* (New York: Praeger, 1979); Robert A.M. Stern, "The Suburban Alternative for the 'Middle City,' " *Architectural Record* (Aug. 1978), 98–100. For a more extensive bibliographical review, see the essay by Muller listed in the bibliography.

8. Lewis Mumford, "Planning for the Phases of Life" (1949), *The Urban Prospect* (New York: Harcourt, Brace, Jovanovich, 1968), 34–35.

9. Recent critiques of this bias of location theory include Ann R. Markusen, "City Spatial Structure, Women's Household Work, and National Urban Policy," in C. Stimpson, et al., eds., *Women and The American City* (Chicago: University of Chicago Press, 1981). The annotated Coatsworth bibliography listed in the bibliography to this book gives a broad overview of literature on women and planning. Especially recommended are four volumes of scholarly essays: Gerda Wekerle, ed., *New Space For Women* (Boulder, Colorado: Westview Press, 1980); Suzanne Keller, ed., *Building For Women* (Lexington, Mass.: Lexington Books, 1981); Susana Torre, ed., *Women in American Architecture* (New York: Whitney Library of Design, 1977); and Stimpson, ed., *Women and The American City*.

10. Chester Hartman and Michael E. Stone, "A Socialist Housing Program for the United States," in Marcus G. Raskin, ed., *The Federal Budget and Social Reconstruction* (Washington, D.C.: Institute for Policy Studies, 1979).

11. Gary J. Coates, ed., *Resettling America: Energy, Ecology, and Community* (Andover, Mass.: Brick House, 1981), 4. He says as 6 percent of the world's population, the U.S. uses 33 percent of the world petroleum output and 36 percent of the metals,; and translates this into 20 metric tons per year per person, half of which ends up as solid wastes!

12. Ruth Schwartz Cowan, cited in Hayden, *Grand Domestic Revolution*, 314, n. 33.

13. *Transit Fact Book*, 1977–78 Edition (Washington, D.C.: American Public Transit Association, 1978), 29. *Motor Vehicle Facts and Figures* (Detroit: Motor Vehicle Manufacturers Association, 1977), 29, 53, 31.

14. For a sound approach see Helga Olkowski, William Olkowski, and T. Javits, *The Integral Urban House* (San Francisco: Sierra Club Books, 1979); and Peter Calthorpe and Susan Benson, "Beyond Solar," in Coates, ed., *Resettling America*, 313–28; for a solar dream house, see Malcolm Wells, "Mac Well's Summertime Blues," *New Shelter* 2 (May/June 1981), 60–69; and David Bainbridge, Judy Corbett, and John Hofacre, *Village Homes Solar House Designs* (Emmaus, Pa.: Rodale Press, 1979).

15. Ray Reece, *The Sun Betrayed* (Boston: South End Press, 1979).

16. Patricia Mainardi, "The Politics of Housework," in R. Morgan, ed., *Sisterhood is Powerful* (New York: Vintage, 1970), 447–54.

17. Michele Zimbalist Rosaldo, "Women, Culture, and Society: A Theoretical Overview," in *Women, Culture and Society,* ed. Michele Zimbalist Rosaldo and Louise Lamphere (Stanford, Calif.: Stanford University Press, 1974).

18. Bonnie Loyd, "Women, Home, and Status," in *Housing and Identity,* ed. James Duncan (London: Croom Helm, 1981).

19. The remedy for "going to pieces" is analyzed by Anne S. Kasper, "Women Victimized by Valium," *New Directions for Women* 8 (Winter 1979–80), 7.

20. Betty Friedan, *The Feminine Mystique* (New York: W.W. Norton, 1963).

21. Adrienne Rich, "A Primary Ground," in *Poems: Selected and New, 1950–1974* (New York: W.W. Norton, 1975), 203–4.

22. Adrienne Rich, "The Fourth Month of the Landscape Architect," in *Poems,* 224–25.

23. Bernice Johnson Reagon, "My Black Mothers and Sisters, or On Beginning a Cultural Autobiography," *Feminist Studies* 8 (Spring 1982), 81–96.

24. Susan Anderson-Khleif, "Housing Needs of Single-Parent Mothers," in Keller, ed., *Building for Women,* 21–38.

25. Anne Cools, "Emergency Shelter: The Development of an Innovative Women's Environment," in G. Wekerle, et al., eds., *New Space for Women,* 311–18. Also see: Lois Ahrens, "Battered Women's Refuges: Feminist Cooperatives vs. Social Service Institutions," *Radical America* 14 (May-June 1980), 40–47; Ann Withorn, "Helping Ourselves: The Limits and Potential of Self Help," *Radical America* 14 (May-June 1980), 24–39; and Renae Scott, "Notes on Race, Mothering, and Culture in the Shelter Movement," *Radical America* 14 (May-June 1980), 48–50.

26. Donna E. Shalala and Jo Anne McGeorge, "The Women and Mortgage Credit Project: A Government Response to the Housing Problems of Women," in Keller, ed., *Building for Women,* 39–46.

27. Killearn Estates, Tallahassee, Florida: I am indebted to Martin Pawley for this phrase, "owner-speculator," used in his *Home Ownership* (London: Architectural Press, 1978), 135.

28. Constance Perin, *Everything in Its Place: Social Order and Land Use in America* (Princeton, N.J.: Princeton University Press, 1977), 32–80.

29. Jon Douglas, Beverly Hills, California.

30. On the FHA, see Wright, *Building the Dream,* 247–48. Levitt was quoted in the *Saturday Evening Post,* Aug. 7, 1954, page 72: "As a Jew, I have no room in my mind or heart for racial prejudice. But, by various means, I have come to know that if we sell one house to a Negro family, then 90 to 95 percent of our white customers will not buy into the community. That is their attitude, not ours. We did not create it and cannot cure it. As a company, our position is simply this: we can solve a housing problem, or we can try to solve a racial problem. But we cannot combine the two." For a discussion of what happened when a Black family did move into the second Levittown, see Gans, *The Levittowners,* 375.

31. Emily Card, "Women, Housing Access, and Mortgage Credit," *Signs: A Journal of Women in Culture and Society* 5 (Supplement, Spring 1980), S215–S219.

32. *Los Angeles Times* (Nov. 21, 1982), VII, 24.
33. Federal National Mortgage Association, "The Baby Boom is Househunting," *Smithsonian* 11 (Nov. 1980), 151; Urban Land Institute, and Council on Development Choices for the 1980s, *The Affordable Community: Growth, Change, and Choice in the 80s* (Washington, D.C.: U.S.G.P.O., 1981), 3.
34. Residential non-farm mortgage debt outstanding, *Statistical Abstract of the United States 1982–83* (Washington, D.C.: U.S.G.P.O., 1982), 512.
35. Diane Henry, "Market Grows for One Room 'Studio' House," *New York Times,* May 3, 1981, Real Estate Section, 1; Barbara Behrens Gers, "The 300-sq.-ft. home and other ideas for the 1980s," *Housing* (Jan. 1981), 72–77; "Teeny-Weeny Condos" (440 sq.ft.), *Los Angeles Times* (Mar. 28, 1982), VII, 27.

Chapter 4. Home, Mom, and Apple Pie

1. An exception is Ellen Malos, ed., *The Politics of Housework* (London: Virago Press, 1980). For a critical look at existing scholarship, see Hayden, *Grand Domestic Revolution,* 306–9.
2. The various approaches are reviewed in Hayden, *Grand Domestic Revolution,* 291–305.
3. Writing from a Marxist-feminist perspective, Heidi I. Hartmann has pioneered the analysis of women's labor time in the home, as the basis for her analysis of the family as a site of class and gender conflict usually ignored by liberal theorists. Heidi I. Hartmann, "The Family as the Locus of Gender, Class, and Political Struggle: The Example of Housework," *Signs: Journal of Women in Culture and Society* 6 (Spring, 1981), 366–94.
4. Laura Balbo, "The Servicing Work of Women and the Capitalist State," in *Political Power and Social Theory* (New York: Basic Books, 1981); "Crazy Quilts: Rethinking the Welfare State Debate From a Woman's Perspective," mimeographed, GRIFF, Milan, Italy, 1981; Laura Balbo and Renate Siebert Zahar, *Interferenze* (Milan: Feltrinelli, 1979).
5. Erma Bombeck, *The Grass Is Always Greener Over the Septic Tank* (New York: Fawcett, 1977), 5. Billed as "the exposé to end all exposés—the truth about the suburbs" this book can be read as a bunch of little jokes, or as an unconscious but revealing indictment of numerous planning and design failures, and housewives' struggles to overcome them. A more serious attack is John Keats, *The Crack in the Picture Window* (Boston: Houghton Mifflin, 1957).
6. Literature on the family is reviewed in Hartmann, "The Family as the Locus of Gender, Class, and Political Struggle," 365–68.
7. Among the traditional family's defenders is Christopher Lasch, *Haven in a Heartless World: The Family Besieged* (New York: Basic Books, 1976).
8. William O'Neill, *Everyone Was Brave: A History of Feminism in America* (1969; New York: Quadrangle, 1971), 358.
9. Betty Friedan, *The Second Stage* (New York: Summit, 1981), 43, 83.
10. V. I. Lenin, *The Emancipation of Women* (New York: Progress Publishers, 1975), 69.
11. Hayden, *Grand Domestic Revolution,* 3–5.

12. August Bebel, *Women Under Socialism,* tr. Daniel De Leon (1883; New York: Schocken, 1971), 338–39.

13. Jane Cunningham Croly, letter to Elizabeth Cady Stanton, printed in *The Revolution* 3 (May 27, 1869), 324.

14. Melusina Fay Peirce, "Cooperative Housekeeping II" (second of five articles), *Atlantic Monthly* 22 (Dec. 1868), 684.

15. Melusina Fay Peirce, "Cooperative Housekeeping III," *Atlantic Monthly* 23 (Jan. 1869), 29–30.

16. Mari Jo Buhle, "A Republic of Women: Feminist Theory in the Gilded Age," paper read at the 1981 meeting of the American Historical Association, 4–7; also *Lake Placid Conference on Home Economics, Proceedings* (Lake Placid, N.Y., 1903, 1907).

17. I use "paradigm" in the sense established by Thomas Kuhn, *The Structure of Scientific Revolution,* International Encyclopedia of Unified Science, vol. 2, no. 2 (1962) (Chicago: University of Chicago Press, 1973); "Second Thoughts on Paradigms," in *The Essential Tension: Selected Studies in Scientific Tradition and Change* (Chicago: University of Chicago Press, 1977), 293–319.

18. Susan Strasser, *Never Done: A History of American Housework* (New York: Pantheon Books, 1982), is an excellent work, dealing with this process in great detail, with constant humor.

19. Ruth Schwartz Cowan, "The 'Industrial' Revolution in the Home: Household Technology and Social Change in the 20th Century," *Technology and Culture* 17 (Jan. 1976), 1–23.

20. Carol Miles, "The Craftsman Ideal of Home Life," includes all these quotations from Gustave Stickeley's *The Craftsman,* typescript, 1981.

21. Christine Frederick, *Household Engineering: Scientific Management in the Home* (Chicago: American School of Home Economics, 1920), 92.

22. Edith Mendel Stern, "Women Are Household Slaves," *American Mercury* (Jan. 1949).

23. Jo Anne Vanek, "Time Spent in Housework," *Scientific American* (Nov. 1974), 116–120.

24. Strasser, *Never Done;* "U.S. Dines Out Despite Prices," Boston *Globe* (Oct. 25, 1978), 75.

25. Edith Evans Asbury, "Col. Harland Sanders, Founder of Kentucky Fried Chicken Dies," *New York Times* (Dec. 17, 1980), 29.

26. "A Big, Big Business," *Southern Exposure* 8 (fall 1980), 36–40; Joseph Lelyveld, "Drive-in Day Care," *New York Times Magazine* (June 5, 1977), 110.

27. Victoria Stevens, "Buy groceries at home with 'rent-a-shopper,' " Toronto *Star* (Dec. 1, 1978), C4.

28. Anne Roberts, "Professional Wife Draws Line At Sex," Toronto *Globe and Mail* (Dec. 19, 1978), 1.

29. Phyllis Battelle, "For $25 An Hour, Anyone Can Rent A Wife," Seattle *Post-Intelligencer* (July 20, 1980), D1; Strasser, *Never Done,* 229.

30. Kristin Moore and Sandra Hofferth, "Women and Their Children," in R. Smith, ed., *The Subtle Revolution: Women At Work* (Washington, D.C.: Urban Land Institute, 1979), 125–58.

31. Douglas Shuit, "Welfare Mothers Face Hard Choice: Work or Stay Home," *Los Angeles Times* (Jan. 18, 1982), 1.

32. Carole Krucoff, "Firms Find Day Care Is Just Good Business," Boston *Globe* (Aug. 24, 1980), 26.

33. Beverly Beyette, "Nurse Recruitment on the Critical List," *Los Angeles Times* (Sept. 30, 1980), Part 5, 1.

34. Nancy S. Barrett, "Women in The Job Market: Unemployment and Work Schedules," in Smith, ed., *The Subtle Revolution*, 88–90.

35. Ari Korpivaara, "Play Groups for Dads," and Alison Herzig and Jane Mali, "Oh, Boy! Babies!" in *Ms.* 10 (Feb. 1982), 52–58.

36. Sarah Fenstermaker Berk, "The Household as Workplace," in G. Wekerle, ed., *New Space For Women*, 70; also see Nona Glazer-Malbin, "Review Essay: Housework," *Signs: Journal of Women in Culture and Society* 1 (Summer 1976), 905–22; Nadine Brozan, "Men and Housework: Do They or Don't They?" *New York Times* (Nov. 1, 1980), 52; Clair Vickery, "Women's Economic Contribution to the Family," in Smith, ed., *The Subtle Revolution*, 159–200.

37. Hartmann, "The Family as the Locus of Gender, Class, and Political Struggle," 383.

38. *Ibid.*, 380.

39. Mainardi, "The Politics of Housework," in Morgan, ed., *Sisterhood Is Powerful*, 447–54.

40. The majority of American men stop paying child support within two years of a divorce settlement, according to Kathryn Kish Sklar, "Women, Work, and Children, 1600–1980," paper read at the Third Annual Conference on Planning and Women's Needs, UCLA, Urban Planning Program, Feb. 21, 1981.

41. Bebel, *Women Under Socialism*, 344–49.

42. Vladmir I. Lenin, *The Great Initiative*, quoted in Vladimir Zelinski, "Architecture as a Tool of Social Transformation," *Women and Revolution* 11 (spring 1976), 6–14.

43. Kopp, "Soviet Architecture Since the 20th Congress of the C.P.S.U.," paper delivered at the Second World Congress of Soviet and East European Studies, 1980, 12–13.

44. Michael Paul Sacks, "Unchanging Times: A Comparison of the Everyday Life of Soviet Working Men and Women Between 1923 and 1966," *Journal of Marriage and the Family*, 39 (Nov. 1977), 793–805.

45. Alice H. Cook, *The Working Mother: A Survey of Problems and Programs in Nine Countries*, 2nd ed. (Ithaca, N.Y.: New York State School of Industrial and Labor Relations, 1978).

46. Carollee Benglesdorf and Alice Hageman, "Women and Work," in "Women in Transition," special issue of *Cuba Review* 4 (Sept. 1974), 9.

47. I was shown this project by planners in April 1980 when I visited China as a guest of the Chinese Architectural Society.

48. Heidi Steffens, "A Woman's Place," *Cuba Review* 4 (Sept. 1974), 29.

49. Geoffrey E. Fox, "Honor, Shame, and Women's Liberation in Cuba: Views of Working-Class Emigré Men," in *Female and Male in Latin America*, ed., A. Pescatello (Pittsburgh: University of Pittsburgh Press, 1973). I visited Cuba in 1979 and also observed male refusal to do housework in many situations.

50. Delia Davin, *Woman-Work: Women and the Party in Revolutionary China* (Oxford, England: Clarendon Press, 1976); Elisabeth J. Croll, "Women in

Rural Production and Reproduction in the Soviet Union, China, Cuba, and Tanzania: Case Studies,'' in *Signs*, special issue on Development and the Sexual Division of Labor, 7 (Winter 1981), 375–99.

51. For a full account see Hayden, *Grand Domestic Revolution*, 66–89, 208–27, 266–77.

52. Charlotte Perkins Gilman, *Women and Economics* (Boston: Maynard and Small, 1898), Hayden, *Grand Domestic Revolution*, 182–205. An early translation of Gilman in an architectural journal is "Le Maison de Demain," *La Construction Moderne* 5 (Nov. 1914), 66–68.

53. Erwin Mühlestein, "Kollektives Wohnen gestern und heute," *Architese* 14 (1975), 4–5.

54. Otto Fick, "The Apartment House Up To Date" *Architectural Record* 22 (July 1907), 68–71.

55. Vestbro, 6–7.

56. *Ibid.*, 8–11.

57. Mühlestein, "Kollektives," 6–8; Vestbro, "Collective Housing," 8–11.

58. *Ibid.*

59. Hayden, *Grand Domestic Revolution*, 230–37.

60. Clementina Black, *A New Way of Housekeeping* (London: W. Collins Sons, 1918).

61. Lawrence Wolfe, *The Reilly Plan* (London: Nicholson and Watson, 1945).

62. Hayden, *Grand Domestic Revolution*, 251–61.

63. Ann Oakley, *Woman's Work: The Housewife Past and Present* (New York: Pantheon, 1974), 227–29.

64. Kay Hanly Bretnall, "Should Housewives Be Paid a Salary?" *American Home* 37 (Feb. 1947), 15–16.

65. Wages for Housework Collective, *All Work and No Pay* (London: Falling Wall Press, 1975), 5; also see Ellen Malos, *The Politics of Housework*, for a full analysis of this movement.

66. Gary B. Trudeau, *Doonesbury*.

67. Nona Glazer, Linka Majka, Joan Acker, Christine Bose, *Women in a Full Employment Economy* (1977), mimeo.

68. Melusina Fay Peirce, "Cooperative Housekeeping, *Atlantic Monthly* 23 (March 1869), 297.

Chapter 5. Roof, Fire, and Center

1. Kenneth Frampton, *Modern Architecture: A Critical History* (London: Thames and Hudson, 1980), 9.

2. Ada Louise Huxtable, "Some Handsome Housing Mythology," *Kicked a Building Lately?* (New York: Quadrangle, 1976), 33.

3. Kathleen Anne Mackie, "An Exploration of the Idea of Home in Human Geography," M.A. Thesis, University of Toronto, 1981, 33. This outstanding essay reviews a wide variety of literature, including Cooper, Jung, Gibran, Raglan, Heidegger, Eliade.

4. *Ibid.*, 33–57, see also Clare Cooper, "The House as Symbol of the Self," in

Proshansky, et al., eds., *Environmental Psychology* (New York: Holt, Rinehart, and Winston, 1976).

5. Francesco Dal Co, *Albitare Nel Moderno* (Rome: Laterza, 1982).

6. Joseph Rykwert, *On Adam's House in Paradise: The Idea of the Primitive Hut in Architectural History* (New York: Museum of Modern Art, 1972).

7. John Brinckerhoff Jackson, "The Westward Moving House," *Landscapes* (Amherst: University of Massachusetts Press, 1970), 10–42.

8. Adrienne Rich, "A Primary Ground," in *Poems: Selected and New* (New York: W.W. Norton, 1975), 203–4.

9. William Nowlin, *The Bark-Covered House, or Back in the Woods Again,* 1876 (New York: Readex Microprint, 1966).

10. D. Hayden, "Catharine Beecher and the Politics of Housework," 40–49.

11. Amos Rapoport, *House Form and Culture* (Englewood Cliffs, N.J.: Prentice Hall, 1969), 54, shows the herrgottswinkel.

12. Charlotte Perkins Gilman, *The Home,* 100.

13. Carol Barkin, "Electricity Is Her Servant," *Heresies* 11 (1981), 62–63; *Architectural Forum* (Apr. 1935).

14. Eric Larrabee, "The Six Thousand Houses That Levitt Built," *Harpers* (Sept. 1948), 84.

15. "Housing: Up From the Potato Fields," *Time* (July 3, 1950), 67.

16. Research by Scott Kinzy, discussed in Philip Langdon, "Suburbanites Pick Favorite Home Styles," *New York Times* (Apr. 22, 1982), Home section, 1.

17. Tom Wolfe, *From Bauhaus to Our House* (New York: Farrar, Straus and Giroux, 1981), 69.

18. Bill Owens, *Suburbia* (San Francisco: Straight Arrow, 1973).

19. Denise Scott Brown and Robert Venturi, *Signs of Life: Symbols in the American City* (Washington, D.C.: Aperture, Inc., 1976).

20. "Quick Facts about the Manufactured Housing Industry," Manufactured Housing Institute leaflet, July 1982; see also *Report of the President's Commission on Housing* (Washington, D.C.: U.S.G.P.O., 1980), xxvi, for slightly lower estimates. The industry estimates are 1977, 24%; 1978, 25%; 1979, 28%; 1980, 29%; 1981, 36%.

21. Patrick H. Hare, "Why Granny Flats Are a Good Idea," *Planning* 18 (Feb. 1982), 15–16; Larry Agran, "Rethinking the single-family home," *Los Angeles Times,* Home magazine (Feb. 14, 1982), 24; Jack Birkinshaw, "Granny Housing Act Weighed in County," *Los Angeles Times,* Westside (Dec. 20, 1981), 1.

22. Henry James, *The American Scene* (1904; Bloomington, Ind.: Indiana University Press, 1968), 11.

23. *Ibid.,* 10.

24. Thorstein Veblen, *Theory of the Leisure Class* (New York: New American Library, 1954).

25. Robert Woods Kennedy, *The House and the Art of Its Design* (New York: Reinhold Publishing Co., 1953), 42.

26. Many examples can be found in the houses published in *Architectural Record* and *Progressive Architecture* in the last 10 years.

27. R. Buckminster Fuller, "The Dymaxion House," *Architectural Forum* 70 (1932); and "The 8000 Lb. House," *Architectural Forum* 84 (1946).

28. Elliott Erwhitt, "A House That Thinks for Itself," *House and Garden* (July 1976). For a really extreme example of high-tech sacred huts, see Gerard O'Neill, *The High Frontier: Human Colonies in Space* (New York: William Morrow, 1977).

29. Joseph Deken, *The Electronic Cottage: Everyday Living with Your Personal Computers in the 1980's* (New York: Morrow, 1981).

30. Robin Evans, "Bentham's Panopticon," *Architectural Association Quarterly* 3 (Apr.–July 1971), 21–37.

31. Taylor Stoehr, *Nay-Saying in Concord* (New Haven: Archon Books, 1978), 100.

32. Bauer, *Modern Housing,* 119–41.

33. Frampton, *Modern Architecture,* 137–38.

34. Competition prospectus, quoted in Vladmir Zelinski, "Architecture as a Tool of Social Transformation," 6–14. See also Barbara Kreis, "The Ideal of the *Dom-Kommuna* and the Dilemma of the Soviet Avant-Garde," *Oppositions* 21 (Summer 1980), 52–77.

35. Filippo Marinetti, "Foundation Manifesto of Futurist Architecture," 1909, quoted in Ian Todd and Michael Wheeler, *Utopia* (New York: Harmony Books, 1978), 131. For another translation, see *Marinetti: Selected Writings,* ed. and tr. R. W. Flint, (New York: Farrar, Straus and Giroux, 1971) 41–42.

36. Alexandra Kollontai, *Women's Labor in Economic Development,* quoted in Zelinski, 10.

37. Kopp, "Soviet Architecture," 26.

38. Le Corbusier, *Towards a New Architecture* (1927; London: The Architectural Press, 1946) 269. See also Peter Serenyi, "Le Corbusier, Fourier, and the Monastery of Ema," *Art Bulletin* (Dec. 1967), 277–86.

39. Nicholas John Habraken, *Supports* (Cambridge, Mass.: MIT, 1964).

40. See Dolores Hayden, "What Would a Non-Sexist City Be Like?" in Stimpson, et. al., eds., *Women and the American City,* for plans, 179.

41. SITE, *Highrise of Homes* (New York: Rizzoli, 1982).

42. Department of the Environment, *Space in the Home* (London: Her Majesty's Stationery Office, 1972), 4–8.

43. Glenn Robert Lym, *A Psychology of Building: How We Shape and Experience Our Structured Spaces* (Englewood Cliffs, N.J.: Prentice Hall, 1980), 20–29.

44. *Ibid,* 45–48.

45. Virginia Woolf, *A Room of One's Own* (1929; New York: Harper and Row, 1970).

46. Torsten Malmberg, *Human Territoriality* (The Hague: Mouton, 1980).

47. Margaret Mead, *Sex and Temperament in Three Primitive Societies* (1935; New York: Morrow Quill, 1980), is a pioneering example.

48. Catherine Bauer, "The Dreary Deadlock of Public Housing" *Architectural Forum* (May 1957), 140ff.

49. *Report of the President's Commission on Housing,* xxiv.

50. Charles Jencks, *The Language of Post-Modern Architecture* (New York: Rizzoli, 1977), 9; see also Lee Rainwater, *Behind Ghetto Walls* (Chicago: Aldine, 1970), and "Fear and the House-as-Haven in the Lower Class," *AIP Journal* (Jan. 1966) 23–31.

51. Personal conversation with Charles Jencks, 1982.

52. Jan Wampler, Columbia Point Project, *Progressive Architecture* (Jan. 1973).
53. Charles Jencks, *The Language of Post-Modern Architecture*, 79–82.
54. Hayden, *Grand Domestic Revolution*, 50–63.
55. *Ibid.*, 64–114.
56. *Ibid.*, 151–79.
57. Ebenezer Howard, *Garden Cities of To-Morrow* (1902; Cambridge, Mass.: MIT Press, 1970); Hayden, *Grand Domestic Revolution*, 230–37.
58. Stein, *Toward New Towns for America.*
59. *Ibid.*
60. Esther McCoy, *Five California Architects* (New York: Praeger, 1975), 58–100. See also Stefanos Polyzoides, Roger Sherwood, James Tice, and Julius Shulman, *Courtyard Housing in Los Angeles* (Berkeley and Los Angeles: University of California Press, 1982).
61. Tinggarden was built by Tegnestuen Vandkunsten of Copenhagen with Svend Algren, Jens T. Arnfred, Michael S. Johnsen, Steffen Kragh, and Karsten Vibild.
62. Francis Strauven, "A place of reciprocity: home for one parent families in Amsterdam by Aldo Van Eyck," *Lotus* 28 (1980), 22–39.
63. Roger Montgomery, "High Density, Low-Rise Housing and Changes in the American Housing Economy," in Sam Davis, ed., *The Form of Housing* (New York: Van Nostrand Reinhold, 1977), 83–111.
64. Urban Land Institute and Council on Development Choices for the 1980s, *The Affordable Community.*
65. Daniel Lauber, "Nothing New in This Housing Report," *Planning* 48 (June 1982), 26.
66. Montgomery, "High Density," 99.
67. *Ibid.*, 110.
68. *Ibid.*, 111.

Chapter 6. Getting and Spending

1. Helvi Sipila, "The State of the World's Women, 1979" (New York: United Nations, 1979).
2. See also a special issue of *Signs,* "Development and the Sexual Division of Labor," 7 (winter 1981).
3. Jan Peterson, speaking at a conference at Smith College, Northampton, Mass., Oct. 1981.
4. Markusen, "City Spatial Structure," 27.
5. Heidi Hartmann, "Capitalism, Patriarchy, and Job Segregation by Sex," *Signs* 1 (spring 1976), 137–69; Hartmann, "The Family as the Locus of Gender, Class, and Political Struggle," 370–72, 377.
6. Nancy S. Barrett, "Women in the Job Market: Occupations, Earnings, and Career Opportunities," in Smith, ed., *The Subtle Revolution,* 31–62.
7. Mary Witt and Patricia K. Naherny, *Woman's Work—Up From 878: Report on the DOT Research Project* (Madison, Wisconsin: University of Wisconsin Extension, Women's Education Resources, 1975).

8. Alice Amsden, ed., *The Economics of Women and Work* (New York: St. Martin's Press, 1980).

9. Robert Goodman, *The Last Entrepreneurs: America's Regional Wars for Jobs and Dollars* (New York: Simon and Schuster, 1980), 38.

10. William Gauger, "Household Work: Can We Add It To The GNP?" *Journal of Home Economics* (Oct. 1973), 12–15.

11. Paul Samuelson, *Economics: An Introductory Analysis,* 5th ed. (New York: McGraw Hill, 1961), 212–37.

12. Gauger, "Household Work," 12–15.

13. *Ibid.*

14. Kay Lehman Schlozman, "Women and Unemployment: Assessing the Biggest Myths," *Women: A Feminist Perspective,* ed. Jo Freeman, 2nd ed. (Palo Alto, Calif.: Mayfield Publishing, 1979), 290–312; Nancy S. Barrett, "Women in the Job Market," 64–79.

15. Rae André, *Homemakers: The Forgotten Workers* (Chicago: University of Chicago Press, 1981), 186–206.

16. Nancy M. Gordon, "Institutional Responses: The Social Security System," in Smith, ed., *The Subtle Revolution,* 223–56. Also see "The Future of Social Security: An Exchange," *The New York Review of Books* 30 (March 17, 1983), 41–57.

17. Gordon, 223–56.

18. Markusen, "City Spatial Structure," 27.

19. Gerda Wekerle, "Review Essay: Women in the Urban Environment," in C. Stimpson, ed., *Women and the American City,* 206.

20. Melanie Archer, "Public Policy and Access to Opportunity: A Time-Geographic Analysis of Constraints on Women's Activity Patterns," M.A. Thesis, Architecture and Urban Planning, University of California, Los Angeles, 1980; Risa Palm and Allan Pred, "A Time-Geographic Perspective on Problems of Inequality for Women," Working Paper no. 236 (Berkeley, Calif.: Institute of Urban and Regional Development, 1974).

21. Markusen, "City Spatial Structure."

22. Martin Wachs, "Issues in Transportation for Women," text of talk at Second Annual Conference on Planning and Women's Needs, UCLA, 1981, 2.

23. *Ibid.,* 2.

24. *Ibid.,* Table 8; Edith Perlman, "Kicking the car habit: Why it's up to women," *Radcliffe Quarterly* 67 (Dec. 1981), 25–26.

25. *Ibid.,* 4; Helena Znaniecki Lopata, "The Chicago Woman: A Study of Patterns of Mobility and Transportation," *Signs: A Journal of Women in Culture and Society* 5 (Supplement, spring 1980), S161–S169.

26. Wachs, table 2.

27. Unpublished paper by Natalie McConnell, including interviews with many rape crisis centers, cited by Wachs, 4.

28. My account of this incident is based on a personal conversation with Prof. Rosenbloom in 1979.

29. U.S. Department of Housing and Urban Development, "Housing and Social Services," transcript of a roundtable, Oct. 28, 1980.

30. Michael Freedberg, "Self-Help Housing and the Cities: Sweat Equity in New York," in Gary J. Coates, ed., *Resettling America,* 272.

31. *Ibid.*, 264.

32. *Ibid.*, 280.

33. Claire Greensfelder, "New Technology Gets Politics," *In These Times* (Dec. 24, 1980–Jan. 13, 1981), 5.

34. "History and Background of the San Bernardino West Side Community Development Corporation," mimeo (San Bernardino, Calif.: Community Development Corporation, n.d.); A.R. Jones, *Westside Community Development Corporation CETA Training Program* (San Bernardino, Calif.: Community Development Corporation, 1978).

35. Nadine Brozan, "Swapping Strategies at Forum on Family," *New York Times* (Aug. 2, 1982), A13.

36. *Id.*

37. "Designed for 24-Hour Child Care," *Architectural Record* (Mar. 1944), 86.

38. *Id.*

39. Sheila B. Kamerman, "Work and Family in Industrialized Societies," *Signs: A Journal of Women in Culture and Society* 4 (summer 1979), 644–45.

40. Mühlestein, 5–9; Dick Urban Vestbro, "Collective Housing Units in Sweden," *Current Sweden*, Svenska Institutet, Stockholm, publication no. 234 (Sept. 1976), (6), 6–7.

41. "Sweden's Model Apartments: Stockholm Building is Wonderful for Wives Who Work," *Life* 18 (Mar. 12, 1945), 112–14.

42. "Bridge Over Troubled Water," *Architects' Journal* (London, Sept. 27, 1972), 680–84; personal interview by the author with Nina West, 1978.

43. Women's Development Corporation, Providence, R.I., mimeographed statement, 1980.

44. *Id.*

Chapter 7. Reconstructing Domestic Space

1. William E. Geist, "A Suburban Tempest," *New York Times* (Dec. 8, 1981), B2.

2. George Sternleib and James Hughes, *America's Housing: Prospects and Problems*, 26–27.

3. *Ibid.*, 59; U.S. Bureau of the Census, *1980 Census of Population and Housing*, 3.

4. Andrée Brooks, "Wide Appeal for Accessory Apartments," *New York Times*, real estate (Jan. 3, 1982), 6.

5. Patrick Hare, "Carving Up The American Dream," *Planning* 47 (July 1981), 14–17.

6. Bill McLarney, quoted by Amory Lovins, in Coates, ed., *Resettling America*, xx.

7. *The Report of the President's Commission on Housing* (Washington, D.C.: U.S.G.P.O., 1982), xxxiv.

8. Mary Jo Bane and George Masnick, *The Nation's Families: 1960–1990* (Cambridge, Mass.: Harvard-MIT Joint Center for Urban Studies, 1980); The Urban Land Institute, *The Affordable Community*, 4.

9. George Sternleib, quoted in *The Affordable Community*, 56.

10. David Morris, "Self-Reliant Cities: The Rise of the New City States," in Coates, ed., *Resettling America,* 248.
11. Robert Lindsey, "Southern California Sets An Example of How to Grow Old in the Sunbelt," *New York Times* (July 10, 1982), 7.
12. David Morris, "Self-Reliant Cities," 248.
13. Robert Goodman, *The Last Entrepreneurs,* 52–75.
14. Morris, "Self-Reliant Cities," 243.
15. On energy costs see Amory Lovins, *Soft Energy Paths: Toward A Durable Peace* (New York: Harper and Row, 1979).
16. Leonard Sloane, "Franchising of Home Repairs," *New York Times* (July 29, 1982), D1.
17. Patrick H. Hare, with Susan Conner and Dwight Merriam, *Accessory Apartments: Using Surplus Space in Single-Family Houses,* PAS Report no. 265 (Chicago, Illinois: American Planning Association, 1982).
18. *Ibid.,* 9–19.
19. *Ibid.,* 6.
20. Morris, "Self-Reliant Cities," 243.
21. Patrick H. Hare, "Rethinking Single-Family Zoning" 34.
22. Patrick H. Hare, "The Nation's Largest Untapped Housing Resource," *Christian Science Monitor* (Aug. 19, 1981).
23. Hare, "Rethinking," 33; also see his "Why Granny Flats Are a Good Idea," *Planning* 18 (Feb. 1982), 15–16.
24. Nancy Rubin, *The New Suburban Woman: Beyond Myth and Motherhood* (New York: Coward, McCann, and Geoghegan, 1982); Karen Lindsey, *Friends as Family: New Kinds of Families And What They Could Mean For You* (Boston: Beacon Press, 1981).
25. Robert Weiss, *Going It Alone: The Family Life and Social Situation of the Single Parent* (New York: Basic Books, 1979).
26. National Congress of Neighborhood Women, "Women's Leadership and Community Development Program," xerox, 1982. (NCNW, 249 Manhattan Avenue, Brooklyn, N.Y. 11211).
27. Marshall Hunt and David Bainbridge, "The Davis Experience," in Coates, ed., *Resettling America,* 366–74; "Four Families Get Together," *Sunset* (April 1983) 258–9.
28. Robert Lake, *The New Suburbanites: Race and Housing in the Suburbs* (New Brunswick, N.J.: Rutgers, 1981); Thomas A. Clark, *Blacks in Suburbs: A National Perspective* (New Brunswick, N.J.: Rutgers, 1979).
29. Hattie H. Hartman, "Rehabbing the Suburbs: Freedom to Change," M. Arch. thesis, MIT, 1982.
30. Gers, "The 300-sq.-ft. home."
31. Raquel Ramati, *How to Save Your Own Street* (Garden City, N.Y.: Dolphin Books, 1981).
32. Dolores Hayden, *Seven American Utopias,* 224–59.
33. Hans Wirz, "Backyard Rehab: Urban Microcosm Rediscovered," *Urban Innovation Abroad* 3 (July 1979), 2–3. See also Donald Shoup, "The Economics of Neighborhood Renewal," UCLA Graduate School of Architecture and Urban Planning, Discussion Paper DP 121, May 1979.
34. Gary Garber, "The Cheyenne Community Solar Greenhouse," in Coates, ed., *Resettling America,* 357.

35. *Ibid.*, 363.
36. Richard Britz, *The Edible City: Resource Manual* (Los Altos, Calif.: William Kaufmann, 1981).
37. Edward T. Hall's *The Hidden Dimension* was one of the first books to alert people to the non-verbal territorial responses of different cultures.
38. Sam Hall Kaplan, "From Renters to Owners: A Success Story," *Los Angeles Times* (June 10, 1982), 5, 1.
39. *Id.;* Elisabeth Virata, "Cooperative Housing in Los Angeles, 1945–1982," unpublished paper, UCLA, 1982.
40. Ronald Lee Fleming and Lauri Halderman, *On Common Ground,* 150. On shared maintenance and its problems, also see Gerda Wekerle, et al., "Condominium Housing: Contradictions in Ownership, Participation, and Control," paper given at Environmental Design Research Association meeting, Tucson, 1978.
41. "Inn for Elderly Proves Workable Idea," *Los Angeles Times,* (Jan. 17, 1982), VII, 23.
42. Catherine Davis, "Business Is Booming," *Historic Preservation* 34 (July / August 1982), 52–53.
43. *338 Harvard Street: A New Option for Living Cooperatively in Cambridge* (Cambridge, Mass.: Cambridge Living Options for Elders / Unihab, Cambridge, Inc.), 1982; The 338 Committee, "Common Area and Shared Living Agreement," mimeo, 1982.
44. Grace Duffield Goodwin, "The Commuter's Wife: A Sisterly Talk by One Who Knows Her Problems," *Good Housekeeping* 49 (Oct. 1909).

Chapter 8. Domesticating Urban Space

1. Susan Saegert, "Masculine Cities, Feminine Suburbs: Polarized Ideas, Contradictory Realities," in Stimpson, et al., eds., *Women and the American City,* S96–S111; Adele Chatfield-Taylor, "Hitting Home," *Architectural Forum* 138 (Mar. 1973), 58–61.
2. Ira Katznelson, *City Trenches: Urban Politics and the Patterning of Class in the United States* (Chicago: University of Chicago Press, 1981), discusses the split between "home" and "work" as an event of political importance but makes no gender analysis.
3. Henri Lefebvre, *La production de l'espace* (Paris: Anthropos, 1974) suggests the political importance of this demand for men. On women's exclusion, see Christine de Pizan, *The Book of the City of Ladies,* tr. E.J. Richards (New York: Persea Books, 1982).
4. See Wekerle's review essay in Stimpson, et al., eds., *Women and the American City,* S188–S214. Also see Claude Enjeu and Joana Savé, "The City: Off-Limits to Women," *Liberation* 8 (July-Aug. 1974), 9–15; Bodil Kjaer, "A Woman's Place," *Architect's Journal* 176 (Sept. 15, 1982), 87. These last two essays from France and from Denmark (published in England) show that the double standard in public places is an international problem, not simply a result of American housing.
5. Carl Degler, "Revolution Without Ideology," *Daedalus* 93 (Spring 1964), 653–70, and also his *At Odds: Women and the Family* (New York: Oxford, 1979).

6. Lyn Lofland notes that in urban sociology, for many researchers, women are "part of the locale or neighborhood or area—described like other important aspects of the setting such as income, ecology, or demography—but largely irrelevant to the analytic *action*. They may reflect a group's social organization and culture, but they never seem to be in the process of creating it. They may be talked about by actors in the scene, but they rarely speak for themselves. They may, like males, suffer from certain structural inequalities, strains or disjunctions, but it is primarily the male figure who struggles against the pain. They may participate in organized groups, but such groups are tangential to the structuring of community life or to the processes of community government. When the researcher's lens pulls back for the wide-angle view, they are lost in the ubiquitous and undifferentiated 'he.' When it moves forward to close, detailed focus, they are fuzzy, shadowy, background figures, framing the male at center stage." "The 'Thereness' of Women: A Selective Review of Urban Sociology," in *Another Voice: Feminist Perspectives on Social Life and Social Science*, ed. M. Milliman and R. M. Kanter (New York: Anchor, 1975).

7. Jessie Bernard, *The Female World* (New York: Simon and Schuster, 1980), takes up the pervasiveness of gender segregation without analyzing this as an explicitly spatial phenomenon, although she is the most perceptive of all feminist sociologists.

8. Lewis Mumford, *The Transformations of Man* (New York: Harper and Row, 1956), 159–61.

9. For a description of one mother's problems in public, see Phyllis Chesler, *With Child: A Diary of Motherhood* (New York: Thomas Crowell, 1979), 149–50, 175.

10. Linda Hollis and Vivian Barry, "Kidspace," Community Design for Family Use exhibit organized in Washington, D.C., 1980, Capital Children's Museum; Colin Ward, *The Child in the City* (London: The Architectural Press, 1960).

11. Quoted in Robert B. Edgerton, *Alone Together: Social Order on an Urban Beach* (Los Angeles: University of California Press, 1978), 4.

12. *Ibid.*, 5.

13. Margaret Gordon, Stephanie Riger, Robert K. LeBailly, and Linda Heath, "Crime, Women, and the Quality of Urban Life," in C. Stimpson, et al., eds., *Women and the American City*, 144–60.

14. Philip Hager, "Safehouses Ease Fears of Aged Residents of San Francisco," *Los Angeles Times*, Nov. 21, 1982, 1.

15. Helena Lopata, "The Chicago Woman: A Study of Patterns of Mobility and Transportation," in C. Stimpson, et al., eds., *Women and the American City*, 161–69.

16. Allan Griswold Johnson, "On the Prevalence of Rape in the United States," *Signs: Journal of Women in Culture and Society* 6 (Autumn 1980), 136–46. Also see Susan Brownmiller, *Against Our Will: Men, Women, and Rape* (New York: Simon and Schuster, 1975), 15; Susan Griffen, "Rape: The All-American Crime," *Ramparts* 10 (Sept. 1971), 26–35; Diane Herman, "The Rape Culture," in Freeman, ed., *Women: A Feminist Perspective*, 469–73.

17. Gerda Wekerle, "Women's Self-Help Projects in the City: Transportation and Housing," paper presented at conference on Social Practice, UCLA Urban Planning Program, Mar. 2, 1979, 5.

18. *Ibid.*, 5–7. On women as providers of urban services, also see Galen Cranz, "Women and Urban Parks: Their Roles as Users and Suppliers of Park Services," in Keller, ed., *Building for Women*, 151–71; "Women in Urban Parks," in Stimpson, et al., eds., *Women and the American City*, 79–95.

19. William H. Whyte, "Street Life," *Urban Open Spaces* (Summer 1980), 2. For a more detailed critique of hassling: Lindsy Van Gelder, "The International Language of Street Hassling," *Ms.* 9 (May 1981), 15–20, and letters about this article, *Ms.*, (Sept. 1981); and Cheryl Benard and Edith Schlaffer, "The Man in the Street: Why He Harasses," *Ms.* 9 (May 1981), 18–19.

20. Erving Goffman, *Gender Advertisements* (New York: Harper Colophon, 1976), 24–27 Nancy Henley, *Body Politics: Power, Sex, and Nonverbal Communication* (Englewood Cliffs, N.J.: Prentice-Hall, 1977), 30; Marianne Wex, *Let's Take Back Our Space* (Berlin: Movimento Druck, 1979).

21. John Berger, et. al., *Ways of Seeing* (Harmondsworth, England: BBC and Penguin, 1972), 45–64.

22. Tom Hayden, *The American Future: New Visions Beyond Old Frontiers* (Boston: South End Press, 1980), 15.

23. Laura Shapiro, "Violence: The Most Obscene Fantasy," in Freeman, ed., *Women: A Feminist Perspective*, 469–73.

24. *Ibid.*, 469.

25. Sheila de Bretteville, "The Women's Building: Physical Forms and Social Implications," in Keller, ed., *Building for Women*, 47–64; "The Los Angeles Women's Building: A Public Center for Women's Culture," in Wekerle, et al., eds., *New Space for Women*, 293–310; "Feminist Design: At the Intersection of the Public and Private Spheres," unpublished, 1982.

26. Lewis Mumford, *The City in History* (New York: Harcourt Brace, 1961), 526.

Chapter 9. Beyond the Architecture of Gender

1. Roger Alcaly and David Marmelstein, eds., *The Fiscal Crisis of American Cities* (New York: Vintage Books, 1976).

2. David Morris, *Self-Reliant Cities: Energy and The Transformation of Urban America* (San Francisco: Sierra Club Books, 1982), 94–95; Ari L. Goldman, "City Shows Off Rotting Structures," *New York Times*, July 28, 1982, B1. Morris, in *Self-Reliant Cities*, notes that Boston's water mains leak one-half of the water they carry; New Orleans' sewers (some purchased second-hand from Philadelphia in 1896) need replacement; 49 of the 163 city bridges in Cleveland need replacement.

3. Denise Scott Brown, "Between Three Stools: A Personal View of Urban Design Practice and Pedagogy," in *Education for Urban Design*, special issue of *Urban Design International* (Winter 1982), 156.

4. Martin Pawley, *Architecture Versus Housing* (London: Architectural Press, 1969), 1.

5. Beverly Stephen, "The Striking 15: Wives on a Crusade," *Los Angeles Times* V (Dec. 16, 1982), 1.

SELECTED BIBLIOGRAPHY

Amsden, Alice, ed. *The Economics of Women and Work*. New York: St. Martin's Press, 1980.

André, Rae. *Homemakers: The Forgotten Workers*. Chicago: University of Chicago Press, 1981.

Ardener, Shirley, ed. *Women and Space: Ground Rules and Social Maps*. London: Croom Helm, 1981.

Bauer, Catherine. *Modern Housing*. Boston: Houghton Mifflin, 1934.

Bebel, August. *Woman Under Socialism*. 1883. Tr. Daniel De Leon, 1904. New York: Schocken Books, 1971.

Bernhardt, Arthur D. *Building Tomorrow: The Mobile / Manufactured Housing Industry*. Cambridge, Mass.: MIT Press, 1980.

Blake, Peter. *Form Follows Fiasco: Why Modern Architecture Hasn't Worked*. Boston: Little, Brown, 1977.

———. *God's Own Junkyard: The Planned Deterioration of America's Landscape*. New York: Holt, Rinehart and Winston, 1964.

Brandwein, Nancy, Jill MacNeice, and Peter Spiers. *The Group House Handbook*. Washington, D.C.: Acropolis Books, 1982.

Britz, Richard. *The Edible City: Resource Manual*. Los Altos, Calif.: William Kaufmann, Inc., 1981.

Burns, Leland S. and L. Grebler. *The Housing of Nations: Analysis and Policy in a Comparative Framework*. London: The Macmillan Company, 1977.

Burns, Scott. *Home, Inc.: The Hidden Wealth and Power of the American Household*. Garden City, New York: Doubleday, 1975. Republished as *The Household Economy: Its Shape, Origins, and Future*.

Clark, Thomas A. *Blacks in Suburbs: A National Perspective*. New Brunswick, N.J.: Rutgers University, Center for Urban Policy Research, 1979.

Coates, Gary J., ed. *Resettling America: Energy, Ecology, and Community*. Andover, Mass.: Brick House Publishing Company, 1981.

Coatsworth, Patricia, ed. *Women and Urban Planning: A Bibliography*. Chicago: Council of Planning Librarians, 1981.

Commoner, Barry. *The Politics of Energy*. New York: Alfred A. Knopf, 1979.

————. *The Poverty of Power: Energy and the Economic Crisis*. New York: Alfred A. Knopf, 1976.

Community Energy Cooperatives: How to Organize, Manage, and Finance Them. Washington, D.C.: Conference on Alternative State and Local Policies, 1983.

Corbett, Michael N. *A Better Place to Live: New Designs for Tomorrow's Communities*. Emmaus, Pennsylvania: Rodale Press, 1981.

Dal Co, Francesco. *Abitare nel Moderno*. Rome: Laterza, 1982.

Davis, Sam., ed. *The Form of Housing*. New York: Van Nostrand Reinhold, 1977.

Deal, Mary, ed. *Planning to Meet the Changing Needs of Women: A Compendium Developed from a National Competition to Identify and Promote Creative Solutions for Women in Urban Environments*. Dayton, Ohio: xerox manuscript, furnished by the editor, 1982.

Duly, Colin. *The Houses of Mankind*. London: Thames and Hudson, 1979.

Duncan, James S., ed. *Housing and Identity: Cross-cultural Perspectives*. London: Croom Helm, 1981.

Edwards, Arthur M. *The Design of Suburbia: A Critical Study in Environmental History*. London: Pembridge Press, 1981.

Ehrenreich, Barbara. *The Hearts of Men: American Dreams and the Flight from Commitment*. New York: Doubleday, 1983.

Eichler, Ned. *The Merchant Builders*. Cambridge, Mass.: MIT Press, 1982.

Faltermayer, Edmund. *Redoing America: A Nationwide Report on How to Make Our Cities and Suburbs Liveable*. New York: Harper and Row, 1968.

Feins, Judith D. and Terry Saunders Lane. *How Much For Housing*. Cambridge, Mass.: Abt Books, 1981.

Fleming, Ronald Lee and Lauri A. Halderman. *On Common Ground: Caring for Shared Land from Town Common to Urban Park*. Harvard, Mass.: The Harvard Common Press, 1982.

Fleming, Ronald Lee and Renata Von Tscharner. *Place Makers: Public Art That Tells You Where You Are*. Cambridge, Mass.: Townscape Institute; New York: Architectural Book Publishing Company, 1981.

Francis, Mark, Lisa Cashdan, Lynn Paxson. *The Making of Neighborhood Open Spaces*. New York: Center For Human Environments, CUNY, 1981.

Friedan, Betty. *The Second Stage*. New York: Summit Books, 1981.

Friedmann, John. *Retracking America: A Theory of Transactive Planning*. Garden City, New York: Anchor Press, 1973.

Gans, Herbert. *The Levittowners: Ways of Life and Politics in a New Suburban*. 1967. New York: Columbia University Press, 1982.

Getzels, Judith, ed. *Planning, Women, And Change*. Chicago: Planning Advisory Service, 1974.

Goffman, Erving. *Gender Advertisements*. New York: Harper Colophon Books; New York: Harper and Row, 1976.

Handlin, David. *The American Home: Architecture and Society, 1815–1915*. Boston: Little Brown, 1979.

Hare, Patrick et. al. *Accessory Apartments: Using Surplus Space in Single Family Houses*. Chicago: Planning Advisory Service, 1982.

Hartman, Chester, ed. *America's Housing Crisis: What Is to Be Done?* Boston: Routledge and Kegan Paul, 1983.

Hayden, Dolores. *The Grand Domestic Revolution: A History of Feminist Designs for American Homes, Neighborhoods, and Cities.* Cambridge, Mass.: MIT Press, 1981.

————. *Seven American Utopias: The Architecture of Communitarian Socialism, 1790–1975.* Cambridge, Mass.: MIT Press, 1976.

————. "What Would a Non-Sexist City Be Like?" *Women and the American City.* Eds. C. Stimpson et al. Chicago: University of Chicago Press, 1981.

Hayden, Tom. *The American Future: New Visions Beyond Old Frontiers.* Boston: South End Press, 1980.

Heresies Collective, special issue. *Making Room: Women and Architecture, Heresies* 11 (1981).

Heskin, Allan. *Tenants and the American Dream.* New York: Praeger, 1983.

Howell, Sandra C. *Designing for Aging: Patterns of Use.* Cambridge, Mass.: MIT Press, 1980.

Jackson, John Brinckerhoff. *Landscapes: Selected Writings of J.B. Jackson.* Amherst, Mass.: University of Massachusetts Press, 1970.

Johnson, Bruce, ed. *Resolving the Housing Crisis: Government Policy, Decontrol, and the Public Interest.* Cambridge, Mass.: Ballinger, 1982.

Institute for Community Economics. *The Community Land Trust Handbook.* Greenfield, Mass.: ICE, 1982.

Kamerman, Sheila B. *Parenting in an Unresponsive Society.* New York: The Free Press, 1980.

Kamerman, Sheila B. and Alfred J. Kahn. *Not For The Poor Alone: European Social Services.* Philadelphia: Temple University Press, 1975.

Keller, Suzanne, ed. *Building for Women.* Lexington, Mass.: Lexington Books, 1981.

Kolodny, Robert. *Multi-Family Housing: Treating the Existing Stock.* Washington, D.C.: National Association of Housing and Redevelopment Officials, 1981.

Lake, Robert W. *The New Suburbanites: Race and Housing.* New Brunswick, N.J.: Rutgers University, 1981.

Lindsey, Karen. *Friends as Family: New Kinds of Families and What They Could Mean to You.* Boston: Beacon Press, 1981.

Lovins, Amory. *Soft Energy Paths: Toward a Durable Peace.* 2nd ed. Cambridge, Mass.: Ballinger Publishing Co., 1977.

Luria, Daniel. "Wealth, Capital, and Power: The Social Meaning of Homeownership." *The Journal of Interdisciplinary History* 7 (Autumn 1976).

Lynch, Kevin. *A Theory of Good City Form.* Cambridge, Mass.: MIT Press, 1981.

Malmberg, Torsten. *Human Territoriality.* The Hague: New York: Mouton Publishers, 1980.

Marris, Peter. *Community Planning and Conceptions of Change.* London: Routledge, 1982.

————. *Loss and Change.* New York: Pantheon, 1974.

Miliutin, N.A. *Sotsgorod: The Problem of Building Socialist Cities.* Tr. George Collins and William Alex. Cambridge, Mass.: MIT Press, 1974.

Moore, Charles, Donlyn Lyndon, and Gerald Allen. *The Place of Houses.* New York: Holt, Rinehart and Winston, 1974.

Moore, Gary, et al. *Recommendations for Child Care Centers.* Madison, Wisconsin: University of Wisconsin, 1979.

Montgomery, Roger, and Daniel Mandelker. *Housing in America.* Indianapolis: Bobbs-Merrill Company, 1979.

Morris, David, and Karl Hess. *Neighborhood Power: The New Localism.* Boston: Beacon Press, 1975.

Morris, David. *Self-Reliant Cities: Energy and the Transformation of Urban America.* San Francisco: Sierra Club Books, 1982.

Muller, Peter O. "Everyday Life in Suburbia: A Review of Changing Social and Economic Forces That Shape Daily Rhythms within the Outer City." Bibliographical essay. *American Quarterly* 34 (1982): 262–77.

Mumford, Lewis. *The Transformation of Man.* New York: Harper and Row, 1956.

National Housing Law Project. *The Subsidized Housing Handbook.* Berkeley, Calif.: National Housing Law Project, 1982.

National Policy Workshop on Shared Housing, Findings and Recommendations. Philadelphia, Pa.: Shared Housing Resource Center, 1981.

Norberg-Schultz, Christian, Makoto Suzki, and Yukio Futagawa. *Wooden Houses.* New York: Abrams, 1979.

Pawley, Martin. *Architecture Versus Housing.* New York: Praeger, 1971.

———. *Home Ownership.* London: Architectural Press, 1978.

Perin, Constance. *Everything in Its Place: Social Order and Land Use in America.* Princeton, N.J.: Princeton University Press, 1977.

Planning and the Changing Family, special issue of the Journal of the *Journal of the American Planning Association.* Vol. 49 (Spring 1983).

Rapoport, Amos. *House Form and Culture.* Englewood Cliffs, N.J.: Prentice Hall, 1969.

Relph, Edward. *Rational Landscapes and Humanistic Geography.* London: Croom Helm, 1981.

Richards, Janet Radcliffe. *The Sceptical Feminist: A Philosophical Enquiry.* London; Boston: Routledge and Kegan Paul, 1980.

Rothblatt, Donald N., and Daniel J. Garr, and Jo Sprague. *The Suburban Environment and Women.* New York: Praeger, Holt, 1979.

Rubin, Nancy. *The New Suburban Woman: Beyond Myth and Motherhood.* New York: Coward, McCann, and Geoghegan, 1982.

Safa, Helen, and Eleanor Leacock, eds. *Development and the Sexual Division of Labor.* Special issue, *Signs: Journal of Women in Culture and Society* 7 (Winter 1981).

Sargent, Lydia, ed. *Women and Revolution: A Discussion of the Unhappy Marriage of Marxism and Feminism.* Boston: South End Press, 1981.

Shared Housing Resource Center. *National Policy Workshop on Shared Housing: Findings and Recommendations.* Philadelphia, Pa.: Shared Housing Resource Center, 1982.

Sklar, Elliot and Matthew Edel. *Shaky Palaces.* New York, forthcoming 1983.

Smith, Ralph, ed. *The Subtle Revolution: Women at Work.* Washington, D.C.: Urban Land Institute, 1979.

Stein, Peter J., ed. *Single Life: Unmarried Adults in Social Context.* New York: St. Martin's Press, 1981.

Stilgoe, John R. *Common Landscape of America, 1580 to 1845*. New Haven, Conn.: Yale University Press, 1982.

Stimpson, Catherine, Elsa Dixler, Martha Nelson, and Kathryn Yatrakis, eds. *Women and the American City*. Chicago: University of Chicago Press, 1981.

Strasser, Susan. *Never Done: A History of American Housework*. New York: Pantheon Books, 1982.

Sussman, Carl, ed. *Planning the Fourth Migration: The Neglected Vision of the Regional Planning Association of America*. Cambridge, Mass.: MIT Press, 1976.

Todd, John and Nancy Jack Todd. *Tomorrow Is Our Permanent Address*. New York: Lindisfarne / Harper and Row, 1980.

Uhlig, Günther. *Kollektivmodell "Einküchenhaus."* Wekbund-Archiv 6. Berlin: Anabas Verlag, 1981.

U.S. Department of Housing and Urban Development. *The Affordable Community: Growth, Change, and Choice in the '80s*. Washington, D.C.: U.S.G.P.O., 1981.

———. *Housing Our Families*. Washington, D.C.: U.S.G.P.O., 1980.

Urban Land Institute. *Affordable Housing: Twenty Examples from the Private Sector*. Washington, D.C.: Urban Land Institute, 1982.

———. *Housing for a Maturing Population*. Washington, D.C.: Urban Land Institute, 1982.

Wachs, Martin. *Transportation for the Elderly*. Berkeley, Calif.: University of California Press, 1979.

Walker, Lester. *American Shelter: An Illustrated Encyclopedia of the American Home*. Woodstock, N.Y.: Overlook Press, 1981.

Weicher, John C., Kevin E. Villani, and Elizabeth A. Roistacher, eds. *Rental Housing: Is There A Crisis?* Washington, D.C.: Urban Institute, 1981.

Whyte, William H. *The Last Landscape*. Garden City, N.Y.: Doubleday, 1968.

Wekerle, Gerda, Rebecca Peterson, and David Morley, eds. *New Space for Women*. Boulder, Colorado: Westview Press, 1980.

Wolfe, Tom. *From Bauhaus to Our House*. New York: Farrar, Straus, and Giroux, 1981.

Women and the City. Special issue, *International Journal of Urban and Regional Research* 2 (October 1978).

Women's Expressions on the Environment: A Commentary to the Exhibition På Vej That Shows the Works of Women Architects, Planners and Artists. Arhus, Denmark: 1980.

Wright, Gwendolyn. *Building the Dream: A Social History of American Housing*. New York: Pantheon Books, 1981.

———. *Moralism and the Model Home: Domestic Architecture and Cultural Conflict in Chicago, 1873–1913*. Chicago: University of Chicago Press, 1980.

INDEX